Up from Serfdom

Aleksandr Nikitenko

My Childhood and Youth in Russia 1804–1824

Up from Serfdom

Translated by Helen Saltz Jacobson

Foreword by Peter Kolchin

Yale University Press New Haven & London

Published with assistance from the
Mary Cady Tew Memorial Fund.

Frontispiece: Aleksandr Nikitenko, 1863. Oil painting by I. N. Kramskoy.

Designed by James J. Johnson and set in Stemple Garamond types by The Composing Room of Michigan, Inc., Grand Rapids, Michigan.
Printed in the United States of America by R. R. Donnelley and Sons, Harrisonburg, Virginia.

Library of Congress Cataloging-in-Publication Data

Nikitenko, A. (Aleksandr), 1804 or 5–1877.
Up from serfdom : My childhood and youth in Russia, 1804–1824 / translated by Helen Saltz Jacobson ; foreword by Peter Kolchin.
p. cm.
Based on Nikitenko's diaries.
ISBN 978-0-300-09716-0 paper

1. Nikitenko, A. (Aleksandr), 1804 or 5–1877. 2. Critics—Russia—Biography. 3. Serfs—Russia—Biography. 4. Russia—Social conditions—1801–1917. I. Jacobson, Helen Saltz. II. Nikitenko, A. (Aleksandr), 1804 or 5–1877. Dnevik. III. Title.

PG2947.N5 A3 2001
891.709—dc21
[B] 00-043866

A catalogue record for this book is available from the British Library.

The paper in this book meets the guidelines for permanence and durability of the Committee on Production Guidelines for Book Longevity of the Council on Library Resources.

10 9 8 7 6 5

To the memory of my husband

Gene Jacobson (1919–1996)

and for

Jovana, Kira, *and* Lani

Contents

Foreword

PETER KOLCHIN

Aleksandr Nikitenko's memoir, *Up from Serfdom,* is a doubly atypical work. Most obvious, it is one of only a handful of surviving autobiographies written by ex-serfs in Russia;[1] students of Russian serfdom do not have access to anything remotely like the dozens of slave autobiographies that shed light on the "peculiar institution" in the southern United States.[2] Equally important, Nikitenko's narrative describes the life of a highly unusual serf. It gives a good—but very partial—picture of the peculiar nature of *Russia's* peculiar institution.

To an American audience, what will probably seem most striking about Nikitenko's memoir is the sharp difference that it reveals between the Russian and American versions of bondage. Four contrasts are especially noteworthy. First, by American standards, Russian serf-holding estates were enormous. Nikitenko's unusually wealthy owners—the Sheremetev family—possessed tens of thousands of serfs scattered across Russia; in 1850, just two Americans owned more than one thousand slaves. Only a tiny fraction of enslaved blacks in the southern United States (2.4 percent) had owners with more than two hundred slaves, whereas the great majority of bound peasants in Russia (80.8 percent) had such owners. Unlike most American slaves, most serfs lived in a world of their own, where their masters were remote figures whom they rarely or never saw.[3]

Second, Russian serfdom lacked the kind of sectional-geographic basis that characterized American slavery during its last half-century. True, serfs were far more prevalent in some parts of the Russian Empire than in others; in the sparsely populated far north and in the vast expanses of Siberia their numbers were insignificant. But throughout Russia's most heavily settled regions serfs were numerous, and everywhere serfdom was legal; there was no Russian equivalent of the free states that held out the promise of freedom to fugitive slaves headed north and that served as a bastion of antislavery propaganda directed south, provoking a torrent of *pro*slavery propaganda in return. Serfs *did* run away in massive numbers, typically heading to the undergoverned borderlands in the south and east, where they hoped to and often did escape the constraints of serfdom. But Russia was not divided into the kind of increasingly antagonistic sections that in the United States eventually went to war over slavery.

Third, Russian serfdom lacked the racial component of American slavery. Whereas in the United States (and the Americas in general) the vast majority of slaveowners descended from Europeans and the vast majority of slaves descended from Africans, most Russian serfholders and serfs shared the same national, religious, and ethnic background. One should be careful not to make too much of this distinction. First of all, there were exceptions on both sides of the Atlantic. The racial character of American slavery was muddied by the presence of a tiny number of African-American and a somewhat larger number of Native American masters, as well as significant numbers of Native American slaves and slaves who were so light that they appeared white by all reasonable definitions. On the borders of the vast Russian Empire, ethnic and religious distinctions between owners and owned were common: in the west and south, Orthodox Ukrainian peasants often had Polish Catholic or Russian Orthodox owners, and in the east conquered nationalities were absorbed into the serf population; readers of Nikitenko's memoir will doubtless note the Ukrainian (or "Little Russian") background of his family and many of the peasants among whom he grew up, and the contempt they sometimes expressed for "Muscovites." Second and more important, as historians have recognized, "race" is a subjective construct rather than a physical reality. In America, racial definitions coalesced only gradually (and differed significantly from those applied in other New World societies): in the seventeenth and eighteenth centuries, colonists routinely confused religious and national characteristics with those that would come to be considered racial, speaking of the Irish as a "wild race" and referring to the Christianity of the settlers rather than their color as legitimizing their free status. In Russia, peasants appeared so different from nobles—especially after Tsar Peter I (1682–1725) forced nobles to adopt European dress and manners, including requiring men to shave their beards—that defenders of serfdom found it easy to argue that the peasants were inherently unsuited for freedom. Indeed, use of this essentially racial argument to defend a "nonracial" system of bondage underscores the subjective character of race in general, and shows how Russians "made" race just as Americans did.[4]

Still, there can be little doubt that racial thought came much more easily to American slaveholders than to Russian serfholders, and proved far more limiting to most American slaves than it did to Russian serfs. Exceptional serfs—like Nikitenko—were able to attend school, socialize with prominent men, and live practically as if they were free; in the southern United States, such opportunities for exceptional slaves were virtually inconceivable. There *were* exceptional slaves whose lives were in some ways as different from those of most enslaved blacks as Nikitenko's was from those of most peasants, but in white racism they faced a powerful additional barrier that did not burden the serfs.

Underlying these three contrasts, the most striking apparent difference between Russian serfdom and American slavery—the greater opportunities enjoyed by the serfs—is both important and at the same time less than meets the eye. Important because a serf such as Nikitenko could lead a life that American slaves could barely imagine. Less than meets the eye because Nikitenko's story is so unusual; indeed, most Russian serfs could no more imagine such a life than could their American counterparts. Lest one assume that most serfs went to school, moved around at will, and hobnobbed with noblemen, military officers, and government officials, it is worth pointing out that most peasants never even spoke to such authorities and that Russian serfs were no more likely to know how to read and write than were American slaves.[5] Nikitenko's atypical experiences reveal both what an intelligent, ambitious, and lucky serf could achieve, and how unlikely such an achievement was.

A brief explanation of the peculiar nature of Russian serfdom may help the reader put Nikitenko's experience in context. Originating in the sixteenth and seventeenth centuries with the binding of peasants to the land, it had evolved by the eighteenth century into something close to—although not precisely the same as—chattel slavery. Owned almost exclusively by noble landowners, serfs could be bought and sold, punished at will, and assigned as much work as their owners deemed fit; the legal authority of serfholders over their human property differed little from that of American slaveholders over theirs. Peasants constituted the overwhelming majority of the Russian population—83 percent on the eve of emancipation—but not all of these were privately held serfs: about half the peasants (although far fewer in the central provinces) belonged to the state or the crown, and traditionally enjoyed greater freedom than those who were privately owned; in very rough terms, state peasants can be thought of as the Russian equivalent of the American South's free blacks.

Although noble serfholders legally owned everything on their estates (including the peasants), they usually provided their peasants allotments of land, which they held and cultivated communally and came to regard as their own. (In one popular peasant proverb, the peasant tells the nobleman: "We are yours, but the land is ours.") Badly outnumbered, nobles usually felt uncomfortable among their serfs and interacted with them as little as possible. Some (such the as Sheremetevs) were absentee owners; indeed, wealthy nobles with extensive landholdings were almost always absentee owners, since even if they lived on one of their country estates they were remote figures to the peasants who lived on their other holdings. Even when they were not absent, most wealthy nobles had little contact with their peasants, with the important exception of their house serfs, and dealt with them primarily through administrative intermediaries that included a hierarchy of managers, stewards, and representatives chosen by the peasants themselves. In practice, therefore, peasants on some estates were able to enjoy a considerable degree of day-to-day self-rule, even while ultimately subject to their owners' authority.

There were two major ways in which landholding nobles exploited their serfs economically. Some serfholders imposed labor obligations (*barshchina*) on their serfs, who were responsible for cultivating both their masters' land and their "own" (which also, legally, belonged to the masters); although masters could require their serfs to perform as much labor as they chose, it became customary to assign no more than three days of barshchina per week, allowing peasants an equal amount of time to cultivate their own allotments. Other serfholders, however, dispensed with barshchina, and instead required their peasants to pay them a stipulated yearly fee (known as *obrok*), in money, goods, or both. Such peasants were free to cultivate their allotments full-time, engage in handicrafts, or hire themselves out for jobs either in their native villages or—with their owners' permission—elsewhere. Obrok was especially prevalent in less fertile regions where noble landowners had little incentive to engage in their own agricultural cultivation, but serfholders were entirely free to decide for themselves whether to have their serfs on barshchina or obrok (or a combination of the two). Although most serfs performed labor for their owners, many masters chose to commute some or all direct serf labor; in the mid-nineteenth century, almost one-fifth of all serfs were exclusively on obrok and more than one-third owed their masters both obrok and barshchina. One advantage of obrok, from the point of view of absentee owners, was that it required less direct supervision of serfs; this was also, of course, an advantage from the point of view of the serfs. Nikitenko, and many of the other peasants he described, were held on obrok.

On a day-to-day basis, most Russian serfs suffered less direct intervention from their owners than did American slaves, and were freer to organize their own lives. Required, unlike most slaves, to provide their own sustenance, they controlled a higher proportion of their time; this was especially true of those on obrok, but even those on barshchina could call half their time their own. This position of relative independence facilitated the emergence of economic stratification, especially among peasants on obrok, with some serfs better off than others and a tiny number acquiring substantial wealth. (From the point of view of serfholders, wealthy peasants could be a substantial asset, because they could be required to pay unusually large obrok fees.) It also enabled the serfs to engage in a substantial degree of self-government through their village commune, a central peasant institution that helped the needy in time of hardship, decided who would fill the military levies through which the government recruited soldiers, and in much of Russia periodically reapportioned land allotments among peasant households to prevent the emergence of excessive disparities in economic well-being. Communal officials, typically elected by male heads of households at a communal gathering, served simultaneously as both the peasants' representatives in dealing with the outside world and as the lowest-level managers of the serfholders' estates.[6]

Although most Russian serfs enjoyed greater freedom than most American slaves, the contrast should not be exaggerated. For one thing, some American slaves were able to experience unusual independence as well. They included a relatively small number of skilled slaves who were allowed to "hire their own time," finding employment on their own and paying their owners a stipulated fee that constituted the American equivalent of obrok, as well as a larger number of slaves who lived in the low country of South Carolina and Georgia, where, under conditions of large estates and widespread owner absenteeism, blacks engaged in an unusual degree of self-management. But elsewhere in the South, slaves who were not as atypical as these two groups were able to secure greater economic independence than has commonly been recognized. American masters, too, frequently gave their slaves plots of land on which they could grow crops and raise chickens, although slaves typically used such plots to supplement the rations they received from their masters rather than to provide their own basic sustenance. Historians in recent years have paid increased attention to what has been termed the "internal" (or "slave") economy, in which slaves were able to sell or trade the products they raised, acquiring small sums of cash that could be used to buy luxuries such as tobacco. This internal economy, which was most pronounced in the Carolina low country, did not generally provide as much economic autonomy to slaves in the American South as was common among those in the Caribbean, let alone serfs in Russia; still, its very existence drives home the important point that the totally dependent status that the law imposed on American slaves did not automatically translate into an equivalent dependence in fact.[7]

It is also important to note the limited nature of the serfs' relative "freedom." Rich and privileged serfs existed; a few became fabulously wealthy, and were able—if their owners agreed, which they did not always do—to buy their own freedom. The Sheremetev family even allowed fortunate serfs to buy serfs of their own, registering them in the Sheremetevs' name so as to conform with the law; in 1810, 165 Sheremetev serfs owned 903 others. But although opportunities for exceptional serfs existed, the vast majority were unable to take advantage of them, and economic stratification was relatively limited. Aside from the truly exceptional, "rich" peasants were rich only in the sense that they were not quite as impoverished as their neighbors. The peasant population as a whole lived on the margin of disaster. Poor, ignorant, and disease-ridden, most serfs worked hard, had little to look forward to, and died young; living in a harsh environment where growing enough to survive was a struggle, and suffering both from their owners' "benign neglect" and from Russia's low level of economic development, serfs had a material standard of living—measured by such criteria as life expectancy and mortality rates—that on average was worse than that of American slaves.

Equally important, the serfs' relative freedom was never secure, because it rested on their owners' convenience rather than on any recognition of rights. Should a serfholder decide that intervening in the serfs' lives *did* suit his or her convenience, there was nothing they could do about it. Nikitenko describes in chilling detail the abusive treatment a neighboring landowner (Avdotya Borisovna Aleksandrovna) meted out on her hapless victims, the kind of treatment that in countless other cases went unobserved and unrecorded. But even the most favored of serfs—like Nikitenko—could never be sure when they would lose their privileges and find themselves the targets of some inexplicable vendetta. More than anything else, it was the arbitrary nature of the serfholder's power that weighed on serfs like Nikitenko, for as they discovered, even the most benevolent patron could turn overnight into an overbearing tyrant. In that respect, serfdom and slavery were the same.

Although the title that Helen Jacobson has given Nikitenko's translated memoir will doubtless remind many American readers of Booker T. Washington's 1901 autobiography, *Up from Slavery*, a more useful point of comparison is the 1845 autobiography *Narrative of the Life of Frederick Douglass.*[8] In many ways, Nikitenko's and Douglass's autobiographies appear strikingly different from each other, and illustrate the evident contrasts between American slavery and Russian serfdom. Douglass was separated from his mother at an early age and was unsure of his (presumably white) father's identity; Nikitenko grew up idolizing his accomplished but stern father and his beautiful, kind, and selfless mother. Douglass often experienced close supervision from his masters, was hired out to a "slave breaker" who viciously tormented him, learned to read and write by ingeniously tricking white playmates into teaching him, escaped to the North by borrowing the identification papers of a free black sailor and taking a train and ferry from Baltimore to Philadelphia, and became a radical abolitionist. Nikitenko experienced little of traditional village serfdom, went to school, became a teacher, associated with prominent intellectuals and nobles, used his influential friends to help persuade Count Sheremetev to free him, and went on to become a professor and government censor. At first glance, it is hard to imagine two more different stories of bondage and freedom.[9]

Despite these very real contrasts, the two autobiographies reveal some notable parallels, both in their authors' personal experiences and in the nature of the social relations of bondage that they describe. Douglass and Nikitenko were highly exceptional individuals, both in the way they experienced bondage and in their unusual talents and ambition. Douglass's privileged positions—from a favored house slave to a skilled caulker allowed to hire his own time in Baltimore—appear unremarkable only when compared with Nikitenko's extraordinary experiences as a teacher and protégé of noblemen who moved in the highest circles; because of their atypicality, the life of "ordinary" slaves and serfs appears only obliquely in their narratives, if not in caricature at least in stereotype. Each portrayed himself—in contrast to the mass of slaves or serfs—as possessing keen intelligence, driving ambition, and an unyielding determination to be free. Nikitenko's "passion for reading" (42) was matched by Douglass's, and in both cases books opened a new world for the young men and fueled their desire for liberty. "The more I read, the more I was led to abhor and detest my enslavers," narrated Douglass. "I would at times feel that learning to read had been a curse rather than a blessing. It had given me a view of my wretched condition, without the remedy. . . . In moments of agony, I envied my fellow slaves for their stupidity" (55).[10]

Like all autobiographies, Douglass's and Nikitenko's were self-representations that must be read in light of the authors' goals and interests; both authors omitted "unsuitable" material, shaped their narratives to their didactic purposes, and adhered to widely accepted literary conventions of the day. Yet read carefully, the autobiographies provide surprisingly nuanced portraits of life in bondage. Although both Douglass and Nikitenko adopted the useful device of showing how bondage corrupted the soul of the masters as well as their human property—Nikitenko: "She owned several hundred slaves, yet she herself was enslaved by wicked inclinations" (22); Douglass: "Slavery proved as injurious to her as it did to me. . . . Under its influence, the tender heart became stone, and the lamblike disposition gave way to one of tiger-like fierceness" (52–53)—both took care to describe kind masters as well as those who were cruel and abusive, to stress the humanity of real individuals even as they generalized about the horrendous overall effects of slavery and serfdom. And both described relatively happy childhoods in which they played with free children, times later remembered by Nikitenko as "moments of utterly carefree happiness" (45).[11]

More than anything else, two major themes unite Douglass's and Nikitenko's autobiographies, both as personal memoirs and as condemnations of slavery and serfdom. The first of these is the arbitrary nature of bondage. No matter how privileged a slave or serf might be, one's position was never secure, for privileges were enjoyed not by right but by sufferance of an unpredictable power. Just as Douglass's autobiography recounts numerous traumatic events that drove home to him the manifest injustice of his status, so too Nikitenko's memoir is filled with examples of the tenuousness of even the most favored serf's privileges; like Douglass, Nikitenko experienced the helplessness that accompanied his "status as a non-person" (154). It was in his accounts of his father's roller-coaster career, however, that Nikitenko most forcefully articulated this theme of the privileged serf's utter dependence on outside forces. "On the one hand," Nikitenko wrote of his father, "he seemed to take advantage of the benefits and assets offered by his independent, even prestigious position. On the other hand, he could be trampled on like a worm" (16). Enjoying a variety of trusted positions, including chief clerk, teacher, and steward, he also suffered periodic sudden reversals when "blind, despotic whim decided everything" (32) and he was thrown into prison, sent into exile, or had his property confiscated. He died a broken man, "dispirited by an awareness of the fruitlessness of his labors" (148). Over and over, like Douglass, Nikitenko reiterated the despair of living under another's arbitrary authority.

The second pervasive theme in these autobiographies is the

way in which the peculiar combination of unusual privileges and arbitrary restrictions bred in their authors an unquenchable thirst for freedom. When Douglass's master allowed him to hire his own time, it made him *more* dissatisfied with his slave status, for "the fact that he gave me any part of my wages was proof, to my mind, that he believed me entitled to the whole of them" (107). Douglass generalized that "whenever my condition was improved, instead of its increasing my contentment, it only increased my desire to be free. . . . To make a contented slave," he concluded, "it is necessary to make a thoughtless one" (103). Nikitenko expressed very much the same sentiment. "Tormented by the thought that the law was still against me, and any day I could become a victim of unforeseen, hostile circumstances" (169), he found that success increased his frustration and sense of injustice; "at times," he wrote, "my craving for freedom and knowledge and for expanding the range of my activities possessed me to the point of physical pain" (169). At last, like Douglass, he made the fateful decision to seek his freedom—not by running away, but by writing Count Sheremetev and asking to be freed.

The manner in which Nikitenko became free clearly differentiates him from Frederick Douglass and other fugitive slaves who escaped to the North. Nikitenko was not a rebel. He beseeched his master for freedom, and was successful in securing it only because of the support he received from exceptionally powerful friends. Their divergent routes *to* freedom presaged divergent careers *in* freedom: Douglass became a fiery abolitionist agitator and a supporter of radical causes that included equal rights for women as well as for black men; Nikitenko became a professor at St. Petersburg University and a government censor, and grew increasingly conservative as he settled into a life of comfortable respectability. By the mid-1860s, when, in the wake of the serf emancipation of 1861, Russia saw the emergence of a variety of radical protest movements aimed at democracy, women's rights, and socialism, Nikitenko was warning against the "shameless radical strivings of this generation" and proclaiming that "the most terrifying kind of rule"—worse than despotism or aristocracy—

"is rule by the rabble." A decade later, an embittered old man, he proclaimed that "the Russian *muzhik* [peasant] is practically a perfect savage. He is crude, ignorant, and lacks any understanding of rights and law, while his religion consists of nodding his head and flailing his arms." Nikitenko was even more disillusioned with Russia's intelligentsia, for if the peasant was "a drunkard and a thief," he was "a far better person than the so-called educated, intelligent Russian," who was "a liar from head to toe."[12]

Still, despite these personal differences between Nikitenko and Douglass and the very real contrasts between Russian serfdom and American slavery, in many ways the basic message of Nikitenko's *Up from Serfdom* was similar to that put forth by Douglass and other American slave autobiographers: bondage was cruel, capricious, and utterly unjust. Even for the favored elite serf, being under a master's power made life fearsome and unpredictable. Nikitenko's words when recollecting his first moments of freedom—"Glory to the Almighty and . . . eternal gratitude to those who helped me to be born again" (201)—recall nothing so much as the song remembered by American slave Annie Harris and echoed a century later by Martin Luther King, Jr.: "Free at last! Free at last! Thank God Almighty, we are free at last!"[13]

Translator's Note

In 1824, thirty-seven years before serfdom was abolished in the Russian Empire, a serf youth, descendant of Ukrainian Cossacks, won his struggle for freedom.

Not many years passed before Aleksandr Nikitenko rose to eminence as a university professor and literary critic. He occupied important posts in the Russian government, served in the censorship department and on government commissions, and was elected to the prestigious Academy of Sciences. And all this Nikitenko accomplished well before 1861, when Tsar Alexander II emancipated the serfs.

In 1818, at the age of fourteen, Nikitenko began to keep a diary. In 1851 he decided to compose an autobiography but completed only this memoir, which I have chosen to call *Up from Serfdom.* His sources were the diaries he kept between 1818 and 1824, his father's correspondence and documents, and the information his parents and grandparents had passed on to him as he was growing up. The memoir ends with his successful bid for freedom in 1824.

In 1888 the Russian newspaper *Russkaya Starina* began publishing the memoir in a series of installments. Book editions were issued in 1893 and 1904. *Up from Serfdom* is a translation of the 1904 St. Petersburg edition, whose editor was Mikhail Lemke.

Though the 1818–1824 notebooks were not preserved, fortunately the 1826–1877 notebooks (except for 1851) survived in copies edited by Nikitenko's daughters, in keeping with instructions he had left for them. In 1955 a three-volume edition of these notebooks was published as *Dnevnik* (Diary) in the Soviet Union. In 1975 an abridged, English translation was published. (*Diary of a Russian Censor: Aleksandr Nikitenko,* abridged, edited, and translated by Helen Saltz Jacobson [Amherst: University of Massachusetts Press]).

Personal and place names with anglicized spelling in widely accepted usage follow that spelling. This particularly applies to certain historical figures. Otherwise, with some modifications, I have used an accepted method of transliteration from Russian to English. My modifications consist of reproducing the sound—that is, pronunciation—of some names and places, and of anglicizing plural endings of some Russian terms.

Russians have three names: a first name, a patronymic, and a family name. The patronymic is formed from one's father's first name. A female adds to her father's name one of these endings: *ovna, yevna, inichna, ichna.* A male adds to his father's name *ovich, yevich,* or *ich.* Russians use patronymics in spoken and written Russian, tacking the patronymic onto the person's first name. Nikitenko uses patronymics frequently in his memoir. For example, he refers to his father's close friend in three different ways: Grigory Fyodorovich Tatarchukov, Grigory Fyodorovich, and Tatarchukov. For readers unfamiliar with Russian customs and literature, it can be somewhat confusing to read a character's full name (first name, patronymic, and family name) on one page and, many pages later, read only a first name and patronymic. One hopes that this note will help readers avoid misinterpreting the patronymic as a family name and puzzling over the appearance of this "new character."

Acknowledgments

I can trace my love of translation to my first day in high school. When I arrived home, I planted myself before my father and announced, “Papa, I can read French,” and I proceeded to read Lesson One to him. He beamed, and I was thrilled by my experience with a foreign language.

Some twenty-five years later, the Russian language bug bit me. I owe the launching of a challenging and fulfilling career as a translator to the late Dr. Robert Magidoff, who was the chairman of the Russian department of New York University. He had invited me to translate a Russian science fiction anthology for New York University Press.

About the distinguished historian Peter Kolchin, who wrote the foreword to this translation of *Up from Serfdom,* I cannot say enough. I remember so well how I first came across his landmark work *Unfree Labor: American Slavery and Russian Serfdom.* After reading a review in the *New York Times,* I immediately ordered the book. Without exaggeration I can say that it was the most thorough piece of research that I had ever encountered. It had taken him some fifteen years to produce that scholarly work. Thank you, Peter, for your enlightening foreword to this memoir.

In 1975 the University of Massachusetts Press published *The Diary of a Russian Censor,* my translation of Aleksandr Nikitenko's 1826–77 diaries, which I edited and abridged from three volumes. It was many years before I found the time to translate the memoir of his serf childhood and youth, but I always knew that I must translate it. The story of his struggle for freedom touched me more than any work I have ever translated. For me it was truly a labor of love. For historians it filled a gap because, as Peter Kolchin lamented in his study of American slavery and Russian serfdom, "There is no equivalent to the Federal Writer's Project interviews (of former slaves) and only a handful of autobiographies were written by ex-serfs."

Nonhistorians, representatives of a broad readership who have read my manuscript and were moved by the memoir, suggested that its anticipated readership be extended to include high school students. Teenagers, especially students struggling against poverty, ethnic and racial discrimination, and other forms of hatred or other overwhelming obstacles, can easily identify and empathize with Nikitenko's moodiness and depression. I am grateful to a school psychologist, Adele Vexler, and two teachers of high school English, Joan Goodman and Roslyn Uzupis, for viewing *Up from Serfdom* as an appropriate and desirable addition to the reading lists for English and social studies courses.

To international literary agent Rosalie Siegel, for whom the placement of my manuscript was as much a labor of love for this memoir as mine was for translating it: thank you, Rosalie, with all my heart.

For the reproduction of illustrations I am indebted to photographer John Blazejewski at the Firestone Library, Princeton University, and photographer Abe Hoffman.

For rescuing me from chronic computer problems and for help in preparing my manuscript on disk, thank you, programmer Peter Jacobson.

I want to express my gratitude to others for the support they have given me, each in a different way. Thank you Barbara Sassone, Professor John Mackay, and Elena Gonikberg.

Last but not least go my thanks to those who put this memoir in your hands: Jonathan Brent, editorial director of Yale University Press, and to the patient, supportive staff of the Press: Lara Heimert, Heidi Downey, Chris Erikson, Mary Pasti, and Aileen M. Novick.

Map 1. The provinces of European Russia in the nineteenth century.

Map 2. The Sheremetevs' votchinas. A votchina is hereditary landed property of a noble. It may contain one or more small villages, large villages, and hamlets.

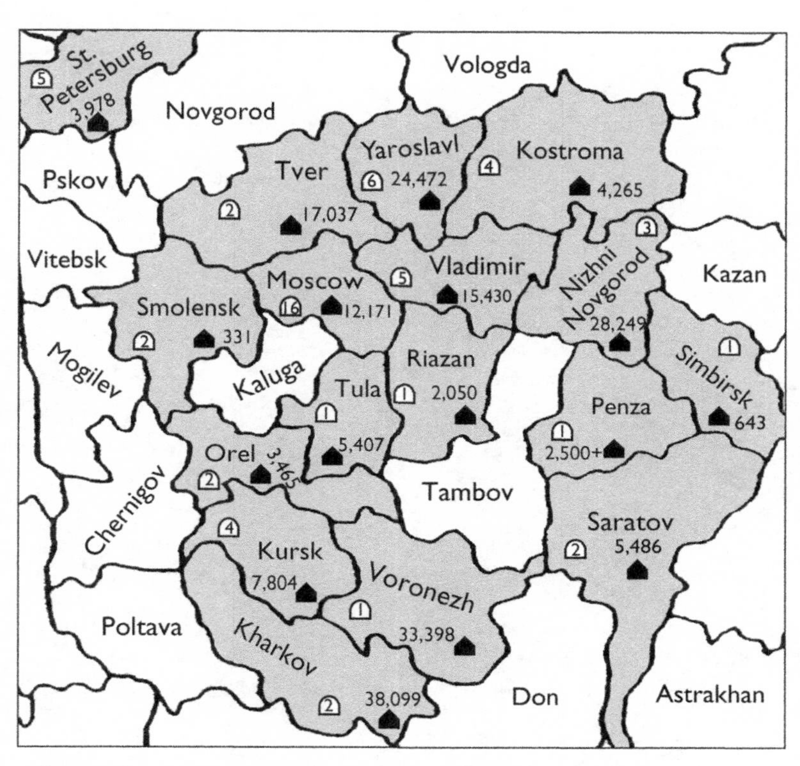

= Number of Sheremetev serfs by province (male and female)
= Number of Sheremetev votchinas by province

Map 3. The Sheremetevs' serfs in seventeen provinces, early nineteenth century.

1

My Roots

In the province of Voronezh, on the Tikhnaya Sosna River, between the small county towns of Ostrogozhsk and Biryuch, is a village, or *sloboda,* called Alekseyevka.[1]

Alekseyevka was settled by Little Russians [Ukrainians], Cossacks, whom Russian policy, in time, forced into serfdom. They certainly didn't foresee this when they responded to a government summons to colonize border lands. Many thousands of Little Russians from Ukraine migrated across the Don River and settled along the Sosna, Kalitva, and other rivers to protect Russia's borders from invasions by Crimean Tatars.[2]

Originally Alekseyevka sloboda was granted to the Cherkassky princes. They passed it on as a dowry to the Sheremetev counts, who owned an enormous number of people in almost every province of Russia. The recent figure of the Sheremetev family's current holdings is said to be up to 150,000 male souls.[3]

In Alekseyevka lived a cobbler, Mikhailo Danilovich, whom the villagers knew by three names: Nikitenko, "Cherevik" (for the ladies' high-heeled boots he made), and "Tinker." Though not a particularly skilled cobbler, he did an honest job on the peasants' boots. This was my paternal grandfather.

How well I remember the old man's genial face, wreathed by a luxurious, gray-streaked beard, his prominent nose, bridged by awkward spectacles, and his kindly, pensive, aging eyes. His arms were covered with bright scars from fights.

Grandfather Nikitenko was warm and kind to everyone, and

Kuskovo, one of Sheremetev's estates.

to me he was especially affectionate. But, oh, how he loved to stop by the tavern. There he might leave his earnings from days of hard work, as well as his sash, cap, and even his sheepskin jacket. When sober, he didn't talk much and was gentle and sensible. But when he had too much to drink, he usually prattled about community affairs, attacked the chaotic state of the village government, and longed for the good old days when the Cossacks were permitted to elect their own hetman [chieftain] to govern them. In this condition he would frighten the wits out of the family. Hurling rebukes, he might back up a verbal lashing brandishing the tools of his trade—a rod and strap.

He was especially grumpy when one of us went to the tavern to fetch him home. Whenever Grandma had a feeling that Grandpa was going to get drunk, she would send a member of the house-

Typical serf dwelling. The huge high oven has three functions: it bakes, it heats the drafty cabin, and its top serves as a warm bed for several family members. Painting by J. A. Atkinson.

hold after him on some pretext or other. Not daring to disobey, he would return, but not without protest.

"Nasty, that's what you are," he would scold his wife on such occasions. "Not an ounce of feeling! I was just beginning to discuss a very important matter with our neighbor when suddenly I heard someone shout: 'Get on home!' The devil only knows when I'll get my thoughts together again!"

Grandmother Paraskaya Stepanovna Nikitenko was a remarkable woman. As the daughter of a priest, she considered herself a member of the village aristocracy and sensed her worth. She confined her friendships and associations to the so-called *meshchane*—small traders, craftsmen, and the like, comprising a caste of the highest class in the sloboda.

Her silver goblet she reserved for ladies who wore fancy hats on holidays instead of cheap kerchiefs, for those who dressed in

Serfs at the local tavern. Lithograph, artist unknown.

coats of fine cloth with gold braid at the waist and sealskin or high-heeled boots. Poor as she was, she adhered religiously to the Little Russian custom of hospitality. She was known for her unusual kindness, for sharing her last few crumbs with the needy. An innate nobility made up for her lack of education and lent dignity to her deeds and actions.[4]

I remember how gracefully she conversed with townsmen, *pomeshchiks* [noble landowners], and literate people.[5] She enlivened her own and other people's stories with clever and subtle remarks, and vividly and coherently described popular beliefs and legends of Catherine II's times. When speaking of the empress, it was always with reverence, her "dear mother Tsarina." She argued and debated vigorously, holding fast to her beliefs. What a fine reputation she enjoyed. To all who knew her, she was known as "clever Stepanovna" or "wise Paraskaya."

Grandfather Nikitenko never attained venerable old age. In his late fifties he drowned while swimming in the river. Grandmother was left with four children, two daughters and two sons. Elizabeth, the younger daughter, a kind and gentle soul, loved me dearly and was my first playmate, although much older than me. Irina, the elder daughter, who behaved badly, often caused her mother much grief. Yet Grandmother almost loved her more than the other children. Vasily, the elder son, was my father.

Grandmother Stepanovna [Nikitenko] had a sturdy constitution. She died at one hundred years of age, with all her faculties intact. About five years before her death, only her vision had begun to weaken slightly.

2

◆•◆•◆•◆

My Parents

A few facts about my father's childhood have come my way. When Father, Vasily Mikhailovich Nikitenko, was eleven or twelve, one of Count Sheremetev's agents arrived in Alekseyevka to select boys for the count's choir. Father had a fine soprano voice, so he was sent to Moscow to join it. Even then the count's choir was famed for its artistry.

At that time Nikolai Petrovich was *the* Count Sheremetev. Like a true noble during the reign of Catherine II, he lived the high life. And that was all he was capable of doing. His name does not appear among the records of a single important event of that remarkable epoch. The only thing his contemporaries can recall about him is a magnificent affair he gave at one of his estates near Moscow for his court when it visited the city. Nor did his position as lord high chamberlain enhance him morally or intellectually. For all his splendor, he remained an insignificant courtier.

Among his numerous vassals he was known as a spoiled, capricious despot, not innately evil but terribly corrupted by his wealth. Drowning in luxury, he knew no law but what struck his fancy. Satiety finally reduced him to the point where he was repulsive even to himself, and he became as much of a burden to himself as he was to others.

Amidst his enormous wealth was not a single object that could give him genuine pleasure. Everything filled him with loathing—valuables, delicacies, drink, works of art, the obsequiousness of numerous lackeys scurrying to anticipate his wishes. And, finally, to make matters worse, nature denied him its most precious blessing—sleep, for which he himself said he would give millions, even half his domain.

About five or six years before his death he fell madly in love with a serf girl, an actress in his own family theater. Although not a remarkable beauty, she was so clever that she succeeded in forcing him to marry her. They say she was also very kind. And only she could soothe and tame this pitiful madman, who considered himself lord and master of many thousands of people but could not manage his own person. When his wife died, he apparently went completely berserk, keeping totally secluded, even refusing to see his friends. He abandoned his young son, Count Dimitry. Empress Mariya Fyodorovna assumed an active role in raising the boy. Although generous to him in other respects, nature endowed Dimitry with no special talents. With all the attention lavished on the young count, he made little progress in his studies or general development.[1]

Anyway, my father became a choirboy when the elder Count Sheremetev was his master. The Sheremetev choir ran a school where, besides studying music, young choirboys learned to read and write. Father displayed an unusual talent for everything he was taught. In his free time he read a great deal and acquired all sorts of knowledge, far above his station in life. He even learned French.

His intelligence, kindness, and talent, as well as his lively and pleasant manner, endeared him to everyone. Soon he became the most popular youngster among his choir mates, and even came to the attention of Count Sheremetev.

Later, Father would recall with emotion and gratitude the attention and affection lavished on him by the famous and unfortunate Degtiaryov. He had died early amidst intense suffering, neither shared nor understood by anyone. Degtiaryov was one of the victims of that wretched state of affairs on Earth where natural gifts are bestowed upon a person as if only to mock and disgrace him.[2]

The combination of talent and slavery ruined Degtiaryov. He was endowed with a real bent for art; he was a born musician. His rare talent early attracted the attention of experts. His master, Count Sheremetev, financed his education. The best teachers taught him music. For further training, the count sent the young serf Degtiaryov to Italy. There his musical compositions earned him a fine reputation. But returning to his homeland, Degtiaryov found a harsh despot. As legal owner of the physical person of this brilliant man, the count wanted to appropriate wholly his creative soul. The master ruled his serf-musician with an iron hand.

Degtiaryov composed many beautiful songs, mainly sacred music. He thought that his musical gifts would win him his freedom. How he longed and pleaded for it. But failing to gain it, the musician turned to drink to drown his misery. He drank large amounts, and often, too. As a result he was subjected to humiliating punishments, whereupon he would again turn to drink. Finally, he died, while composing moving prayers for the choir. To this day some of Degtiaryov's compositions are well known to lovers of church music.

In the meantime, my father's voice had changed. He was already seventeen, and, in keeping with custom in the count's administration, he was sent to one of the count's estates to do clerical work. The post was in Father's native village. His abilities and conduct were considered so outstanding that despite his youth, he was assigned the important position of chief clerk of Alekseyevka.

Alekseyevka was a vast, well-populated sloboda of some seven thousand people. Moreover, considered part of it were some ninety large and small hamlets in the area, which raised the figure to over twenty thousand.* A dual administration governed the sloboda. Some officials were appointed by the count: a bailiff; chief clerk, and solicitor. The others were elected by the sloboda commune. These were called *atamans*. Together these two groups of officials constituted the administration of the count's lands, and the head clerk of the count's chancery was in charge. There was

*For 1799–1800, the total number of male and female serfs was 33,398.

one more authority, the *mir* [commune assembly], which was responsible for discussing financial affairs, calling up recruits for military service, and dealing with other such matters on the count's lands related to general welfare and order.

This was the way the administration was organized to function, but in practice it worked out differently. All administrative power was actually concentrated in the hands of the count's agent or steward, but the power behind the community's mainspring and direction lay in the hands of the wealthy serfs, the so-called meshchane. They were mostly involved in trade, and many possessed considerable capital—anywhere from one thousand to two hundred thousand or more rubles.

Their main trade was in grain, tallow, and skins. As for their ways, nothing good could be said about them. These characters were degenerate Little Russians, ridiculed as renegades who had picked up nothing but vices from the *Moscals.** Inflated by their wealth, these Little Russians had contempt for those below them, that is, for people who had less than they. The meshchane swindled like crazy and owed their prosperity to crooked deals.

They lived ostentatiously, trying to imitate town-dwellers, dressing in elegant *zhupans* [a kind of jerkin worn by Poles and Ukrainians], and mixing Little Russian with Russian style. Frequently they threw drinking parties. Their homes were decorated lavishly but without taste. Wives and daughters strutted about in expensive cloaks of fine, smooth-textured woolens, *ochipoks* [caps] on their heads and gold-stitched apron skirts. They flaunted necklaces strung with large, expensive coral intermixed with silver and gold crosses and ducats.

Real Little Russians, their customs and ways, were to be found almost exclusively in hamlets outside Alekseyevka. There you could meet temperaments of true Homeric simplicity, goodhearted, honest folk, displaying that selfless hospitality for which Little Russians have always been famous. Thievery, deception, and Muscovite audacity and swindling were unheard of among

**Moscal* was a pejorative for Muscovite.

them. To Little Russians, Moscal—embodying all these characteristics—was a swearword.

In their patriarchal simplicity, these good-hearted farmers, unfamiliar with so-called civilized vices and moderate in their demands, would have lived very contentedly had not the meshchane oppressed them. After all, these peasants held the finest of allotments distributed by the mir, and paid a small quitrent to the pomeshchik. Unfortunately, here too, as often happens, wealth meant power at the service of some for the oppression of others.

The meshchane hurt these peasants by employing various devices, like trying to subject them to their authority, seizing small plots of productive land and woods, or by foisting on them community burdens that the meshchane were unwilling to bear. All this was done with impunity. The count's agents thought only of how they could enrich themselves. As for the elected representatives of the people or the commune assembly, they came from those same meshchane, who had at their disposal the elections as well as the votes in the commune assembly.

In the sloboda lived one more special class of people, the skilled artisans: tailors, cobblers, coopers, blacksmiths, and the like. They no longer worked the soil, but peddled their wares at village and town fairs. Running into Muscovites as they plied their trades, these artisans adopted their audacious manner, and for the most part were first-rate swindlers.

This was the kind of society to which Father was first summoned to live and work. He arrived in Alekseyevka in 1800 or 1801, when he had just turned eighteen. From the meshchane he received a cold welcome. Because of his youth, they scorned him and considered him unworthy of participating in the administration of the commune. They soon calmed down, however, when they realized that in my father they had an obedient tool. But Father had other things in mind. Nature had endowed him not only with special talents but also a passionate, noble heart.

Father was the kind of person fated to devote his life to struggling against the disorder around him and, in the end, to become its victim. As I explained earlier, he had acquired quite a bit of ed-

Female serf. Artist unknown.

ucation on his own, but to his misfortune, the intellectual and moral chasm between him and the people with whom he lived and on whom he depended was enormous. His education was haphazard, hardly relevant to his occupation. Lacking practical meaning, it only fired his imagination, filling his head with ideas that clashed with reality. And so it could not help him navigate the chasms and mire through which he was fated to pass. His education served as a brilliant and unanticipated, but dangerous advantage in his destiny.

My father had absolutely no understanding of his situation. From the miserable fate of that gifted serf-composer, Degtiaryov, he learned nothing. The heroes of stories and novels inhabited Father's world; he knew nothing of real life or the doers in the real world. He valued only what he found in the lofty spheres of reality or in his fantastic and strange embellishments of it. From his very first step in life, he rushed headlong to embrace the ghosts of valorous deeds, whose very names were unknown on the count's lands.

Soon after Father assumed his new post as chief clerk, he became convinced that brute force and wealth, not humanity and justice, played the main role in deciding people's affairs and fates. At that time he imagined that providence had chosen him to give his country a new social order, to strike a balance between the privileged and the poor, and to establish a system in which the poor could always find a way of defending themselves against the whim and tyranny of the privileged. That is, he undertook a task that no one else on earth had successfully tackled. So obsessed was he with the idea that he threw caution to the winds, forgetting that he was ill-equipped for the struggle against evil.

Suspecting Father of being a secret agent of the count, the rich meshchane were very upset at first. Their gloom vanished quickly when they saw they were dealing with a hotheaded, inexperienced youth who would be easy to handle. They calculated that it was only necessary to let his fervor build up a little more and wait patiently for the appropriate moment to strike.

In the beginning the local aristocrats still hoped to curb the unwelcome reformer by employing other tactics—peaceful ones. They wanted to marry him off to one of their kin and, by involving him in family matters, make him more compliant. But Father defied them all. Indeed, he rushed into marriage, but to someone of *his choice*.

Here's how it happened. One evening he was crossing the bridge over the Sosna River. A herd of cows and sheep was returning from pasture for the night. As usual, a crowd of women surged forth from the village to meet them. And in the crowd was an attractive, modest-looking young woman who caught my father's eye. From a friend he learned her name and that she was the daughter of a tailor of humble means who made sheepskin coats. His name was Yagnyuk. Father's fate was decided: the maiden's enchanting face possessed him.

Three days later he told his parents that he wanted to marry her. Grandmother Nikitenko was horrified when she learned that her son's intended wife was not the daughter of a rich meshchane but of a poor, obscure tailor.

Father was an important figure in the sloboda; first, because of his administrative position, and second, for his many talents. His Moscow education made him a real gentleman. All this gave his mother grounds to count on a far better marriage for her son. For a daughter-in-law she had hoped to have the daughter of some wealthy member of the sloboda's upper crust. To keep the young man from an unequal marriage she tried everything—she argued, pleaded, exhorted. All in vain. The romantic meeting, the girl's beauty, and her very poverty compelled the young man to stand firm.

But in his determination to marry Katrya, the girl of his choice, he did not follow Little Russian custom. Instead of sending matchmakers to the girl's parents, he approached them himself. They were Little Russians of the old school, in whom the spirit of former Ukrainians had not died. Honest and kind-hearted, they had nothing in common with the depraved world of the tradesmen and artisans. Farming was their chief occupation, but in his youth Yagnyuk had learned to sew sheepskin coats. And now he earned extra money with this skill, so his family always managed to get by.

My future Grandfather Yagnyuk and his family lived on the shore of the Sosna River, in a small, whitewashed hut with a thatched roof. Behind their dwelling, sloping down to the river's edge, bloomed their kitchen garden, with rows of cabbage, peas, beets, corn, and a variety of flowers. How strikingly beautiful were the luxuriant carnations and gigantic sunflowers, the poppies in a riot of colors, the aromatic tansy, marigolds, bluebells, ginger, and cornflowers. Later on, the kitchen garden suffered from my forays, especially where sweet peas curled around supple, long stamens. Across the river, opposite the kitchen garden, stood the cherry orchard, which was Grandmother Yagnyuk's paradise when she was a young girl. And later, her daughter's. Finally mine, too. There, in a dense grove, stood apple, cherry, and pear trees laden with fruit through summer and autumn. The joy of my childhood. More about that later.

Now, back to my story.

The elderly parents of my future mother were struck dumb when they learned why such an important guest as the chief clerk—my future father—had come to see them.

"How can it be," exclaimed the old woman, "that our Katrya would become your wife? What kind of match would that be? We are poor and simple folk, and you are an educated fellow, a gentleman, and a handsome one to boot. Katrya has nothing, honest to goodness, only some skirts, slips, a few kerchiefs."

My father burst into some exalted prose. Naturally, the old woman didn't understand a word of it. But in the end they decided to summon Katrya and ask if she would agree to marry the chief clerk, Vasily Mikhailovich Nikitenko. Bewildered, trembling and blushing, Katrya replied that she would do whatever her parents wished.

About three weeks later the wedding took place, to the secret displeasure of the bridegroom's mother, and to the astonishment of Alekseyevka's upper crust, who from then on hated the renegade and became more determined in their intentions to ruin him.

It is a difficult task to sketch a portrait of my mother from stories passed down to me about her youth and from my own memories. She was a remarkable woman. Life gave her nothing but suffering. Yet, with a rare dignity, she trod her hard path and went to her grave with the halo of a righteous woman.

In her youth she was known as a beauty, and I still remember her that way. Her delicate, regular features reflected her gentleness. As she matured, her manner and bearing acquired a special gracefulness and majesty. She was taller than average and had a

Serf wedding. Artist unknown.

fine figure. Her soft, black hair lay around her high forehead. Most striking of all were her dark brown eyes, in which shone so much tenderness and goodness.

Whoever met Mother could not help but like and respect her. She had no education but possessed those fortunate abilities that help a woman adjust easily to the customs, habits, and ideas of a different, more refined social circle. In his intellectual development, my father was far above her. Recognizing this, my mother respectfully deferred to him. She tried to understand his views and sympathized, if not with his quixotic impulses and the play of his fantasy, then with the noble aspirations that forged his character.

Mother was endowed with boundless native intelligence, which never failed to develop and grow stronger with the passage of time. It was remarkably reliable and sound, devoid of haughtiness and subtle without affectation. In it she always found a solid anchor, where her husband's more venturous but less flexible mind easily found the ground slipping away from under it.

My father's life was like a frail canoe tossed by waves from side to side, from one extreme to the other. He was a plaything of the strangest fate, a fate full of contradictions and bitter disappointments. On the one hand he seemed to take advantage of the benefits and assets offered by his independent, even prestigious position. On the other hand, he could be trampled on like a worm. Although a heroic figure for his broad intellect and talents, and for the pride with which he stood up for his human dignity, he was a poor actor in the role which befell him.

In Father's relations with people there were many contradictions. Chance constantly pushed him into contact with people whose formal education and social status were superior to his own. Yet they willingly treated him as an equal and many of them became his close friends. I have in my keeping some of my father's correspondence, which shows the respect and sympathy these people had for him.

This was the milieu my mother entered, equipped only with a fine heart, a sound mind, and feminine instinct. She adjusted to an alien environment and was able to combine the rigorous execution of the responsibilities of her sex with the demands of an unusual situation. In the kitchen, at the spinning wheel, wielding a needle and thread, my mother was a zealous worker, cook, seamstress, and nursemaid to her children. Moreover, she could be seen conversing sedately with the town's important figures, modestly but at ease, as if she had always lived among them. In general she handled everything simply and appropriately. I can't say that her conversation was brimming with wit, but she spoke interestingly, often flavoring her speech with original Little Russian humor.

But Mother's chief strength lay in her heart and character. She was the embodiment of kindness and selflessness. Of course she knew there was evil in the world. She herself had experienced it. But she simply couldn't understand how anyone could do evil, how anyone could do anything but good. No one could compare with her endurance and courage in the face of the blows fate delivered. Everything that can poison a life befell her: mental anguish, poverty, deprivation, persecution, and the roughest and most terrible shocks. Calamities and misfortunes, it seemed, argued over which would finally overwhelm the fine, noble soul of this woman, who was guilty only of living. But who witnessed the depth and pain of her sorrows? Perhaps only God, to whom she poured out her heart in quiet, humble prayer, not asking why, as a result of what laws, such a heavy yoke was placed on her.

In the course of time, hostile circumstances produced changes in my father's character. He grew more distrustful of people. His view of life became skeptical and, of his own fate, gloomier and more alarming. Meanwhile, my mother's character continued to develop. Under the pressure of misfortune, it only grew stronger and became fully formed. Raised as she was among simple, ignorant folk, it is remarkable that in her religious beliefs my mother shunned superstitions and prejudices that so often are embraced as gospel. Her good sense correctly distinguished the honest and reasonable from the contrived and superficial. In Mother's eyes, only good morals and manners were important, not blind obedience to custom.

On the other hand, my father's religious beliefs, like all his ideas, were strikingly original but full of contradictions. For example, he greatly admired Voltaire but was rather troubled by the author's skepticism. Still, Father was pious and spoke only with respect of "divine matters." He certainly never scorned church rituals. For any important event in our family life, he always invited the priest to say prayers, although often it was hard to find the money to pay him. At prayers he always worshipped reverently. In their wake, he would scoff again at Voltaire's antireligious attacks, especially at the philosopher's derision of priests and monks.

3

◆•◆•◆•◆

Father's First Attempt to Introduce Truth Where It Wasn't Wanted

After the wedding, Father took his bride to his parents' home, believing he could continue living there as before. But soon this turned out to be impossible. His mother could not forgive him for a marriage that had shattered her dreams. And as a woman who spoke her mind, she made her displeasure with her daughter-in-law very clear. Naturally, the young woman, my future mother, became the butt of Grandmother's wrath. Neither the maiden's youth, beauty, nor total submissiveness could assuage Grandma Stepanovna Nikitenko's feelings.

Father could either remain a silent witness to the undeserved insults and humiliation heaped daily upon his young wife or move with her from his parents' home. He chose to leave.

His salary was low, but so was the cost of living in Alekseyevka. Since the needs of the couple were modest, setting up a household of their own was not too difficult. Father's youth, relative contentment in a loving home, and, chiefly, his satisfaction with small pleasures and a faith in the future created an environment in which, for a time, he considered himself happy. You could call this stage of Father's life his golden, idyllic period. But the idyll was short-lived. Rapidly it turned into a drama whose sad denouement left him at death's door.

It didn't take long for Father's social activism to take shape. From the very beginning of his employment as chief clerk he assumed the role of defender of the weak and enemy of the power-

Serf blessing his son, who has been conscripted for army service. Lithograph, artist unknown. State Historical Museum.

Seeing off a serf conscripted for army service. Lithograph, artist unknown. State Historical Museum.

ful. A series of incidents began that revealed his dialectical skill in disputing unjust claims and his determination to pursue evil. This intensified the vigilance of his enemies and roused their anger. A bitter battle began. Unfortunately, Father stood completely alone. It never occurred to him to acquire allies. In his youthful inexperience, he thought that it was enough to raise one's voice on the side of truth, and victory would be assured. Even later in life, he learned nothing from experience.

The Russian government declared a new drive for compulsory military service. Count Sheremetev had to supply a specific number of conscripts from the peasant community on his estate. The authorities manipulated the draft so that the grown sons of wealthy folk were exempt from this community burden. So it fell to the poor to bear it. Many families were deprived of their sole support, and even married men were called up. Such injustice angered my father.[1]

Father submitted an impassioned plea on behalf of a widow whose only son, her sole provider, was taken from her. But his protest was futile. Then he wrote directly to the count to expose all the recruiting abuses.

There was a terrible uproar. As was customary, the count sent inspectors authorized to investigate disruptions and take measures to prevent their reoccurrence. And what did these esteemed guardians of morality do? First they accepted enormous bribes from the guilty. Then they declared them innocent, practically saints. They labeled my father a slanderer, discharged him from his post, and threw him in prison to await the count's orders.

But Father did not accept his fate. He figured on tricking his enemies and getting his own report to the count before his accusers did. How could he manage this? As an important criminal, he was guarded closely and was not allowed to have paper, pen, or ink.

But my mother, permitted to see the prisoner, sneaked the supplies to him during one of her visits. Folding some paper into a small wad, she smuggled it in under her cap. In those days Little Russian women wore a very roomy headdress with an expandable top. There she also concealed a pen. And ink? Mother slipped that to him inside a thick chunk of bread!

Two days later Father's letter describing his persecution was on its way to Count Sheremetev. Before Father's opponents had a chance to gather their wits, a strict order arrived to hold off on the case, release the prisoner, and send him to the count in Moscow. There, Father would personally present his version of the episode. What a blow this was to my father's opponents, while it filled him with great hopes. These quickly dissipated.

True, the count heard him out, but he lent a more willing ear to the calumny of his opponents. They declared that Father had a restless, disturbed mind and that he was more concerned with the welfare of mankind than with the count's. In the end my father was bound in chains and returned to the sloboda, where he was to live under the surveillance of the local authorities. From the moment he set foot in the village, a series of misfortunes, humiliations, persecutions, and deprivations began.

First of all, Father had to think about earning his daily bread. He made a mental inventory of everything he had learned during the years he had spent in the count's choir in Moscow, where choirboys also received an education. Adding this to the knowledge acquired on his own from books, he decided to put his small capital to use.

In a small village about fifteen versts* from Alekseyevka lived the mistress of an estate, Avdotya Borisovna Aleksandrova. This memorable individual, a type found among Russian *pomeshchitsas* [noblewomen landowners] at the beginning of the nineteenth century, deserves more than a footnote in my memoirs. Besides, she was my godmother. How well I remember her now, some forty years later. Tall, rather buxom, with a coarse face and masculine bearing, she had a brusque, dictatorial manner that left an unpleasant impression. Although not particularly wealthy, she lived like a noblewoman. She entertained a great deal, especially the officers from a regiment quartered nearby. Rumor had it that she

*One verst equals 0.66 miles or 1.067 kilometers.

treated them to substantial food and drink, as well as her fading charms. Her education did not go beyond reading, writing, and learning to dress and behave as befits the mistress of an estate. Nevertheless, she was full of pretensions. Living in idle luxury, she had little to do with the management of the estate and ran the household with the help of a steward, butler, housekeepers, and the like.

This feudal lady possessed all the characteristics of a despot. She owned several hundred slaves, yet she herself was enslaved by wicked inclinations. Scourge and fright to those unfortunates under her power, she was a holy terror to the house serfs in particular, simply because she had more contact with them than with serfs working outside the manor house.

My recollections of her are limited to my childhood. I vividly remember how she personally thrashed her favorite housemaid, Pelagaya, with a rolling pin and boxed the ears of other servants.

In the maidservants' room. Lithograph, artist unknown.

She punished her other housemaid, Dunyasha, by shaving her head and forcing her to parade around the house for several days with a bar around her neck. She flogged all her female serfs with nettles. No one was outraged by this kind of behavior. It was perfectly acceptable in those days.

The mother of four children, Avdotya Borisovna managed to get permission for my father to move to her estate, to work as a teacher in her home. So, about two years before I was born, my parents moved to Udarovka. If I am not mistaken, that was in 1802.

The village was famous for its picturesque surroundings. The manor house stood on a high hill overlooking the Tikhnaya Sosna River. A magnificent stand of trees, including a variety of fruit trees and enormous oaks, lined the slope from the hilltop to the bank of the river. On the opposite side of the river lay a lush, flowery meadow adorned with clusters of almondleaf and daphne willows. A water mill stood by one of the graceful bends of the river. Here the water foamed and bubbled, and the distant sound of falling water reached the very top of the hill. The village, facing the manor house, fanned out along the hillside. The mistress of the manor housed my father and his bride in a small but tidy cottage next to an orchard. And it was here that I came into the world, in 1804 or 1805, in the second or third year after my parents had settled in Udarovka.

4

◆•◆•◆•◆

My Early Childhood

Although I can reach back into my toddler years, my memory retains only the most prominent features of people and events. Yet these recollections are very sharp and vivid. I can picture people, events, and places as if I were experiencing them now. Probably my earliest memories go back to age three—and even two. One is of feeling utterly miserable when I was ill with smallpox and was wheeled around the garden in a carriage. The other is of a hunchbacked lad, Tretyak. I was terrified of him, probably because of his pathetic appearance, although there was nothing frightening or repulsive about it.

I don't know why I wasn't vaccinated against smallpox. I suppose vaccination at that time was not as extensive in the provinces as it is today. This circumstance nearly cost me my life. I was stricken with an unusually virulent form of smallpox, but perhaps I owe my present good health to it. At a very early stage of my life the disease cleansed my body of its most powerful and destructive juices, and to this day barely noticeable scars remain on my face.

I was my parents' second child. Their firstborn, a daughter, died before she was two. I was born in March, on the twenty-first day, a day that my father took as a lucky sign. In those parts, this date marked nature's revival. Snow melts, rivers throw off mantels of ice, streams flow through mountains, water bubbles and whirls through hollows and ravines. Barely perceptible fuzzy verdure bursts into bloom on trees, and the first blue flowers peep through fields. The air rings with the song of skylarks. Trumpeting cranes,

Serf family. English engraving, first quarter of the nineteenth century.

sounding like French horns, head toward us in V-formation on their migration from the far South to a joyous East.

At my christening my godparents were pomeshchitsa Aleksandrova, the Udarovka proprietress; and Prince Zhevakhov, a captain or lieutenant in the cavalry who was very fond of my father. According to my mother I developed into a healthy, sturdy child, whose appearance others often admired. My godmother was very affectionate to me and treated me with sweets. I began to walk and talk at an early age, and my physical development proceeded at a normal rate.

I don't know exactly how long my father worked for pomeshchitsa Aleksandrova, perhaps three or four years. His life there was rather peaceful. From the pomeshchitsa and her children to the lowliest house serf, everyone loved him. Later I got to know the two young Aleksandrovs, son and daughter of the Udarovka lady of the manor. They spoke with gratitude of my father as the individual to whom they owed their development and the small store of knowledge that their modest education had given them. These pupils of my father were so unlike their impetuous and cruel mother. They were simple and good folk, without lordly or feudal ways.

Father's obligations to pomeshchitsa Aleksandrova came to an end. From his earnings he had saved enough to buy a small cottage in his native sloboda. How vividly I remember this modest refuge of my childhood, a pretty, cozy, Little Russian dwelling of two tidy rooms, consisting of a kitchen and pantry. The roof was covered with reeds, a measure of some prosperity, as cottages of other farmers lay modestly beneath straw. On the homestead stood a large barn, stable, chicken coop, and a shed for cows and sheep.

Of all the structures on our land, the gate captured my interest most of all. Above it, as is Little Russian custom, a pigeon house had been put together, where a great number of pigeons built nests and bred their progeny. I spent a lot of time visiting these lovable, graceful creatures, and they didn't avoid me. My appearance at the pigeon shed did not frighten the birds but pleased them enormously. I never went there empty-handed. Fluttering about and crowding around me, pecking corn from my hands, the birds were absolutely unafraid and trusting—like children with a sweet tooth flocking around a housekeeper as she emerges from the pantry laden with gingerbread cakes, nuts, and other sweets.

All God's creatures held a fascination for me. I had a great friendship with Garson, a venerable old dog who guarded our homestead conscientiously. And there was a large white cat, a pretty thing, but an awful rogue and thief. His antics drove Mama and the cook wild. The kitchen and the pantry were the targets of his raids. He would loot the foodstuffs and completely ignore the mice.

Our family wasn't the only victim. Our neighbors also suffered from his expeditions. One family had stored in their attic a bast bag of pork lard rendered for the holiday. That rogue contrived to nibble through the bag. He bored an opening in it, shaped like a door, and created for himself a sort of lodging with full board. Gradually the lard disappeared, and the cat put on a lot of weight. Soon all that remained of the lard was a hollow shell. The eve of the holiday arrived. The head of the household climbed into the loft, counting on the treat for himself and his family for the next day. He went up to the bag and out jumped the cat. The lard? Gone, every bit of it.

Complaints about this feline thief rained down from all sides. Finally the neighbors decided to hang him. And they did. But evidently they didn't tie the noose tight enough or they removed it too soon, and he revived. As everyone knows, crafty professional thieves are lucky. Some kindhearted people turned up and pleaded with the neighbors to forgive the cat in the hope that he had learned his lesson. For the next three or four weeks the cat behaved well but then he returned to his old ways. They hung him a second time. And this time, to make sure, they left him hanging on the rope a full two weeks. I was unaware of my little friend's misbehavior and cried bitterly at losing him. He had always been so eager to play with me!

Behind our homestead was a fair-sized piece of land, which my father expeditiously transformed into an orchard. He planted cherry, apple, bergamot [a pear-shaped orange], and pear trees, as well as oaks and maples. All this he designed with a skill that left our neighbors surprised and envious. However, Father did not live long enough to enjoy the fruits of his labors.

Teaching was still his main source of income; it was a skill that rescued him whenever he found himself in dire circumstances. The Little Russians at that time displayed a far greater interest in learning than did the Great Russians. If Little Russia, before its unification with Russia, was more educated than it is now, it's not surprising. In my day every fair-sized village had a school, maintained mainly by clerical sextons.[1]

The curriculum in these schools was divided into four parts.

The first part covered the ABCs. Letters were pronounced in the old style: *az, buki, vedi,* and so on. From syllables the children progressed to the Book of Hours, then to the Psalter, and last of all to writing. Some schools taught only reading. At the conclusion of each part of the curriculum, the pupil brought the teacher a jug of milk pudding. The pupil's parents, in addition to paying a contractual fee, rewarded the teacher with a bundle of *bubliks* [bagels] or a knish. Those who were a little better off gave the teacher a lamb, maybe a sack of flour or wheat, and the like.

Regardless of the pedagogical method used in those schools, all instruction was backed up by lashes (with three or four thongs) and by rulers for blows on an upturned bare hand. Saturday was the most important day in school life. On Saturdays naughty pupils were punished for mischievous acts performed during the school week, while pupils who were completely innocent of wrongdoing received punishment for possible future misbehavior.

However, there were schools where general flogging was not mandatory. The school that my father established was one, and its teaching methods and atmosphere differed from the norm. There, the children learned to read from books printed in the Russian language. In other schools children learned to read from prayer books in Old Church Slavonic, such as the Book of Hours and the Psalter. Also, all of my father's pupils had to study writing and arithmetic. The birch rod took the place of the whip, and was very rarely used, and only in extreme cases. The meshchane, the highest class in the sloboda, sent their children to my father's school, and, generally, so did those inhabitants who were concerned about their offspring's education. In addition, we had boarding pupils from distant homesteads, even from the town of Biryuch.

The tuition fees Father received were not large, but he supplemented them with income from produce he raised on our land. Besides, in our region basic necessities were inexpensive. We lived comfortably with refinements hardly known to others in the sloboda. We drank tea. For our dinner some dishes were prepared and served town-style. Father wore frock coats and tails. Mother wore a kerchief round her head like a townswoman instead of a colorful Little Russian cap. And instead of a paneled skirt and corset stays, she wore a German garment of rather ridiculous cut—a so-called long dress. Me they clothed in a little frock coat.

Father was a stickler for dress, even at home, and Mother willingly conformed. What's more, he had a penchant for luxury and had no idea how to save for a rainy day. No sooner would our financial situation show signs of improvement than things would appear in our home that, in a pinch, one could very well manage without. And the entertainment of "good folk," a sign of Little Russian hospitality, grew more frequent and lavish.

None of this really improved our family's well-being, but Mother's good sense and frugality were an effective counterweight to Father's extravagance. Nevertheless, he was very moderate in respect to his own person. He neither drank wine nor cared for any strong drink. He was content with a small glass of liqueur before dinner. He loved sweets, fruits, jam, and various imported delicacies but ate them in moderation, enjoying them more for their quality than their quantity.

The delectable image of a chap called Sidork will never leave me. Every year, on his winter sales route from Moscow, Sidork carted heaps of gingerbread, *pastilas,* raisins, and similar treats. He always dropped in to visit us on the way to the pomeshchiks who were his customers. If Father had money on hand, the man resumed his journey with a considerably lighter sleigh.

My recollections of this stage of my childhood are incomplete and fragmentary. I remember that I learned reading and writing along with Father's other pupils. I also spent lots of time with Grandmother Stepanovna [Nikitenko]. At that time she succeeded in almost completely diverting my attention from my other grandmother, *Babusa* Emelyanovna, as she was called in Little Russian. I remember playing "feathers" with my Aunt Yelizabeta, pretending we were geese, ducks, and chickens. But most of all I loved going hunting with Father. Often the whole family would go to the woods nearby, where Father had discovered a beautiful spot we called Elfin Meadow. There, in the shade of a magnificent oak, we drank tea and gathered medicinal herbs for Father. Having some knowledge of healing, he dried the herbs for medicines.

I can hardly describe the pleasure these outings gave me. I wasn't old enough to consciously appreciate the beauty of nature, but was instinctively drawn to it. I was completely happy in the fields and woods and always willingly traded play with other children for a solitary stroll far from human habitation. Generally I didn't care to have lots of friends, but I developed warm friendships with one or two boys to whom I had taken a real liking. At times I was overwhelmed by the urge to perform daring deeds, but this was due more to a lack of understanding of danger than innate courage. Once I tried to shave and accidentally cut my hands. To this day traces of this unsuccessful attempt are still visible.

On another occasion, I stole out of the house and ran down to the river. There stood a boat that had not been tied to a mooring. In an instant I was in it. The boat floated away from the shore and was pulled along by the current. Fortunately Mother was nearby in the kitchen garden. When she saw me in the middle of the narrow but deep river, waving my little hands joyfully, she was scared to death. Somehow she managed to talk me into sitting quietly and then summoned a worker for help. The man swam to the boat and set me ashore safe and sound.

But my crowning exploit was one that nearly burnt down our house and could have set the entire countryside afire. Father was an ardent hunter. Watching him in action inspired me, and I decided I would shoot birds, too. One day, when he wasn't home, I jumped at the opportunity. I took down his gun from the wall, loaded it, and went outside. There, on a pussy willow, a flock of sparrows were chirping merrily, and they became the object of my desire. To get a good shot at my target, I climbed up to the roof of our cottage and fired. From the priming-pan of the gun, sparks hit the thatched roof, and if not for the presence of workers nearby, a disaster would have occurred. As soon as they saw what I had done, they rushed to the roof and doused the fire before it could spread. When Father returned and heard about my prank, he gave me a licking he knew I would never forget.

In general you couldn't call me a brat because I wasn't bold or wild. Probably because Father was so strict with me, I was timid and shy. I was easily carried away, drawn by some passion or predilection. I did things that, for daring, far surpassed the usual pranks played by my contemporaries.

5

Exile

Father was peacefully occupied working his plot of land and teaching the local inhabitants to read and write. He was unaware that misfortune was about to strike. He no longer held an official position in the sloboda and was not involved in community affairs, but his enemies continued to regard him with suspicion. He had been a witness to their lawlessness, although he now kept silent about it. They were nevertheless determined to get rid of him. I don't know what pretext they concocted to discredit him in the eyes of Count Sheremetev, but suddenly an order came from Moscow to confiscate all our belongings and exile us to one of the count's estates in a remote region of Smolensk Province. There we settled in the village of Churilovka, in Gzhatsk County. This was the usual punishment the count's agents meted out for real or imagined misdeeds.[1]

This undeserved blow threw poor Father into despair. In an instant it destroyed the bit of comfort that his years of honest labor had won for us. There was no investigation, no trial: blind, despotic whim decided everything. Little Russians are attached to their homeland. They mourn separation from its clear, balmy skies and fruitful fields. They fraternize reluctantly with the Moscals. This sudden, fatal exile tore my parents from their native home, from bounteous nature that had responded so generously to their selfless love.

For some reason that I can't remember, the count's manager also summoned me to the office. The whole scene is still vivid in my mind. My father, in a simple, uncovered sheepskin coat, is standing in the middle of a filthy room. His face is pale, his lips are trembling, and his eyes are filled with tears. Probably he has just received the count's sentence. Meanwhile, at home everything was topsy-turvy. The authorities were confiscating our belongings . . . Then I see all of us in a spacious covered sleigh. On one side of me sits my morose father. On the other side is my mother, holding in her lap a year-old baby bundled in a short sheepskin coat. This was Grisha, her second son.

Two guards accompanied us to Churilovka. Etched in my memory is the image of an enormous man with a sullen face and extraordinary strength called Zhurba. For fun he broke horseshoes, thick iron keys, and bent a silver ruble with his fingers. Still, he was as kind and simple-hearted as a child. Especially amusing were his antics whenever a string of sleighs loaded with merchandise headed toward us and blocked our way. They didn't always move to the side as quickly as Zhurba wished. Taking matters into his own hands, he grabbed each sleigh by the corner and, one after another, overturned them into the snowdrifts. The bewildered drivers only scratched their heads, exclaiming, "Good heavens!" Although he was one of our guards, Zhurba's behavior amused me, and his kindness and warmth gave my parents some solace.

I have no idea how long we rode, but at last we arrived at our place of exile. Before us stood a small hamlet of about thirty homesteads. Poking up through a snow-filled ravine, they looked like clumps of swampgrass or rotten haycocks. Behind them stood a forest of murmuring pines. The landscape evoked an inexpressible despair.

With a sinking feeling, Father and Mother crossed the threshold of the smoke-filled cabin where they were assigned to live under the same roof as its owners. The cramped, smoky quarters, the presence of cattle, the typical Moscovite sloppiness—legendary to Little Russians—left my parents depressed and disgusted. But in a mass of evil, there is always a mite of goodness concealed, and you must not shut your eyes to it. Everything around us looked dreary and ugly, but in the background of this gloomy scene, a

Serf dwelling. Engraving from the Le Prince collection.

more comforting phenomenon quickly emerged. The area residents gave us a hearty welcome. They didn't treat us as despicable exiles but as people who had been unjustly punished.

The inhabitants of Churilovka lived in the woods, isolated from the main avenues of communication and manufacturing centers, thus retaining a kind of primitive honesty and generosity.

They waged a cruel struggle with the North's inhospitable earth, literally sweating blood to wrench from the soil the meager grain to feed themselves. But hard labor and poverty went hand in hand with a feeling of brotherhood and compassion for those more destitute than they were. Thanks to them we did not feel as lonely in exile as expected.

Gradually we adjusted to our new home. Our nearest neighbor was a very old but active woman, in whose cabin I quickly became a daily visitor. She was a better housekeeper than her neighbors, and she got the heat going so early that it was almost smokeless all day. I was especially pleased with this, as we absolutely could not get used to the smoke in our cabin. For some reason there were very few young girls in Churilovka. I can remember two in all. They pampered me but I preferred the good-looking one, Domna, with her rosy cheeks and pug nose. Even now I can picture her clearly.

I was about six or seven years old, but I had already learned to read and write. For the first half-year in Churilovka my studies were at a standstill. It was my fault, because during the winter I had acquired a new skill, weaving *lapti* [bast shoes]. I was terribly proud that I wore shoes I had made myself. And with them I kept up with the other boys when we played and ran about in the deep snowdrifts. When summer came I picked mushrooms, gathered sorrel—my only delicacy at that time—and collected young fir cones, whose reddish color and subtle, resinous fragrance were so appealing.

After we'd spent almost half a year in Churilovka, our situation improved significantly. Father made friends with local pomeshchiks. Some of them asked him to tutor their children. Pomeshchik Pyotr Grigorovich Markov, from a hamlet called, I think, Andronovo, became especially friendly with Father. I believe Andronovo was about fifteen versts from Churilovka and the same distance from the chief county town of Gzhatsk. Pomeshchik Markov managed to get permission from the local authorities to let my father live on his estate. We were delighted to accept his invitation, although not without regret on leaving the good folk of Churilovka.

In Andronovo, Markov settled our family in a bright, clean, smokeless dwelling—a former bathhouse. Father tutored Markov's son and daughter according to a fixed schedule of days and hours. In addition, he rode to other pomeshchiks' homes to give lessons. I recall him speaking very highly of one Mikhail Stepanovich Aleksandrov, a pomeshchik from the village of Zvezdunov. This man had a grown daughter whom Father tutored. For me it was a real holiday each time he returned from there. Usually he arrived home with a sack full of apples or with peaches or apricots. Zvezdunov had bountiful greenhouses, and after each lesson Father's pupil never forgot to send me a treat.

In Andronovo a basic change took place in my social relationships. I didn't go around with the village boys but associated with the children of pomeshchiks who visited Andronovo often or went there for lessons. I studied with these boys and played with them.

My father and mother kept a sharp eye on me. They worried that I might develop bad habits and tried hard to shield me from bad influences. It's not surprising that I was polite and obedient. Probably my obedience was due to the frequent floggings I received. Despite Father's iron hand, I was a lively, bright boy.

I had certain family responsibilities, such as minding my little brother Grisha, who then was about two. I tended him no worse than any nanny. But once he gave me an awful scare. Our yard was on a hill overlooking a pond. That day Grisha raced down the slope and, arms flapping, flew into the pond. Scared to death, I rushed in after him. Fortunately the water wasn't deep and, though it wasn't easy, I dragged him safely to shore.

Barely had our family gotten on its feet when a new disaster struck. We lived next door to the manor-house kitchen. The autumn was warm and dry. Then, one afternoon, a fire broke out in the kitchen. Instantly the flames spread to adjoining structures, engulfing our modest refuge with its straw roof. My parents were resting after dinner and were unaware of the danger threatening them. Fortunately the pomeshchik saw the fire and literally pushed them out of the burning house. Still half asleep, they were confused and hastily grabbed some unimportant things. The fire consumed everything we owned. But the manor house was saved.

When the fire broke out, my brother and I were playing outdoors. I grabbed Grisha's hand and started to run, not knowing where I was headed. Suddenly we found ourselves in the forest. It was late evening when our rescuers found us crying, trembling with fear and shivering from cold. Father and Mother were left utterly destitute. But this time, too, good folk helped them. Markov gave us a new dwelling and some clothing and household utensils. Other pomeshchiks followed his example. But what touched us most was the kindness of the good people of Churilovka. For several days after the fire, folk from that poor, tiny hamlet kept coming to Andronovo, hauling supplies for us on wretched-looking horses. Soon our new home was overflowing with pieces of canvas, sacks of flour, spools of thread; with everything these people had earned by the sweat of their brow. And all this was offered so simply, so sincerely, with such warmth, that Mother wept each time they appeared, and again when she bade them goodbye.

The second winter arrived, and our second year in exile passed. Father recovered from the fire. He had many pupils, and our financial situation was not bad. But my parents were consumed with nostalgia for their native land and the thought that they were nothing more than exiles. Father, especially, yearned for Alekseyevka, for its sweet-smelling fields and copses. Besides, no matter what the cost, he wanted to clear his name.

In the meantime, the old count had died. He left an only son, Dimitry. As a minor, the child was placed under guardianship in St. Petersburg. Among the guardians were Senators Alekseyev and Danaukov and other people of position and influence. But Mariya Fyodorovna, the wife of Paul I, assumed the role of chief guardian of the young count.

With these changed circumstances, my father planned an extremely daring act. Until this point he had written many letters to the young count's guardians, complaining of undeserved persecution, but never received a reply. Now he decided to appeal to the tsarina herself and, through her, seek justice. He wanted to return to his native home, but to return with honor and dignity. For that reason, among others, he asked the authorities for permission to appear in St. Petersburg for a personal discussion of his case.

Father's friends, thunderstruck by the audacity of a direct appeal to the tsarina, tried to dissuade him. But he entertained an unshakable faith in the goodness of her majesty, whose name was pronounced with love everywhere in Russia. Stubbornly he went ahead with his plan. He sent a letter to St. Petersburg, supported by the signatures of Gzhatsk pomeshchiks who testified to his impeccable conduct. I still have a copy of his letter. Its sincerity, energy, and literary language are striking. Father was very adept with the pen. Later on he often had occasion to write and compose business documents for himself and others that were considered exemplary.

My father's trust in the tsarina was not misplaced. At the end of the winter, instructions arrived from the count's guardians that directed the local authorities to return us to our native home. In addition, in keeping with my father's request, permission was granted for him to journey to St. Petersburg to present his case in person.

My parents' spirits soared. Our patrons, the Gzhatsk pomeshchiks, were utterly delighted with the success of my father's bold undertaking and arranged a respectable send-off for us.

Our preparations for departure didn't take long. Once again we set out on a winter journey. To the farewell wishes and blessings of our dear Churilovka friends, we departed for Alekseyevka.

6

◆•◆•◆•◆

Home from Exile

Father's return to his native soil was a real triumph. His enemies were glum, but the other inhabitants of the sloboda expressed their pleasure for all to hear. The Little Russians are known as a poetic people. No matter how insignificant an occasion or event, they love to set it to music. On our return we learned that they had composed a special song about us when we were sent into exile. But I can only remember the first two lines:

> Oy, the latest modes are reported,
> Vasilka to icy waters was deported.*

Now the song was replaced by congratulations and hearty welcomes, showered upon us from all sides. When we entered the sloboda the first person we met was one of my father's best friends, Father Petry. At first instant the priest was dumbfounded. Then he stopped his horses and rushed to kiss us, all the time interjecting thanks to God. We had to tear ourselves from his embrace.

After we settled in and Father rested a bit, he began to prepare for a new journey—to St. Petersburg. The count's office staff received orders to give Father money for travel expenses, and was told not to rush him or limit his freedom. He decided to wait until the spring because of his poor health. Although my father had a

*Vasilka = Vasily, Nikitenko's father.

sturdy constitution and was only twenty-seven, the troubles of exile and Churilovka's cruel climate had taken their toll. He began to fall ill frequently. Sadly, this would not prove to be the worst bane of his existence. As for the journey to St. Petersburg, the provincials of that time viewed it like a journey to the end of the earth. Everyone bade him farewell as if it meant goodbye forever.

Probably my mother was left without any means of support. Now she had three children to care for: a third son, Semyon, was born just before Father's departure. I remember that in his absence we led an existence of want and deprivation, barely having enough to eat each day. Our belongings, which the count's agents had confiscated when we were sent into exile, were not returned to us. Our home had been given to strangers and was finally destroyed. The orchard that Father had lovingly planted was torn up, leveled to the bare ground.

All that remained was the right to part of the income from a mill to which Father and his partners had acquired exclusive rights before he was exiled.[1] Now the partners disputed Father's right. Litigation began, whose outcome would depend wholly on those same hostile agents in the count's office.

At first, the deacon of one of the sloboda churches sheltered us. He gave us cramped but clean quarters. We were desperately poor. The best of our possessions, all the farewell presents the Gzhatsk pomeshchiks had given us, gradually disappeared. Mother sold them in order to feed us.

Now I was dressed no better than other peasant lads: a large shirt, rarely changed, and a pair of drawers tied with a woolen sash. For very special occasions, I was clothed in a nankeen vest over my everyday clothes, with strict instructions not to stain or tear it. Because I went barefoot, my feet were covered with cuts and scratches. In Churilovka I had learned to weave bast shoes, and I gladly would have worn them here. Had I chosen to go outdoors in them, the other children most certainly would have thrown stones at me, because Little Russians had not yet adopted this kind of footwear.

When Father was here, at least my education followed a spe-

Serf youth. Oil painting by A. G. Venetsianov.

cific routine. Scheduled hours were devoted to studies, or at least reading books. Afterward, I would watch my little brother or help Mother with household tasks. Strict punishment awaited me for any prank, even the most innocent, as well as for the slightest mistake in reading or writing. Father never indulged me in anything. He always had the rod ready to use on me. Only on very rare occasions did he show me affection. Still, this didn't mean that he didn't love me or my brothers. He was embittered by misfortune, and this caused him to become extremely strict, harsh, and impatient. But to some extent my father's innate impetuous temperament was partly responsible.

His inner world was full of worries. His mind always gravitated toward the lofty and sublime, but bitter reality kept him dependent on the most worthless people and his most petty needs. This contributed to his erratic behavior and discontent. Family life did not seem to satisfy him. To sweat, to work solely for his daily bread, was not what he wanted of life. He aimed at life's loftier goals. But for him there was no such role to play, and he remained unemployed and almost unable to feed us. This inner discord could not help but affect my father's relationship with the family. As the eldest child, I more often than anyone was subjected to the outbursts of his morbid anger. At the same time he was proud of me and pinned great hopes on me.

With his departure for St. Petersburg, I found myself, as they say, at liberty. Father did not instruct Mother to send me to the sloboda school. He feared, not without reason, that I was more likely to pick up bad ways at the school than learn something worthwhile. To tell the truth, there was nothing I could have studied there because the only subjects were reading and writing, and I already could read and write as well as the schoolmaster himself. Mother could not educate me further.

But about this time I began to develop a passion for reading. Father had a substantial collection of books, and I could freely follow my penchant. I read indiscriminately, everything I could lay my hands on, preferring fairy tales and stories to textbooks. In any case, this diverted me from the rough play of my contemporaries and prevented me from becoming a street urchin. Simultaneously, another penchant began to surface—the urge to become a writer. I poured out my thoughts and feelings on any scrap of paper I could get ahold of. I put them in the form of letters to friends, who, of course, never received them. And if they had, they wouldn't have been able to read them because they read poorly or not at all.

In this way, unconsciously, I began to live my own inner life and seek changes in it that my outside life did not give me. Among the circle of children with whom I mingled, I enjoyed a certain kind of respect. We weren't close friends, and they, without any desire or effort on my part—at least in that period of my childhood—easily fell under my influence. I wasn't considered a bold or cunning lad. Nor was I a leader in their games or pranks. Among my peers I was known only as the most "learned." Even among the grown-ups I acquired this reputation, and some of them—including our host, the deacon—commissioned me to teach their children to read and write. Mother was not particularly happy about this, feeling that my work was a kind of remuneration for the shelter given our family.

Among the people who touched my life during that period, I remember well the old priest, Father Stefan. He was terribly eccentric, good-natured, but inclined to be impetuous and obstinate. Once he got into a fight in church with the deacon. He was brought to trial, but a timely bribe at the consistory rescued him from misfortune. A jolly fellow and a rake, he visited us often, saying he'd come to cheer us up.

At that time my favorite activity was to assist during divine services. How proud I felt when I appeared before the parishioners with candlesticks in my hands during the ceremony of the Gospel or when I passed the censer to the deacon. With what pleasure I performed the duty of a bellringer! I never missed a service, requiem, or christening. During each of these rituals, there was a task for me, such as reading the Psalter or something similar. For such deeds I received a reward, a few coins or a string of breadrings. How this inflated my self-esteem, making me feel as if I were on a par with deacons, sextons, readers, and bellringers, whom, at that time, I considered very important people.

Of all the other activities I enjoyed, none gave me as much pleasure as hanging around the kitchen garden and the little cherry orchard on the other side of the Sosna River. In their love for me, both my grandmothers—Emelyanovna and Stepanovna—tried to outdo each other. My mother's mother, Grandma Emelyanovna, due to her modest opinion of herself, yielded first place to Grandma Stepanovna, who occupied a higher position in the sloboda and associated exclusively with the wives of priests and tradesmen. Grandma Emelyanovna timidly expressed her affection for me, believing that I, "such an educated lad, such a fine boy, who wears a waistcoat on Sundays, even boots now and then, and is respected by sextons and deacons—almost a young gentleman," was above her kin's claims to my affection. She felt that the right to show affection and receive mine belonged only to Grandma Stepanovna.

Simple-hearted Granny Emelyanovna hadn't the slightest suspicion that on her side lay an enormous advantage. Her kitchen garden, with its bed of peas and cherry orchard, had won me over, whereas Stepanovna shunned everything related to rural life. She was a town-dweller and didn't give a care about the state of her kitchen garden. It was overrun with tall weeds, and bushes of nightshade threatened to take over. Her yard was the picture of desolation, while Emelyanovna's left quite the opposite impression. It was full of life and movement. A cow on a tether mooed, a foppish rooster strutted among the chickens, a gander strolled sedately with its goslings, ducks wallowed in a puddle, a frisky goat ambled along some logs.

I loved both grannies. In the summer, especially, I preferred the less prosperous one but better manager. When I visited Grandma Emelyanovna, the poor old soul was beside herself with joy. In turn, I felt more relaxed and free in her home than anywhere else. There wasn't a corner of her cottage that I was forbidden to explore. And when I was in her garden, the beds of peas and flowers were all mine to enjoy.

I can see it all now. The cherries were ripening. My beloved granny and I climbed into a little boat and crossed to the other side of the river, to the orchard. There Emelyanovna tied a jug around her waist and filled it with fresh berries. And I scrambled up a tree and sat on a branch like God's bird and enjoyed myself to my heart's content. Now and then the voice of an old man warned me not to break the branches, but more important, not to break my neck or, like a new Absalom, get myself hung in the tree. From time to time I heard the jingling of a rattle that the watchman used to chase away the ruthless cherry starlings. Like dark thunder clouds, these birds descended on the orchard and, if you let them, in no time at all stripped the trees of the ripest berries. To some extent the rattle limited their bold forays.

It was hot. Not a leaf stirred. We settled down for dinner in the shade of a fruit tree or beneath the watchman's shelter. We kept a watchful eye on the curd dumplings in sour cream and on the lard and mutton. In the evening the family gathered to catch fish and crayfish in the river. On the bank they built a fire and made supper from the catch. Afterward, old-fashioned fun took over when Galya, wife of Grandma Emelyanovna's eldest son, and Anna, an energetic, beautiful young woman, turned these peaceful meals into lively affairs. Anna was an expert at running her household, and was an excellent cook, but she wasn't averse to flirting, having a jolly good time, and behaving capriciously. Either she was teasing me or hugging me. One minute we were the best of friends, the next we were quarreling.

Recalling these rural scenes, I am transported again to a time when I experienced moments of utterly carefree happiness. And now, so many years later, reading Homer's *Odyssey,* I relive my early years among my beloved farmers. In them are—or at least were during my childhood—characteristics identical to the primitive simplicity and purity of Homer's heroes. The figures of Eumaeus, the old man Laertes, Telemachus, and the old nurse are more meaningful to me when I look at them through the customs and ways of my own people, the Little Russians. This Slavic tribe, like most other Slavic tribes, could not or did not know how to create for itself an independent existence, although it tried so hard, at least, in 1648, when Khmelnitsky led a revolt against oppressive Polish rule.[2] But in Little Russians, more than in northern Slavs, indigenous Slavic characteristics have lived on—love of nature, and the peaceful ways of rural life.

7

◆•◆•◆•◆

Father Returns from St. Petersburg

The whole time Father was in St. Petersburg we received only bad news from him. He had arrived there safely, had been well received by the young count's guardians, but soon felt the pernicious effects of the northern climate. He began to feel poorly, and held out for a long time—then finally he wrote Mama that his only hope for relief was to return home, to his native soil, as quickly as possible.

In the middle of September a covered wagon, looking as if it had made a long journey, halted in front of our cottage. In the wagon lay Father, so exhausted that he had to be carried inside. Weeping, my mother rushed to his side, convinced that she had only to close the eyes of her dead husband. But so powerful was the life-giving force of his native air, that a week later Father was able to rise from his bed and stand firmly on his feet. But he never fully regained his health. Sores appeared on his hands and feet that would heal for a time, only to open up again.

His health required his constant attention, and he treated himself. He had a pile of excerpts copied from medical books, and all sorts of notes relating to his own and other people's experience. Based on these sources he prepared medicines, which were no worse than those available from provincial pharmacists. Mostly he made them from herbs and the roots of vegetables. In this way he built up a rather complete home pharmacy for his family and others as well. He never refused to help anyone, and his advice, always gratis, often produced cures in several kinds of uncomplicated ailments.

Father's material circumstances hardly improved. But in St. Petersburg he had achieved his goal. The inquiry about his case confirmed his own testimony. Senator Alekseyev, one of the young count's guardians, played a sympathetic role in the final outcome. He listened favorably to my father's explanations and spoke with him time and time again, quite informally and frankly. In the end the senator suggested that my father remain in St. Petersburg, where he promised to help him get established. Of course this could have changed my father's life and the whole family's, too. But poor health drew him back home. Nevertheless, with Senator Alekseyev's help, he succeeded in winning complete independence from the authorities on the count's lands and the right to live where he pleased. He thought about moving the family away from this place, which had become hateful to him because of the humiliations he had experienced.

His presence in St. Petersburg led to a satisfying resolution of another problem. The litigation over the mill was decided in my father's favor. The court ordered the partners with whom he had leased the mill to pay my father all profits and expenses due him according to his calculations. Altogether it was a rather large sum. Although his partners were fairly well-to-do, they succeeded in making my father feel sorry for them, and he agreed to accept as full payment a mere four hundred rubles in bank notes.

Father's partners advised him to speculate, to buy up hay harvests with a view to selling the mowed grass later at a profit. Unfortunately, Father knew very little about speculation and he relied on a shrewd manufacturer who turned out to be a first-class rogue. All the money ended up in a partner's pocket, and Father was stuck with piles of rotten hay scattered among different meadows.

This unsuccessful venture had its good side, too. It took Father and me on delightful trips to hamlets and fields where we often spent the night beneath the sky on freshly cut, fragrant grass.

The sites where we bedded down left an indelible impression on me. No pen can convey the enchantment of the peaceful steppes. Everything around us had an air of graceful simplicity and exuded an elusive charm that I felt with all my being. The chirping of grasshoppers on the sweet-smelling grass, the flutter of wings as birds flew through the evening dusk, the mewing of a quail, the glow of fires built by the mowers, twinkling stars in the limpid heavens, and, finally, sounds of life fading and blending into the solemn silence of a balmy southern night. All this had an indescribable effect on my adolescent heart. How peacefully I fell asleep beneath the gentle glow of the stars! How fresh and cheerful I awoke when the first rays of the sun, unobstructed by walls or curtains, fell directly on my face.

As I mentioned earlier, Father loved to hunt. From St. Petersburg he brought a setter and an English gun with a hunting device. Never was he in such high spirits as when pursuing pigeons in the woods or ducks by the river and around lakes, where they nested in the rushes in large numbers. That's where we nabbed the culprits who plundered our cherry orchards—the starlings, whose tasty meat we valued so highly. During hunting season we always had roasted meat on our table, as well as borscht and a thin gruel made with the game Father had shot. This was a great help to Mother.

Most of the time I accompanied Father on his hunting trips, both on water and in the woods. Occasionally we ventured far into the steppe, hunting for great and little bustards. Weary from the long trek, we halted at the first apiary or melon field we came upon. We sat down next to Uncle* [the watchman] in his shelter of branches and straw, took provisions from our knapsack, and the three of us satisfied our hunger. Uncle supplemented our meal with a honeycomb or warm, ripe melons and watermelons glittering like gold in the sun-drenched field.

During these excursions I was in a state of bliss, although my role was not an easy one. My arms and shoulders were so loaded down with bird kills and all kinds of baggage that I felt like a pack beast, a donkey. Sometimes we would cross a recently harvested field, and this was awfully hard on my bare feet. Sharp fragments

*"Uncle" is a term of address by children to any male of mature age.

left from the harvest scratched and cut them. But all this was minor compared to the pleasure that our setter Valetka and I experienced when, after the shots, we raced to pick up dead starlings or catch downed ducks in the reeds.

Quite often we'd get caught in a thunderstorm, like one that I remember vividly. The air was heavy and still. Nothing stirred and it was dead quiet. Seething life gave way to an oppressive languor. Nature waited tensely as a blue-gray storm cloud crawled slowly from the edge of the horizon. It expanded, swirled, and spread out along the horizon. Arched arrows of lightning darted across the sky, came closer, grew brighter. The remote rumble of thunder grew louder and crackled more. Suddenly we heard a deafening clap overhead and saw dazzling streaks of light. The heavens were bursting. Rain gushed down. Through the downpour we couldn't make out anything around us. We were scared, but it was thrilling and exhilarating.

We had anticipated the storm and found refuge in a woodcutter's shelter. How delightful everything looked and felt afterward! How clean and fresh the air! How fragrant the woods and fields! Leaves and grass sparkled anew. Again grasshoppers chirped, butterflies fluttered, and birds twittered. You felt as if a new spring had burst out all around. You could feast your eyes on it forever and still not get enough of this miraculous vision. Nor could you ever become sated with the sounds of joyous life.

Now, back to my story about riding with my father around harvested meadows. One trip nearly cost me my life. Father had acquired a frisky horse and hitched it to a two-wheeled cart, and he drove everywhere in it. How I longed to sit up front and drive the horse and cart. Although he rarely yielded to my desires, this time, as luck would have it, he agreed. To my indescribable joy, he handed me the reins. An earlier rain had left the seat very slippery, and somehow, while urging the horse on, I slid off. Instantly I tumbled under the cart along with the reins. The horse was young and spirited, and sensing that something was amiss, she rushed to one side of the road and, like an arrow, dashed through the field. Father was paralyzed with fear. He heard me scream but did not see me. My clothes caught on the wood coupling-bolt of the cart, and I was dragged along the ground. There was no way to stop the horse and, in my fright, I grabbed the reins and held on to them for dear life. Fortunately, the frightened animal only ran and did not strike me with its hooves. Otherwise I would have been done for. At last a strong jolt knocked me to the ground and the coupling-bolt broke off. Still between the shafts, the horse kept running alone another half-verst.

Crazed with fear for me, Father leaped from the cart, sure that he would find my dead body, but he saw me already on my feet, almost unharmed, though terribly frightened. He could not believe his eyes and for a long time kept feeling me to make sure that I was really whole. Not a single limb was injured. There was only a cut on my left cheek and a nasty abrasion on my left leg from hitting a rock. We managed to repair the coupling-bolt, and connected it to the cart shaft and front axle. Driving the cart at a walking pace, we dragged ourselves to a neighboring farmhouse, where we received a cordial welcome and rested a while.

The local farmers were very fond of my father. They never forgot how he had suffered in his fight for their rights and interests. One who stands out in my memory is a venerable old man by the name of Gromovoy, who lived in the hamlet Krivaya Beryoza. He had a huge family of sons, daughters, grandchildren, and great-grandchildren, among whom he circulated like a genuine patriarch. Gentle and somewhat pompous, he enjoyed the respect of his large family, who considered him their head, and remained with him out of a sense of duty. All his sons were literate. One served in the military and had already achieved the rank of non-commissioned officer. Another studied under my father and also planned to join the army. Gromovoy was wealthy. He owned herds of cows and sheep, two windmills, an apiary, and a huge orchard. He welcomed and treated us as close friends. Father and I often spent whole days at his place. And whenever we left he always loaded our cart with all kinds of produce from his fields, orchard, and apiary.

The unsuccessful hay operation had left my parents destitute again. Now they had neither house, land, nor the tools to win their bread by physical labor. Father sought employment as steward of an estate or, since he was well versed in the law, as a solicitor. But nothing opened up. Once again he had to turn to teaching to earn a living. This time, too, the Little Russians, with their love of learning, did not leave him without pupils. And once more our life followed the same course as before—Father's lessons day after day and our constant struggle with poverty.

Before long a new source of distress burdened my poor mother. Father's romantic, restless soul struggled like a caged bird. He was forever dashing off somewhere searching for something and, not finding it, he would become despondent and irritable. His passionate nature enticed him away from home. And when temptation presented itself elsewhere, he hadn't the strength to resist it.

Chance drew Father into a close friendship with a young widow from a neighboring farmstead. She was a striking beauty, a southern type, with an oblong face, dark golden complexion, raven hair, and eyes "as clear as day and dark as night." I don't understand how she could have been born in our region; she looked more like a native daughter of Spain's Andalusia. She had spent two years in St. Petersburg and Moscow, and there acquired a certain refinement, which enhanced her beauty and natural grace.

Her husband's health was very poor, and he turned to my father for advice. One look at him told my father that the sick man was beyond help—he had consumption [tuberculosis]. Not wishing to upset the patient before the proper time, Father began to visit him and prescribe herbal potions. Then one day he took me along. It turned out that we arrived just in time to hear the sick man's last breath. For the first time I was face to face with death, and the gloomy scene made an indelible impression on me. A priest, my father, and one other person stood around the dying man. The wife sobbed as she leaned over the head of the bed. I stood in a corner of the room and, scared and curious, watched what was happening. The sick man had received his last rites. His breathing was heavy and irregular. For a long time he tried to speak but couldn't. Finally, he turned to the priest and said:

"Have you finished everything?"

This effort was his last. His eyes closed, and he stopped breathing.

"It's all over," said Father. "Now that's *philosophy* for you!" he said, putting the emphasis on philosophy. The priest was intelligent and learned, and Father and he often discussed and argued about philosophical subjects. What struck me most in the entire scene was the dying man's tranquility. Thus, for the first time, I imagined death to be more a solemn event than a terrifying one.

Even after her husband's death, my father continued to visit the beautiful widow, who gradually became accustomed to seeing in him her only friend. They became intimate. For a long time this made my mother's life miserable. But magnanimously she concealed her pain, never burdening his already depressed spirits with complaints and reproaches. Usually she suffered in silence, without a murmur, finding solace in the execution of her duties.

Meanwhile I was growing up with nothing special happening in my personal life, which was subject only to the inevitable uncertainties springing from poverty. For my parents our impoverished circumstances were hardly conducive to focusing on their children's development. We weren't raised, we simply sprouted. Whatever developed in me did so independently, without the efforts or influence of others. I grew like a seedling in a forest. When days are warm and clear, it sprouts and turns green. A frost hits—the leaves wither and fold and the flower ready to blossom falls off.

As for my morals, I must say that my mother concerned herself with them to a certain degree. And I, of course, am obliged to her for my first notions of honesty and duty. But for the most part, I was left to my own devices and increasingly became wrapped up in myself. When I had unpleasant encounters with people, I'd detach myself from them as quickly as possible. I'd run to the barn and hide deep in the hay, endure my distress there, then begin building fantastic castles in the air. Children's noisy games generally didn't attract me. In a crowd of other boys, I felt awkward and lost. But alone with a friend of my choice, I was lively, cheerful, and inventive.

Observing my hunger for learning, Father began making me read serious books. But my interest in what he gave me to read flagged rapidly because most of the books were dry textbooks, sometimes beyond my comprehension. For example, he'd give me an edition of a Russian history book intended for use in public schools and say, "Go on, read it. It'll do you more good than those shallow books, and it's better than running around outside."

So I sat and read about the Poles and other Slavic tribes—the Drevlyane, Kriviche, Vyatiche . . . What strange names! I flipped through the pages: battles and more battles, princes charging one another with swords . . . But my mind was elsewhere. Like a free bird I flew through a bewitched kingdom where I was omnipotent ruler and tsar.

8

◆•◆•◆•◆

1811
New Place, New Faces

Father waited a long time until he finally found a desirable position. In Boguchar county lived Marya Fyodorovna Bedryaga, a wealthy pomeshchitsa, the owner of two thousand souls. She offered my father the position of steward of her estate, where she too resided. The conditions were favorable, particularly in light of our family's circumstances at that time: a thousand rubles per year, plus housing and food. We packed up quickly and left Alekseyevka in the summer of 1811. I was seven years old.

Our journey was very pleasant. We left with light hearts and bright hopes for the future. And our route took us through one of the most attractive regions. Between Biryuch and Boguchar, about two hundred versts to the south, are the most productive plains in the world. Irrigated by numerous tributaries of the Don River, and set among picturesque, sloping hills dotted with tidy Little Russian cottages, the plain is striking in its lushness. From the rich, black earth a farmer's returns are multiplied one hundredfold.

The only blemish in this region is the absence of forest, but nature is not to blame. The soil here kept producing plenty of woodlands and finally gave out when reckless pomeshchiks, unconcerned about the future, destroyed the forests. Nor did they spare ancient oaks, hundreds of years old.

The population of this territory was Little Russian. The peasants suffered beneath the yoke of serfdom. If a master was wealthy

Serfs delivering provisions to their pomeshchik. These peasants are on obrok, which means they pay quitrent to their pomeshchik in cash or kind. Oil painting by M. M. Zaitsev.

Dinner break during haymaking season. Oil painting by A. I. Morozov.

and owned several thousand serfs, they suffered less oppression because most of them were tenant farmers on *obrok*—paying quitrent in cash or kind. The serfs of smaller pomeshchiks were on *barshchina* [the corvée]—paying their masters in labor. Nevertheless, serfs on barshchina were subject to the capriciousness of stewards and bailiffs. On the other hand, small pomeshchiks literally sucked out the strength and birthright of unfortunates in their power. Neither time nor land was at their disposal. Serfs of wealthy pomeshchiks were consumed by barshchina and were at the mercy of the pomeshchik's greed and arbitrariness. In addition, sometimes there was inhuman treatment, and often cruelty was accompanied by debauchery. The pomeshchik could enjoy every beautiful woman or daughter of his vassals with impunity, like sampling a watermelon or other kind of melon from his melon field.

Of course, here too, as everywhere, there were exceptions where serfs received better treatment. But in general, conditions were as I described. People could be bought and sold wholesale or in small numbers, by families, or singly like bulls and sheep. Nobles weren't the only ones buying and selling human beings. Tradesmen and rich peasants were engaged in this as well, registering serfs in the name of an official or aristocrat who was their patron.[1]

Owners could treat their serfs as they pleased but were not allowed to kill them. Words like this—"The other day I bought a wench," or sold a boy, coachman, lackey—were uttered as callously as if a cow, horse, or suckling pig were being discussed.[2]

Tsar Alexsander I,* during the humanitarian phase of his reign, talked about improving the lot of his serf-subjects, but attempts to limit the pomeshchiks' power vanished without a trace. The nobility wanted to live in luxury befitting its station. The aristocratic way of life was notorious for wild extravagances and self-indulgence. And the serfs did not understand that other moral pursuits existed for them besides submission to their master's will,

*Tsar Alexander I (1775–1825) reigned from 1801 to 1825.

Two pomeshchiks negotiating the sale of serfs. Oil painting by N. V. Nevrev.

Serfs on sale at a market fair. Oil painting by K. V. Lebedev.

or that there was more to life than a smoky cottage, a piece of black bread, and kvass.

So we arrived at our destination, Pisaryevka sloboda, a village of two thousand residents. It was about thirty versts from the chief county town of Boguchar. A deep ravine divided Pisaryevka into two equal parts. The smaller, with four or five hundred people, was called Zayarskaya Pisaryevka, and it belonged to Marya Fyodorovna Bedryaga's brother, Grigory Fyodorovich Tatarchukov. In addition he owned several farmsteads and a vast amount of land.

You couldn't call Pisaryevka picturesque. It lay on a flat stretch of land along the Boguchar River, on whose bank stood several small and large farmsteads and the unremarkable chief county town bearing the river's name. The manor house, an old wooden structure, was dilapidated and unsightly. The pomeshchitsa kept talking about rebuilding it, but from year to year postponed it, and finally moved to another house. A vast orchard sloped to the river's edge. Across the river towered a wine distillery. At that time Little Russian pomeshchiks, exercising their right to operate a winery, considered a distillery an economic necessity.

We were assigned a rather cozy outbuilding near the manor house. The first few days we were weary with boredom. We still hadn't any friends. We were the object of curiosity and, as we found out later, of snooping. Every morning Father went to see the pomeshchitsa, returned home late, and immediately buried himself in figures and ideas related to the management of her estate.

His first meeting with pomeshchitsa Bedryaga was a stormy one. He found her estate in terrible disorder and the peasants ruthlessly plunged into ruin. Due to poor management, the estate failed to produce the revenues it could yield. What income it did generate the owner secured at the expense of her peasants, exhausting them with backbreaking labor and punishment.

Father took on the job of putting everything in order, increasing the pomeshchitsa's income and restoring the peasants' wellbeing. But he demanded a free hand to accomplish his aims. Marya

Fyodorovna didn't like this. Willful, a true lady of the manor, she followed only her own whims and caprices and could not imagine that any creature on her land would dare breathe and move against her will.

Her stupidity wasn't innate, and instantly she recognized in Father a man of talent, intelligence, and perseverance. Without giving in to him, she wanted to take advantage of his services in such a way that at least it would appear, as before, that she was solely in charge. However, necessity compelled her to yield. She gave Father full authority and promised not to interfere.

But the deal didn't last. These individuals, my father and pomeshchitsa Bedryaga, evidently were not cut out to work together in harmony. Sooner or later they would clash and a break would occur that would be painful for both sides, especially for my father, a poor man of low status, while Marya Fyodorovna had wealth and prominence in provincial society.

Actually, pomeshchitsa Bedryaga was no worse or better than most of the landowning gentry of that time. Many called her cruel, and indeed she was, but only to the extent that ignorance and unlimited power made most Russian nobles behave cruelly in those days.

She was past fifty and neither pretty nor ugly—nothing about her was engaging. There was something ruthless and repulsive in her face. She almost never smiled, and in her scowling, glowering look one would be hard put to find a hint of feminine tenderness. In dealing with people she was always so irritable, as if she were perpetually angry. But with people she needed, Marya Fyodorovna could be gracious—as much as her innate austerity and haughtiness would allow. She was very generous with promises but miserly when it came to fulfilling them.

The ugliest aspect of her character was her habit of spreading malicious gossip. She was either at odds with or suing her neighbors. Acquaintance with her rarely ended without a summons to court. All kinds of solicitors buzzed around her. Most of them had scanty knowledge of the law and only flattered her and bungled her affairs even more.

Proprietress Bedryaga willingly took on the most foolish projects if she thought they would increase the size of her property and her influence in the county or improve the management of her estate. Anyone who proposed such a project would gain easy access to her but not enjoy her trust for long. A swindler, of course, would quickly show himself, but Bedryaga would get rid of him only to fall into the hands of another. An honest man, however, would have a hard time gaining her favor and confidence.

At the same time as my father struggled to get her to agree to measures to her advantage, the stupid Jewess Fyodosya easily wheedled permission from her to do the same kind of things. The result was disastrous. Subsequently, both the pomeshchitsa and my father had a hard time untangling the mess the woman had caused.

Marya Fyodorovna Bedryaga was obsessively busy. Her room looked like the office of a professional. Her desk was piled with papers, and the overflow was stacked on the floor. Without fail she spent several hours a day with pen in hand, surrounded by her worthy advisers or listening to informant Fyodosya's secret reports. Rarely did Marya Fyodorovna receive visitors who had not come on business, and she didn't go out. She had a huge staff of servants, about ten of whom were housemaids.

From morning until night these poor devils trembled in fear of displeasing their mistress and incurring her wrath. When the inevitable happened, it usually ended with the errant one being turned over to a certain Stepan Stetska. This lame old man was a trusted household serf who was in charge of a stable with a whole collection of birch rods. Woe to the unfortunates who fell into Stetska's hands! He was a master and enthusiast of flogging, especially of girls, and they were terrified by the mere sight of him.

Many of the maids were pretty, including one by the name of Khristina, who played a role in my childhood. Misery befell the hapless girl, who could not resist the tender lure of love, and because of this was subjected to every conceivable torment. Marya Fyodorovna was an implacable champion of morality and con-

Beating of female serf with birch switches, a punishment ordered by her pomeshchik. Painting by J. A. Atkinson.

demned her housemaids to eternal chastity. She did not allow them to marry.

The tyranny here, as everywhere, did not achieve its aim. Secretly the girls had liaisons. The stronger the attraction, the more strictly it was forbidden them and the more hopeless loomed their future. They worried mostly about becoming pregnant but in most cases managed to avoid motherhood.

Marya Fyodorovna had a daughter and two sons. The daughter, Kleopatra Nikolayevna, was married to some Cossack general by the name, I think, of Denisov. While the mother's maliciousness was moderated by selfish considerations and egoism, the daughter's knew no limits. Kleopatra Nikolayevna was malicious to the core; she had neither passions nor vices that, for the want of better qualities, would temper or, rather, dilute her cruel nature. At heart she was not stingy or vain, but she was inclined to harm everything that could feel injury, to poison everything she touched. Several months after the wedding, her husband drove her out. She returned to her mother and installed herself there to be a scourge and plague to her mother. No one but Marya Fyodorovna with her callous disposition could tolerate the presence of such a monster.

Marya Fyodorovna's sons were not much better than the daughter. Both men served in St. Petersburg. The older one, Samuil, later worked as chairman of the criminal tribunal in Voronezh, and his violent temper amazed even the most unbridled pomeshchiks. He flogged people to death. This man was not a judge, but an executioner. They say he never took bribes. Marya Fyodorovna's other son, Fyodor, was notorious more for his craftiness than his maliciousness, and he led a dissolute life.

So this was the haven to which the vicissitudes of life delivered our frail canoe. But, I repeat, nestled somewhere near evil you can always find a bit of goodness. Therefore it's not so surprising that the same soil that produces a Bedryaga sometimes produces an individual with a vastly different type of personality.

As I mentioned earlier, Marya Fyodorovna's brother owned the Zayarskaya section of Pisaryevka sloboda. Grigory Fyodorovich Tatarchukov was an eccentric person with lots of quirks. Yet he was intelligent and kind. At that time he was well past sixty. He had not received a sound education because it did not exist in Russia in those days. But, fortunately, nature had endowed him with many talents and something that was rare at the time—humane aspirations.

Where such people sprang from in the middle and end of the eighteenth century, and how and where they acquired their philosophy, is interesting. The blow Peter the Great's herculean hand had delivered to ignorance roused these people. Still, they were a rarity, and from time to time such individuals flared like sparks struck from flint. Unfortunately, they had no support.

Catherine II yearned for fame. What appealed to her was the

idea of humanizing people, which eighteenth-century philosophers had succeeded in making attractive to rulers as a path to glory. She nurtured intellect, talent, science, and art, believing that Russia needed these things no less than political power and that this path would win her a place in history alongside Peter the Great. In the wake of Catherine, the kind of people we're talking about also felt the spirit of the times. Unaware of the terrible abyss between an idea and its fulfillment, between striving for and attaining one's goal, they naively read Voltaire and the encyclopedists. They avidly devoured everything printed and published in Russian. And a substantial amount was published then, at least in comparison to earlier times. Sumarokov, Novikov, Kurganov, and, even to this day underestimated, Fyodor Emin and Kheraskov—to say nothing of Lomonosov, Fonvizin, and Derzhavin; all offered plenty of food for thought. There were even readers for judicial treatises on the administration of justice or the works of Plato, translated by Sidorovsky and Pakhomov.[3]

Of course, none of this led to anything positive, but at least it got people thinking and introduced the reader to ideas about a better order of things, to the habits, customs, and lives of peoples who were ahead of us in education. It was people of a progressive bent who participated in this movement. They were liberals—not as we define liberals today. You might even call them negative liberals. They didn't create doctrines or utopian ideas about changes in the Russian political system but were content with the conviction that the moral and intellectual climate in Russia was subject to rapid improvement. They believed that everything from the pre-Petrine era had decayed and that Russia would stride rapidly along the path of enlightenment.

Grigory Fyodorovich Tatarchukov was this kind of person. He and Father were close friends. I saw him often and heard his conversations with my father, many of which are still imprinted in my mind.

He was of average height and slightly round-shouldered, probably due to his habit of walking with his eyes cast down. How different his face was from those of most of our pomeshchiks. Theirs were lifeless and dull or flaunted a devil-may-care attitude. The expression on his face was an intelligent one, touched with a shade of irony. This man was a thinker. You could see it in his large, gleaming eyes. His gentle, imperturbable nature came through in his smile, although Tatarchukov rarely smiled.

The grace and nobility of his person absurdly clashed with the strange cynicism his manner of dress presented. Grigory Fyodorovich always wore the same tobacco-smudged, greasy, ragged nankeen frock coat covered with every conceivable kind of stain. This garment was always unbuttoned and his shirt displayed. How this aroused my childish sense of shame! He couldn't even button the broad breeches-flap on his pantaloons in the correct order. On one side, slung across his shoulder, dangled a large, ugly bag that he called a tobacco pouch. And the pipe sticking out of his mouth was removed only when he ate or slept.

Judging from his clothes, you would think that this fellow standing before you was some Plyushkin—like the character in Gogol's *Dead Souls*—whose stinginess crossed the boundary of decency and common sense. At the same time, Grigory Fyodorovich was generous, utterly incapable of petty thrift, and, in everything except his own person, he observed cleanliness and loved elegance and comfort. His serfs were exceptionally well clothed and maintained. Although his home was not fancy, it was very presentable. The garden, which he had planted himself, was tastefully arranged. Everything on his estate attested to Grigory Fyodorovich's high level of development. He towered above his peers in all respects, if you don't count his slovenly attitude toward his personal appearance.

In view of that attitude, so much the stranger seemed Tatarchukov's penchant for the fair sex. Old age didn't hinder his indulgence in amorous adventures. The diversity of these affairs appealed to him, and he retained his weakness for women until the day he died at the age of eighty.

When he was seventy-two or seventy-three he married again, this time the young, attractive Baroness Wolf, and had a daughter by her. From his first wife he had two daughters and three sons.

One son went into military service, another studied at Moscow University, and the third, a boy of thirteen, was preparing to enter some educational institution.

Grigory Fyodorovich Tatarchukov's estate consisted of six hundred serfs instead of the thousand he was supposed to receive when his father died. Through court proceedings, his sister, Marya Fyodorovna, succeeded in wresting four hundred serfs from him, a circumstance that he took stoically. He didn't like his sister, and not because she had fleeced him, but because her feelings for people and her ideas were completely opposite his.

Grigory Fyodorovich was content with his situation and, what's more important, everyone was content with him. His peasants adored him; all in his domain lived a comfortable life, free of oppression. There wasn't a single instance of his humiliating someone. With an awareness and conscientiousness rare in those days, he often said to my father: "The peasants don't owe me anything. On the contrary, I owe them everything, since I live by their labor."

Tatarchukov had been in government service, but didn't stay long and retired with the rank of ensign. He hadn't a drop of ambition in him.

He held out no hope for radical reforms because his understanding of the deeply rooted evil in the social system of that time convinced him that basic state policy would paralyze any privately sponsored measure directed toward change.

Confronted by such an order of things he could see only one approach: he felt that he must always do good among those open to his influence. And this he did nobly, unselfishly, untiringly, unperturbed by ingratitude—if he encountered it—and without expecting praise from anyone.

9

◆•◆•◆•◆

Our Life in Pisaryevka, 1812–1815

Father plunged into his new job with enthusiasm. The pomeshchitsa and peasants quickly felt the positive results of his conscientious labor. Some noticed how order had been restored where they hadn't seen it for many years; others felt a slackening of oppression and, though living in poverty and ruin, began to feel some hope for their future. Marya Fyodorovna had to admit that she was indebted to my father in many ways. Finally convinced of his honesty, she entrusted him to manage her estate. And so she decided to go on a journey that she had been planning for a long time: a trip with her daughter, Kleopatra Nikolayevna, to Don Cossack villages where they would visit her daughter's husband. She hoped to reconcile them but mainly wanted to get her daughter off her hands and foist her off on somebody else.

They departed, leaving my father in charge of the estate. Pomeshchitsa Bedryaga was absent almost a year. And if that interim wasn't the happiest time for our family, at least it was a period of independence and tranquility.

Meanwhile, a social circle developed in Pisaryevka that was remarkable for that remote region of the steppe. Father and Tatarchukov formed a close friendship. As I mentioned earlier, Grigory Fyodorovich Tatarchukov had just married a young, pretty, and educated girl, Baroness Wolf. With her mother and two sisters, she had come to Pisaryevka for a visit and, before long, captured her host's heart.

The Wolf baronesses were German aristocrats, boasting kinship with the famous Field Marshal Laudon.[1] But they had become impoverished and were now living on the dwindling remains of what had once been a considerable fortune. It wasn't love that inspired Baroness Yuliya to give her hand in marriage to Grigory Fyodorovich. It was the pressure of poverty, which had become increasingly painful and persistent. Besides Yuliya and two other daughters, her elderly mother also had four sons. One served in the military and was in no position to help the family. Two youngsters were students in the cadet corps, and the eldest of the four, an idiot, lived with the mother.

Yuliya was no ravishing beauty but was quite good-looking. I remember her vividly. A brunette of average height, she had a dark-complexioned, expressive face. Her stately bearing and manner were striking, distinctly setting her apart from the provincial ladies of the manor. She had just turned twenty, and her husband was past seventy.

And what a husband! True, he was one of the most intelligent and generous of men, but he smelled like a goat. Even after his marriage he went around all the time in that same greasy frock coat and drooping pantaloons. Slung across his shoulder dangled that same ugly sack. It was not easy to cut through a seventeen-year layer of dirt and uncover the gem beneath, and even less so for a young, inexperienced woman. Nevertheless, for a long time she had no ties elsewhere. But in the end, life with this satyr was repulsive and after many stormy domestic rows, Yuliya left him and went to Moscow. Before her departure, however, she bore him a daughter.

As I mentioned earlier, Tatarchukov had two daughters from a previous marriage—Lyubov and Yelizabeta. Both were stout, rosy-cheeked, and clumsy. However, they were so intelligent and pleasant that you forgot about their homeliness, especially the younger one, Yelizabeta. Her angelic, gentle manner captured everybody's heart.

My father and mother were welcomed like kin in this family circle. We lived a short distance from each other, so that the two

Moscow. E. Buttura, artist. A. Boullionier, engraver.

The eve of Napoleon's invasion of Moscow. Martinet, artist. Reville, engraver.

Moscow in flames during the War of 1812. Martinet, artist. Couché, engraver.

The Kremlin throne room after the fires. Desnoyers, artist. A. Boullionier, engraver.

families were almost constantly together, and soon new faces joined us.

Napoleon's army had occupied Moscow, and its inhabitants streamed into Russia's interior, seeking refuge wherever they could. Tatarchukov's second son, Aleksei, had just graduated from Moscow University and hurried home to his father for a brief stay. Brief because he wanted to serve in the People's War against Napoleon. Three other Moscow refugees, escaping from the enemy, joined Aleksei in his flight to Pisaryevka. They were Moscow University professor of Greek Semyon Ivashkovsky and his wife, and a young man, a relative—Mikhailo Ignatyevich Belyakov, a junior scientific assistant at the same university. All found refuge at the home of the old man, Tatarchukov.[2]

Frequent visitors to our circle were the village priest, Father Ioann Donetsky, a very intelligent man, and his charming wife.

Thus, in Pisaryevka, a circle of cultured people took shape, the likes of which the province hadn't seen during its entire existence. This circle was destined to live through some very dramatic situations. Passions ran high, and some intimate relationships ended in disaster. We experienced joy together, but our tears were even more abundant.

I can picture vividly the people who participated in this Pisaryevka drama. From the observations of individual characteristics that my childish eyes captured then, it all comes together now to form a complete portrait of the people and events stirring our tiny village world.

I've said enough about Grigory Fyodorovich Tatarchukov. So on to the others in our circle.

Professor Ivashkovsky resembled the scholars of olden days. Devoted to amassing isolated facts, he lost sight of the overall picture. His philological research did not go beyond the painstaking gathering of material, which seems to have left him wondering what to do with his collection of data.

Tall and round-shouldered, he walked hunched over, as if looking for something beneath his feet. Rarely did a smile light up his face, which from constant immersion in the ancient classics seemed to have set into a never-changing, serious expression. But then, he was always as kind and open-hearted as a child. Utterly incapable of deception, Professor Ivashkovsky didn't suspect that he was a constant victim of it. His wife deceived him, as did his servant and students.

Professor Ivashkovsky developed close ties to my father. When the professor left Pisaryevka and returned to Moscow, he began a warm correspondence with Father. In one of his first letters, he enclosed a poem he had composed about the expulsion of the French armies from Russia. I have never seen it published anywhere and am quoting a small part of it, fixed in my memory, as a sample of the poetry in which, expressing their joy of deliverance from Napoleon, poets and would-be poets hastened to practice their art.

The fearsome hour has struck, the celestial court has spoken.
Dark clouds have concealed a once-radiant horizon.
Russia! Where is your world, the majesty of your beauty?
Among sovereign powers, your star has dimmed.
I see only how enemies sow villainy in you.
With flame and sword, their ferocity is stamped.
Sorrow overflows our land; death, cries of pain, fear
In hearts filled with despair.
Where once we had sung the praises of good deeds,
Greed and insolence rages.

Moscow, you too were subjected to terrible misfortune:
Within your walls, the evil Gaul exults in his victory.
He thinks, having captured you, all of Russia is conquered
And with glory, he has become its absolute ruler.
And Europe, astounded, dreams with him,
Enticed by the dawn of his coming victories. . . .

Continuing in the same style, the poet talks about the humiliation of the French, their expulsion and Russia's victory. But I don't know the rest by heart.

Mikhailo Ignatyevich Belyakov, a junior scientific assistant in the natural sciences division of Moscow University, was a pleasant-looking young man and, it seemed, less interested in the pursuit of knowledge than in having a good time.

When Moscow University reopened after Napoleon's massive destruction, Professor Ivashkovsky worked there for a long time and published a Greek-Russian dictionary. But Belyakov, who had married Tatarchukov's eldest daughter and had gone with her to Moscow, somehow or other disappeared in the crowd of this capital city.

Rumors circulated that he drank, went through his wife's dowry, and finally did her in with his nasty treatment of her. He outlived his wife by many years. When I knew him in Pisaryevka, he was still an unspoiled, decent young man. At the beginning, he was good friends with my father, but after his marriage he grew snobbish and no longer deigned to associate with ordinary people.

But the pearl of the Pisaryevka circle was Tatarchukov's son Aleksei, who, at that time, was preparing to enlist in the ranks of defenders of the Fatherland. Here was a youth with a clear mind and pure heart. Everyone loved him dearly. A kind of romantic friendship developed between my father and him. Aleksei Grigoryevich Tatarchukov was twenty years old and my father was past thirty. With such a difference in ages, one would hardly expect to find mutual interests that would bring them together. But the world in which this Pisaryevka circle revolved was something special, woven of enthusiasm and mutual admiration, so there was absolutely no place in it for plain common sense.

Love invaded this circle of worthy souls and ravaged many a heart. First to fall in love was old Tatarchukov, who was captivated by Baroness Yuliya. His love had a simple solution: marriage. Right on his heels, my father was consumed with love for her. His love was romantic, and had a fateful effect on his future.

How my father's passion for her originated, and whether Yuliya herself encouraged it, I do not know. Perhaps, bored by her unnatural marriage, she accepted more favorably than she should have the adoration of a man who was still young and capable of strong, deep feeling. But she wasn't your ordinary coquette and hardly encouraged her admirer with deceptive promises of mutual affection. And Father won nothing from her except sympathy. In this affair his love was purely ideal, and this explains how she got on with him while living amicably with her husband.

Having barely crossed the threshold of his father's home, young Aleksei Tatarchukov fell madly in love with Baroness Wolf's middle daughter, Karolina. A courtship seemed natural. Both of them were young and beautiful and without ties. They could have been happy. Nevertheless, for some reason, the young girl responded indifferently to the youth's passionate feelings, and he carried his unrequited love to the grave.

Love swept through Pisaryevka like a contagious disease. Soon Mikhailo Belyakov fell under the spell. He declared his love for Tatarchukov's eldest daughter, Lyubov Grigoryevna. However, in this case, most of his passion was not for the lady, but for her dowry. The lady was no beauty but was reputed to be the heiress of one hundred serfs. Not a paltry number for a poor junior scientific assistant who had arrived empty-handed from Moscow, except for some books by Carolus Linnaeus, the Swedish botanist and naturalist, and by the French naturalist and author Georges Leclerc, Comte de Buffon.

Spinning off in various directions, these love affairs became woefully complicated. They ensnared and entangled everyone in this tiny rural enclave to the point where the rest of the world ceased to exist. In this game of love only two parties were lucky. One was the old man Tatarchukov, who won the hand, if not the heart, of his special beloved. The other was Belyakov, who initially encountered resistance from the father of his lass, and in the end married Lyubov Grigoryevna.

All these people got together every day, either at Tatarchukov's or my father's house. They played cards—"Boston" [whist]—had friendly discussions, basked in the warmth of affectionate glances from their goddesses, danced, and listened to music.

At one time pomeshchitsa Bedryaga had her own orchestra, composed of serfs. When it disbanded, the retired artists scattered in all directions. Some took to the bottle and went on binges, others occupied themselves with rural chores.

Father was a musician and played the psaltery very well. No matter how modest our possessions, we always had a musical instrument in our household. He collected a group of absentminded virtuosos and somehow managed to get them and their instruments to work harmoniously.

Here was the group he assembled: Ivan, a one-armed French horn player; Bibik, a violinist and conductor; and another violinist, Trofim. He was a young fellow and my friend. For the prize of prunes and gingerbread Trofim was always ready to strum a song that, for some reason, I loved so much: "On the Bridge, the Bridge, on the Kalinovo Bridge." The group also had bassoonists, flutists, and cymbalists. If your mouth wasn't busy blowing your instrument, you sang along with two or three other songsters. The rest of the crowd harmonized with them. Thus, in the small room serving as our parlor, dining room, and foyer, proper concerts were performed. Most often, and always to my indescribable delight, they played "Ring the Victory Bells."

But suddenly a cruel blow struck our group. Young Aleksei Tatarchukov fell ill. He caught a cold, developed a fever, and died in a few days. His death crushed the old man. This was his favorite son, in whom he saw the best part of himself. My father delivered a graveside eulogy, and for a long time could not get over Aleksei's death. And everyone who knew the young man deeply mourned his premature end.

With the passage of time, the distress in our community caused by this sad event gradually subsided and gave way to the normal course of human affairs. We returned to our former pursuits and pleasures. The only thing that changed after this was our meeting place; we met at our home instead of Tatarchukov's.

It is rather strange that at this time, when Russia was experiencing the powerful shocks of Napoleon's invasion, so many were indifferent to the fate of the Fatherland. With the exception of young Tatarchukov, this was true of our intimate circle and the entire surrounding community.

Neighboring pomeschiks and townspeople often visited Father. True, everyone bore the burdens generated by the People's War without complaint. They supplied and equipped recruits at great personal expense. Yet I did not detect in their conversations a sign of deep interest in the events of the time. Evidently everyone was interested solely in their own affairs. The mention of Napoleon's name evoked awe rather than hate. The nonchalant attitude of our community toward the disaster hanging over Russia was startling. This may have been due in part to the distance of the theater of war: they said the enemy wouldn't get here so fast!

But I think the main reason was apathy, characteristic of a people estranged from participation in society's affairs, as Russians were then. They were not accustomed to discussing what went on around them and unconditionally obeyed the orders of the authorities. In this Pisaryevka maelstrom of lovers' sighs, effusive pronouncements and antics—sometimes witty and romantic, sometimes childish—my own childhood passed without any intellectual and moral guidance, other than my mother's supervision. She alone, amidst the general giddiness, maintained presence of mind.

Soon I found a friend, a boy two years older than I. He was the son of a retired official. My friend's name was Andryushka. He had a delightful face, rosy cheeks, very fair skin, and was as gentle and sensitive as a girl. He grew very attached to me, although I irritated him often with outbursts of my hot temper. The years rolled by and in time Andrei Andreyevich [Messarosh] married, became a councillor of state, retired, and now is one of my best friends. Unpretentious, with common sense and a warm heart, he remained as poor as he had been at the start of his official career. He acquired nothing except, as government functionaries say, "a lapel pin for irreproachable service, and hemorrhoids for his backside." In short, he kept completely clean of bureaucratic slime.

Andryushka and I got along beautifully. Generally, for people I liked very much, my feelings knew no bounds. At that time Andryushka wasn't the only one who captured my heart. Among Marya Fyodorovna Bedryaga's housemaids was a very pretty one, Khristina, whom everyone called Khristinushka. Graceful, with a soft complexion quite untypical of country people, and with an expressive, intelligent face, luxuriant hair, and gentle manners, she was thoroughly charming. Khristinushka had just turned seventeen. Imitating Pisaryevka grown-ups falling in love so irrepressibly and nonsensically, I lost no time kindling a passion for her. I followed her everywhere, like a shadow, and caught her glances. Looking upon me as a child, which indeed I was, she didn't deny me hugs, but with cunning scrupulousness gave them only as rewards for my constancy, for example, or for some other reason. But nothing gave me more pleasure than playing cards with her—"Kings," especially.

Oh, what pangs of jealousy I suffered! My friend Trofimka, having captured me with his violin rendition of "On the Bridge, the Bridge, on the Kalinovo Bridge," was not indifferent to the presence of the young girl, who, on her part, clearly showed a preference for him. But both were careful not to provoke my jealousy, for I was the "young gentleman" who often was very helpful to them.

At that time my friend Andryushka and I had almost no formal education. You couldn't call it teaching when someone thrust an arithmetic textbook or Russian history book into our hands and ordered us to sit down and read. We didn't have a teacher because they couldn't get one from anywhere; my father, busy managing the estate, could not devote much time to us.

Meanwhile, my passion for reading grew with every day—not for textbooks but for novels. I read a lot of them, and the most ridiculous ones at that. I don't recall how I got hold of such books, but there was no shortage of them. Besides, I was hardly ever without my songbook, and, being in love, I would memorize and copy in a notebook love songs like these:

> Hear the cry
> Of my distress.
> I must comply
> With my mistress.

or:

Doleful lyre, do spread
Moaning plaintively,
What cruel Timira said:
She no longer loves me.

and so on . . .

Besides literature, Andryushka and I took to painting. From somewhere we obtained paints, and in some miraculous way, copying from postcards, we painted Cossacks armed with lances, also horses, goats, birds, and trees. Nothing fazed us.

And then there was another activity that kept us occupied. In the winter we would snare birds in the orchard, which we considered great fun.

Generally, left to ourselves, we made no intellectual progress; but, on the other hand, we passed the time very pleasantly. To our credit, I must say that we always behaved decently, never abusing our freedom.

My passionate nature and eccentricities found an outlet in my love for Khristinushka and in scribbling. And did I scribble! Most of all I liked to do it in the form of letters. I wrote them to imaginary people and to real people but never sent them.

In these letters, I wrote effusively about my love of nature, and my reflections on friendship and love. For the most part, my writing was inspired by imagination. Lacking guidance, my mind idled or it took off in one direction—the world of fantasy. Like a plant growing poorly, failing to branch out in all directions, for the time being my mind didn't expand, fed only with ideas picked up randomly from books that were almost as stupid as I was.

I was eleven when my father decided to think seriously about my education. This was very timely. Our financial situation had improved so much that it was possible to send me to an urban school. Father planned to send me to Voronezh, with Andryushka, whose parents had entrusted my father to arrange the journey. At that time Belyakov was still on good terms with Father, and, wanting to return the favors he had received from him, he offered to take us to Voronezh and enroll us in the county school.

Without delay we were equipped for the journey. It was painful for me to leave my parents' home. Abounding in neither comforts nor joy, it was the only life I knew. It broke my heart to say goodbye to my dear, indulgent grandmothers, Auntie Liza, and my incomparable mother. Seeing me off, she cried and gave me a blessing for the new life I would begin so far from her.

What also bothered me a lot was the prospect of living among those Moscals. As a real Little Russian, I had an aversion to them. Their customs, clothing, dwellings—all aroused my childish dislike.

As soon as we reached Voronezh, Andryushka and I parted. He went to live with his married sister. And I, along with several friends—Little Russian boys, thank goodness—was placed as a boarder with a meshchanin, Kalina Davidovich Kleshcharev.

Two days later, clutching a sack containing a sugarloaf, a pound of tea, and a square bottle of Kizlar vodka, I was presented to the inspector of the county school, Pyotr Vasilyevich Sokolovsky. I don't know if Belyakov's recommendation or the gift was responsible for the gracious reception I received and for my immediate placement with pupils in the so-called lower division.

10

School

There I was, almost two hundred versts from my family, living among Moscals and attending school—all unusual experiences for me. Naturally timid and shy, I had a hard time adjusting to a new way of life and new people. Moreover, I was terribly homesick for my native land. They say that all Little Russians in foreign lands suffer some degree of homesickness, and some even die from it. So it was no surprise that I fell ill. For several weeks I had a raging fever and turned into a real skeleton. My illness was kept from my mother. Otherwise, nothing would have stopped her from traveling to Voronezh to care for me.

This agonizing interlude left me with indelible memories of the treatment I received from the doctor's assistant. Instead of making me feel better, he only increased my suffering. He dosed me with emetics, which didn't work and tormented me beyond description. In the end, I could not bear the sight of his moon-shaped, though genial, face, with its immobile, leaden stare. Even his thick, brownish flannelette frock coat repelled me. The sight of it sickened me no less than a dose of his medicine.

My landlord, Kalina Davidovich Kleshcharev, in whose care I was entrusted, observed the fruitless efforts of the doctor's assistant. And so he decided to call in a self-taught doctor, a simple fellow, known for his successful treatment of fever.

This fellow prepared a dark-red mixture and instructed me to take two teaspoons of it every day. Like magic, the fever vanished.

Either the fever itself was sick of racking me or the medicine was really effective. Anyway, I recovered quickly and started school.

Anxious and fearful, I entered the building for the first time, but I had worried unnecessarily. I knew far more than required for admission to the class to which I was assigned. I knew the four basic arithmetic operations, I read quickly and intelligently, and I wrote neatly without the aid of lines to guide me.

Nevertheless, I sat down timidly at a designated desk and gazed reverently at the teacher, who was wearing a nankeen frock coat. Any moment I expected his mouth to spew pearls of wisdom, which my head would not be able to accommodate. But from the mouth of poor Ivan Fyodorovich Klemantov nothing came out except the most ordinary things, like $2 \times 2 = 4$ and $3 \times 3 = 9$. Now and then he would call pupils to order, and occasionally he would discharge a volley of more or less expressive oaths at naughty or lazy ones.

However, Ivan Fyodorovich was very kind, and he conscientiously performed this thankless job, which barely kept him from starving to death. He was fair and indulgent with his pupils, but no one noticed or valued this. Besides, unlike most teachers at that time, he was not a drunkard.

In general, the Voronezh county school deserves some credit. As we shall see later, its pervasive climate was superior to that of other schools. The education and morals of its faculty were well above the usual level. Of course, their teaching methods reflected the routine prevailing everywhere in those days, but they treated their pupils with a humanity unparalleled for the times. Considering the unenviable personal lot of the teachers, they deserved even more credit for their humanity. The community gave them no encouragement, and the compensation they received barely covered their daily bread. What kind of progress is conceivable under such conditions!

I started school halfway through the course, in the winter—December or January—I don't recall exactly when. Still, I rose rapidly to the top rank of students. What helped enormously were all the things I had picked up back home, although my home studies were certainly haphazard.

So going to class, and even being its best student, was easy for me. And I had plenty of free time at my disposal. As before, I spent it reading whatever I could get my hands on and daydreaming of my beloved native land. Khristinushka quickly faded from memory, but absence from my family and my homeland only made my heart grow fonder.

Now and then my thoughts carried me back to my Little Russian world. I see white peasant cottages peeking through cherry orchards, and dark-complexioned villagers in tall sheepskin hats, ringlets of curly hair brushing their temples, teeth gripping short tobacco pipes beneath drooping mustaches. Before me flash hazel-eyed maidens in multicolored skirts, wives in white coats, pouches dangling from the waist . . .

From afar, how attractive our house and the surrounding scene appear to me! I even feel nostalgia for the chickens wandering about our yard, and for their leader, a rooster, an impudent and pugnacious fellow with a helmet-shaped red comb boldly quivering above his bill. In my mind's eye, dove-colored wings streak by, and I, following the flight of pigeons on high, am transported into our oak forest and the trembling, feathery grass of the steppe.

Here at school, so far away from my home, what a joy it was to happen upon a caravan of carts harnessed with oxen! Alongside strut the carters in their tar-stained shirts. Armed with rods, they urge the oxen on, shouting "Hey, hey, *tsob, tsobe*" no less lethargically than the oxen's feet move. Sometimes you ask, "Sirs, where are you from?" With baited breath you await their reply. If you hear the words "from Boguchar," you're ready to fling your arms around them and the oxen, too.

Before I knew it, summer vacation had arrived. Packing all my stuff in a sack, I climbed into a Little Russian cart and, with a light heart, set out on the homeward journey to my family. On the way I had to stop over for several days in Alekseyevka to pick up Grandma Stepanovna. From there we would continue together to

Pisaryevka. Now my joy knew no bounds. Oh, the delights that awaited me at Grandma Stepanovna's! Embraces, affection, cherries, watermelon! And I must confess that the latter two items played no minor role in my dreams of vacation pleasures.

On this occasion reality lived up to my dreams. From both grandmothers and Aunt Yelizabeta flowed the riches of their hearts, orchards, and kitchen gardens. I spent several wonderful days with them. Finally, I set out for Pisaryevka, not only with Grandma, but with Aunt Liz, the first friend of my childhood.

We traveled for four days, resting and sleeping in all sorts of places—by a river, in a field, at the edge of a forest, next to an apiary or melon field. Evenings we built a fire, cooked gruel and dumplings with lard, and had supper. After supper we ate a dessert of cucumbers and cherries. Watermelons hadn't ripened yet.

We slept under the open sky, in the cart, under the cart, or in the fragrant grass. And so we rested, if not on a bed of roses, at least of flowers.

Nights were delightful. Warm, gentle. Not a sound to be heard to remind us of human habitation nearby. But the night air was alive with ceaseless murmuring and whispers, with the buzzing and chirping of insects in the grass and foliage, with the shriek of quail and the breath of the wind . . .

Enjoying the charm of these days and nights, little did we suspect that grief awaited us at home. Instead of the noisy and joyous welcome we had anticipated, we were met by long faces and an ominous, anxious bustling, as if something highly unusual was about to happen. Mother emerged from the cottage in tears, pale and distraught. Embracing me, she began to sob bitterly.

Father was hopelessly ill, and we had arrived in the midst of preparations for the administration of extreme unction.

I entered the room where he lay but was not permitted at his bedside. Frightened and confused, I huddled in a corner and wept softly.

Gradually outsiders filled the room, all with mournful faces and many with traces of real grief. I was particularly struck by pomeshchitsa Bedryaga's appearance: she stood there perfectly composed, cold but obviously concerned. The priest arrived and began to administer the last rites.

During the entire ritual Father lay there motionless and evidently unconscious. Everyone left. Only family members remained, in nervous expectation of that dreaded visitor—Death. But late that evening a miracle occurred. Father regained consciousness, mumbled a few words, and fell into a quiet, salutary sleep. The following morning he awoke refreshed and, to the family's joy, rapidly made a complete recovery.

With the exception of this unfortunate episode, which ended happily, everything was fine at home. At this time the pomeshchitsa's regard for my father and her trust in him had reached an apogee. And not without good reason. Besides his management of her estate affairs, which she valued, Father had rendered her chivalrous assistance in a situation that was terribly sad for such a willful, ambitious lady.

I had mentioned earlier that pomeshchitsa Marya Fyodorovna Bedryaga and her daughter had journeyed to the Don, where the daughter's husband lived. The purpose of the trip was twofold. She wanted to reconcile her daughter with her husband and resolve her own personal differences with her son-in-law. But new clashes flared between Bedryaga and the son-in-law. Their relationship worsened, and the Cossack general finally thought up a purely Cossack approach to bridling his mother-in-law and his wife.

He transported them to a distant farmstead and kept them prisoner there. No matter how they raged, they could not free themselves. They were too well guarded and unable to communicate personally or in writing with anyone. Finally, after many fruitless attempts, they succeeded in informing my father of their captivity and begged him to come and free them.

Inclined toward romantic adventures, Father willingly undertook to help them. Stealthily he made his way to the site where they were imprisoned, got friendly with the guard, bribed him, and finally was allowed to see them. After that he managed without difficulty to conduct them from the house where they were held, seat them in a prearranged carriage, and deliver them safely to Pisaryevka.

When they entered her estate, Marya Fyodorovna ordered the driver to stop at the church. Making the sign of the cross, she announced for all to hear that she owed her reappearance on God's earth to my father alone. She solemnly swore never to forget this. How she kept this promise, we shall soon see.

Vacation days flew by. I was back in school in Voronezh. Now I was in the senior class, and this was the beginning of a new chapter of my life.

My studies went very well, and before long I achieved the rank of star pupil, occupying the first desk, initially as class auditor. Later I was appointed class censor, an omen, as it were, of my future career as a censor in government service, where I endured so much adversity, and where disaster threatened me daily in the performance of my duties.

In our school only the best students could become auditors. Their role was to make lists, or *notati,* each morning when the pupils arrived at school, and to check their industry and grade them for it. For this Latin letters were used: *pn* for *prorsus nescit* (pupil knows nothing); *ns* for *nescit* (knows almost nothing); *nt* for *non totum* (knows half); *nb* for *non bene* (not good); *er* for *erravit* (with errors). The most desirable grade was *s* for *scit.*

Taking the notes from the auditor, the teacher handed them to one of the pupils—usually the tallest and burliest, who executed the sentence meted out to lazy and remiss pupils. Armed with a ruler, he went around the classroom, starting from prorsus and ending with erravit, giving each victim's palms a specific number of whacks. Erravits received only a verbal reprimand.

The title of censor was considered the highest school honor, and only the best student could receive it. He was responsible for proper behavior in the classroom. He saw to it that silence and order were observed before the teacher arrived and in all other instances where large groups of students gathered. In a special notebook he recorded the names of pupils who were disorderly or violated decorum. In due course he presented the notebook to the teacher for inspection. To the miscreants the teacher doled out one or another punishment—blows with a birch rod or whacks with a ruler across the palm of the hand.

From my very first steps in school, I wanted more than anything else to become a censor. And when I advanced into the senior class, my obsession gave me no peace.

What I just said about my obsession reminded me that I forgot to mention events that propelled me to star-pupil ranking in the senior class. Here's what happened when my summer vacation had ended, and I was scheduled to return to school in Voronezh.

Due to various circumstances, Father had been unable to send me back to Voronezh on time. I had to wait until I could get a ride with someone going there. A long time had passed before I managed to get transportation, and I had arrived at school almost two months after the beginning of the term.

I was way behind in my studies, and it was very hard to catch up with my schoolmates. Having fallen behind in my work, I was dropped back from the first bench to the third. The position of censor had slipped away from me, and my self-esteem suffered cruelly. Egged on by my pride, I tackled my studies with such zeal that I quickly caught up with the class and again found myself on the first bench.

My schoolmates eagerly supported my efforts to become their leader. For the first half of the year, the censor was a chap by the name of Loginov, who was not popular with the students. They were just as anxious as I was to have him dethroned.

Two more weeks passed. Loginov committed a very serious school offense and was moved to the fifth bench, or, as the boys put it, "he was sent to the country to churn butter." At the same time, of course, he lost the job of censor. Then, according to the rules, it was given to me. I rejoiced, and with me my classmates, who disliked my predecessor for the biased and unscrupulous manner in which he had exercised his authority.

To the credit of my teachers and classmates, I must point out that Loginov was the son of relatively wealthy, influential parents, while I was a mere pauper. I didn't even have money to buy textbooks, so I copied the lessons from the books of classmates who were better equipped than I.

Having attained a position of authority, I did not betray my schoolmates' trust in me. The same ambition that drove me to be first among them now aroused a strong desire to gain their obedience, not by instilling in them a fear of the teacher's authority standing behind me, but through the strength of my will and humble character. Therefore, the main instrument of a class censor—the notebook for recording names of guilty students—was an empty threat in my hands and was never turned over to the authorities.

My approach appealed to my classmates, and with rare exceptions they willingly went along with me. As a result, order and silence in our class were always exemplary. If the boys quarreled it was settled among ourselves and went no further. Bare-fist bouts, very popular then, and not proscribed by the authorities, also improved their image. A code was introduced barring punches aimed at an opponent's nose or any part of the face; blows could be delivered only to the hardiest parts of the body. Any attempt to take an opponent by surprise was sternly censured. Only victory achieved through skill and honest strength was considered valid. I must admit that I didn't fare too badly in these bouts.

We had street scuffles, too, with the wards of the Department of Military Orphans. These boys, being raised for military service, were the sons of deceased soldiers and military settlers. We feuded constantly and rarely encountered each other without getting into a fight. Although my authority as a censor outside of school was very limited, I jealously defended the honor of my comrades. I endured no little fear, and took great pains to keep them from getting battered faces and black eyes.

There were two sports I liked best. One was *lapta:* I could bat the ball hard and far. The other was sprinting. At both of these, none of my classmates was my equal. I hated the game of *svayka;* the idea of tossing a spike to the center of a circle drawn on the ground didn't appeal to me. As for *ladizhka,* I was awful at the game.[1]

The students came from all kinds of families. Often, on the same bench, you would find the son of a secretary, the son of a high official, and the son of a serf; a boy from a wealthy merchant's home, who rode to school in an elegant *droshky* [uncovered carriage] pulled by a well-fed horse, could be found by the side of a poor child with an ill-fitting frock coat, full of holes, barely covering his threadbare linen breeches. Here, too, sat a Ukrainian lad from Biryuch or Ostrogozhsk, the son of a Cossack or military resident, with a perky forelock on his head and wearing a working-smock of dubious color.

Despite such variation in social class, the children at the school fraternized freely, and among them there were no pretensions or jealousy. What did confer status was academic excellence; those who were handier with their fists or more skillful at ball games won the most admiration.

The credit for this egalitarian climate goes to the teachers, whose impartial attitude toward the students encouraged a spirit of equality.

With the exception, perhaps, of the unusual conscientiousness of our faculty, pedagogical methods in our school were no better or worse than those used in all Russian schools of that time. We studied Holy Scripture, some universal history, Russian grammar, arithmetic, physics, natural history, the elements of Latin and German, and the duties of an individual and a citizen. Our faculty knew only one way to teach, that is, they forced us to memorize short textbooks.

The most curious among us recognized the deficiencies in this approach to education and tried to compensate for it by reading on our own. Before I arrived here, I had acquired a passion for books, and now devoured everything I could get my hands on.

Novels, historical works, and biographies of famous people were the delight and chief interest of my life. Plutarch's work fell into my hands, and he became my favorite author. Socrates, Aristotle, Philopoemen (liberator of Syracuse), and Diocletian in turn were so captivating that I spent whole hours thinking about their courage and dreaming of how to become like them. In my mind's eye I pictured a map of a nonexistent country with its province and city names borrowed from the ancient world. I was the ruler, and in my head I composed an entire history of my kingdom, which I structured according to the plan of Plato's *Republic.*

At times my vivid imagination carried me away and found an outlet in impassioned speeches. I imagined I was an orator at a Roman forum or an Athenian marketplace in ancient Greece. In a burst of noble indignation I threatened the enemies of my country or fervently fought for freedom and human dignity. My enthusiasm spread to my schoolmates, and a new game was born, called "Heroes and Orators."

Novels excited me no less. These were mainly translations, and most were poorly written, utterly lacking in character development. What captivated me were romantic adventures and the portrayal of passionate emotions. Quivering with excitement, I followed Ann Radcliffe, the English novelist of tales of terror, into the dungeons. And I was simply intoxicated by the French writer La Fontaine.[2]

I didn't gain very much from these books. In fact, for a long time after reading Ann Radcliffe's novels, I was afraid to be alone in a dark room. And as a result of reading La Fontaine, each time I met a woman I quickly raised her on a pedestal and fell in love with her.

I gave vent to my emotions in passionate and, I daresay, nonsensical letters to my parents. One of my friends, Ryndin, would lend an ear to all my drivel. Although a simple-minded lad, he was kind, well behaved, and always listened agape to my grandiloquent nonsense. Favoring him as my loyal follower and comrade-in-arms, I inundated him with speeches and messages.

While my head filled with all kinds of heroic feats and romantic foolishness, I neglected the demands of sober reality, ignoring what I viewed as mundane and unimportant. Considering my modest financial situation, this attitude was wholly unjustified. I didn't know how to be thrifty or neat, and I simply wasn't interested in practicing either of these principles. Often I preferred to do without some necessity rather than bother acquiring it or taking care of it.

The less scrupulous of my schoolmates, especially those with whom I shared living quarters, observing my disinterest in acquiring material benefits and comforts, used my possessions as if they owned them. No wonder that by the end of each school year I returned home poor as a church mouse. It cost my mother no little effort to conceal my misdeeds from my father. After scolding me a bit, she always managed to provide me with what I needed by paring her own needs to the bone.

Our school consisted of three classes, but for some reason the youngest group wasn't called a class. It was called the lower division. There were three teachers, one for each class. Fyodor Ivanovich Klemantov, whom I've already mentioned, taught the lower division. Nikolai Lukyanovich Grabovsky and Aleksandr Ivanovich Morozov taught the two upper classes. The inspector was Pyotr Vasilyevich Sokolovsky.

I don't know where Sokolovsky received his education. Grabovsky graduated from Kharkov University, and Morozov from Voronezh Seminary. All of them were respectable people and intellectually stood far above the positions they occupied. Only dire necessity had bound them to a thankless teaching career in a provincial backwater. But Morozov, being much younger, later succeeded in better arranging his life. Sokolovsky boarded students and also gave private French lessons, which helped him and his family live rather well. He had written and published a book on French grammar. He was a kind old fellow, though a bit hot-tempered. In a burst of anger he would scold a schoolboy, only to soften an instant later, and that would be the end of it. He simply didn't have the heart to follow through with severe measures against a miscreant.

Grabovsky, too, gave French lessons privately, and he translated a book from French.

Morozov was much younger than his two colleagues. He wrote poems, dressed in the latest provincial fashion, and strutted about with elegant manners. His father, a decorous archpriest in one of the wealthiest villages, gave his son some financial support. So Morozov lived comfortably. But, apparently tired of teaching in the county school, Morozov waited for the opportunity to switch to something more productive, which with his talents he had a perfect right to expect.

Later on, after serving in other government departments, Morozov returned to teaching. By that time I had managed to get somewhere in life and was in a position to offer him assistance. Being on friendly terms with D. M. Knyazhevich, administrator of Odessa District schools, I was able to intercede on behalf of my former mentor. As a result, Morozov became an inspector at one of the schools in that district. My effort to help Morozov was the least I could do to acknowledge gratitude to a man who had shown the most selfless interest in a poor schoolboy.

My achievements at school pleased him, and when one of my poems happened to fall into his hands—around this time I began to scribble verses!—he took a serious interest in me. The poem, a kind of sentimental appeal to nature, was nothing more than a display of the good intentions of an eleven-year-old schoolboy. But it was enough to inspire Morozov to apply himself more zealously to the development of the gifts he thought he saw in me. He offered to give me free lessons at his home—and not in grammar, which he taught at school. The lessons were for the science of what was then called poetics. Without a full course of study in this intricate science, poetic creation was considered unthinkable.

Twice a week I began to go to Aleksandr Ivanovich Morozov's home. But my study of poetics was short lived. I proved to be thoroughly incapable of mastering poetic meter. I simply didn't have the ear for it. My father, a fine musician, was determined to develop in me a taste for music. But this too failed. In poetics and in music, meter and measure were an overwhelming obstacle.

During my first year at school in Voronezh, when my father's situation had vastly improved, he could afford the luxury of hiring a music teacher for me. At the beginning I bravely set to work and took violin and piano lessons. But, oh my God! What torments these two instruments caused me. My teacher was known as a fine musician and person but very impatient. Anyone who hit a wrong note or confused a sharp with a flat invited trouble. And that's just what I did. Since the violin was my teacher's favorite instrument, it was the main cause of his fury with me. The indignant maestro's bow would leap from the strings and furiously trill along my fingers, which, as a result, were always bruised.

I liked music very much, but obviously it didn't like me. Still, I finally managed to strum a few Scottish dances, waltzes, and little songs. And that's as far as I got, especially since my father's circumstances had changed and he could no longer afford to pay for lessons. I happily sold the violin and squandered the money immediately on raisins, dates, figs, and the like.

When I studied poetics, the outcome was the same. I was hopelessly lost among iambs, trochees, spondees. Finally Morozov became convinced of my ineptitude, but even then his zeal did not diminish. He castigated me, saying that even in prose one could be a poet, and he set me to mastering rhetoric.

Here things went better. Tirelessly, I kept scribbling, and my mentor criticized and discussed my "compositions" with endless patience. What drivel poured from my pen at that time. The stuff I came up with! Yet, for the most part, Morozov concentrated on logical flow and grammatical correctness rather than on content.

Time ran its course, and my education at the Voronezh county school approached an end. Around June 25, 1815, I took my finals.[3] Then, as the top student, I delivered two speeches from the rostrum: one, in German, on "Honesty," the other, in Russian, on "The Temple of Fame of Russian Heroes."

I was awarded a diploma and a certificate of merit, receiving them from the hands of the bishop himself, Bishop Antony of Voronezh and Cherkask. His Grace embraced me, patted me on the back, blessed me, and, handing me the documents, smiled and said, "Clever lad! Continue to study and behave well, and you will be a fine man."

In his time Bishop Antony had played a prominent role in our region. At his prime, when he was about forty, he was truly a handsome man. He was also known as a great wit and sharp fellow, but his ways were far from pastoral. He loved the "beau monde" and was very obliging and courteous, especially with the ladies. Since he was so well mannered and harmed no one, people turned a blind eye to some of his behavior. But toward the end of his tenure in Voronezh he did something nasty, which turned public opinion against him. In one of the towns under his jurisdiction, he fired a rural dean whom everyone respected and replaced him with his own good-for-nothing brother.

Thereafter, Antony fared badly. He was transferred to another diocese, where he soon suffered a stroke. His health deteriorated, and he retired to a monastery, remaining there until the end of his days.

Around that time there was another clergyman who conducted himself in clerical matters and secular adventures exactly as had Antony. This was Methody, archimandrite of Akatov Alekseyevka Monastery. I met him only once, at a friend's home. Methody exhorted me to be very pious and to devote myself even more zealously to the study of Latin and Greek. Had the archimandrite not reeked from wine, his exhortations would have been incomparably more persuasive.

I was only thirteen when I graduated from the county school. How sad I felt to part with my schoolmates. But more painful than anything else was the knowledge that I would not be allowed to join the boys who were preparing to enter high school. For me its doors were inexorably closed.

Here, for the first time, I had to face the terrible curse that hung over me because of my social status, which later caused me so much suffering and almost drove me to suicide.

My teachers, Grabovsky and Morozov, sympathized deeply with me and contrived a way to help me. Had their plan materialized, I don't know what the consequences would have been for me, but for them it could have been disastrous.

All the boys had gone; some went off on vacations, others left school for good. I stayed longer in Voronezh, hoping to pick up less expensive transportation to my home. My heart was heavy!

Suddenly I received a letter from Grabovsky. He wrote that he had discussed my situation with other teachers at the school and then conceived a plan that might help me gain admission to the high school. His proposal? He suggested omitting my social status on the graduation certificate. But, on a list that had to be submitted to the director of the high school, I would be called the son of a collegiate registrar. In a burst of magnanimity, they had decided to resort to forgery.

Grabovsky persuaded me to go to the director immediately. What dear people! In their simple-heartedness, they didn't think of leaving themselves a loophole. But, in this letter to me, they had put themselves in the hands of a boy who, in his naiveté, could easily spill everything or through carelessness lose this dangerous document.

Despite my thirteen years I instinctively understood that I had to keep my mouth shut, and I decided to confide only in my father.

11

◆•◆•◆•◆

Fate Strikes Again

Shortly before I graduated, I heard that my father had run into new troubles. In his letters to me, he had said nothing about this. However, I knew that he was no longer in Pisaryevka, but living in Dantsyevka, crown land in Boguchar county.

During my studies in Voronezh, this wasn't the first time that I had been convinced of the unstable and unenviable nature of my father's existence. I remember another occasion, when he had gotten involved in a court case in Voronezh. He had traveled to Voronezh to speak personally with the governor, or rather with Senator Khitrovo, who was then conducting an audit of the province. What transpired between them, I do not know. Later I heard only that he had words with the governor.

Father was hotheaded and, despite previous encounters with the law, still believed that it was on the side of honest people. So he was not afraid to exercise his rights before the authorities. He refused to acknowledge that he lived in a country ruled by bureaucratic tyranny; that for a poor peasant like himself it was inappropriate to claim a right which no one truly possessed, and he least of all.

In any event, the governor was enraged and had Father thrown into prison on the grounds that he was in Voronezh without a residence permit, although he really didn't need one because my parents' residence was in the same province.

I remember how I trembled with fear when a soldier appeared

at the apartment where I was staying in Voronezh. He told me that my father was in prison and wanted to see me. My heart was in my throat. I followed the soldier and found my father locked up in a prison cell with thieves, swindlers, and other rogues.

Father disliked displays of affection and even at home, within the family, would not permit any effusions of the heart. Restraining my feelings, I sat down alongside a red-haired fellow—a peasant—on a plank-bed in the corner. Finally, unable to contain myself, I burst out crying. My tears touched a woman near me. With deep sympathy, she began to console me.

"Don't cry, dear child," she said. "Don't cry. You're still little. You'll see, this will pass."

On the upper bunk sat an old man with a gray beard who mumbled to himself. This was a Georgian priest, brought here from Tbilisi for participating in some uprising or conspiracy. In a grating voice, in broken Russian, he told me not to cry, assuring me that it was all a lot of nonsense, and that my father and I ought not to be so distressed.

All this took place in a dark, filthy, smelly cell. In his poor state of health, my father could not remain there long without serious consequences. He gave me a ruble and instructed me to go to the sergeant and request a transfer to quarters where "refined" people were held.

In my childhood, the mere sight of a police uniform was enough to plunge me into despair. I sensed that it portended something ominous; whenever I encountered a policeman on duty at his booth or a noncommissioned police officer, I bolted from them in good order. So you can imagine how fearfully I set forth to present Father's request. In those times, fortunately now remote, the police were indeed far worse agents of tyranny and force than we have today.

But on this occasion, my fear turned out to be unwarranted. The police officer accepted my ruble and promised to fulfill my request. Soon enough my father found himself in a rather bright and tidy room with only one roommate—a provincial official accused of stealing some file. The room was furnished with two similar beds, and my father made himself comfortable on one of them.

I visited him every day, and after several weeks he gave me a new assignment. This time I had to deliver a letter in person to Senator Khitrovo. Again I was carried away by my imagination, painting a series of images: the senator, yelling at me, stamping his feet, orders his servants to throw me out, and I end up in jail. After all, I thought, anything could happen to a small, insignificant creature like me!

But I had no choice. I had to go. Arming myself with courage, I set out. I entered the senator's antechamber, and there stood a police officer—not the one I already knew to some extent. Instinctively I drew back. But even police officers are not all alike. As I learned later, this officer, the father of a large family, was touched by my pitiful, frightened face. He hastened to cheer me up. And when it was my turn to enter the senator's office, he put an end to my hesitation at once by pushing me deftly through the doorway.

The senator read my father's letter and exclaimed gloomily, in words that made no sense to me:

"That's his problem to solve."

And that was it. Father, too, was puzzled by the senator's response. However, about ten days later, the governor ordered the return of my father to Boguchar—he was deemed guilty, nevertheless, of having willfully absented himself from the county without a pass, but the governor did not subject him to any further punishment.

It's time to explain how my father came to move from Pisaryevka—which belonged to pomeshchitsa Bedryaga—to Dantsyevka, located on crown lands. Further, I'll explain what caused the impoverished circumstances in which I found my family when I finished school.

Marya Fyodorovna Bedryaga had a very short memory for the vow she had taken in front of the church: a vow that she would never forget the good deed rendered by my father. This power-hungry lady of the manor couldn't bear to have anyone in her entourage acting on his own, even when it was in her interest. The notion that her business manager conducted himself too independently consumed her.

For his part, my father was not one to yield without a fight, especially when he was sure he was right or when his honor was involved. He had undertaken the task of putting Pisaryevka in good order on one condition—that the pomeshchitsa, who had made such a mess of running her estate, would give him a free hand. The result of his freedom from her interference clearly justified his demands. Marya Bedryaga's income had doubled, the peasants' conditions had improved, and excesses, the chief cause of the estate's decline, were significantly reduced.

The parasites in her retinue, unscrupulously exploiting her wicked propensities, couldn't accept the new order of things. They didn't miss an opportunity to turn the pomeshchitsa against her loyal, conscientious servant.

Especially active in this regard was the Jewess Fyodosya, an awful mischief-maker, whom I mentioned earlier. Sometimes when my father had things out with Marya Fyodorovna, he simply couldn't control his hot temper. Fyodosya never failed to exploit such incidents and spread malicious gossip. The pomeshchitsa grew increasingly impatient with the secondary role imposed on her, a situation produced by a combination of various circumstances and her own laxity. More and more she expressed her dissatisfaction and made impossible demands.

Father held out for a long time. Finally he couldn't take it and decided it was better to quit this well-paying position than tolerate Madame Bedryaga's capriciousness and the snooping of her minions. One fine day, armed with a thick notebook, he appeared before Marya Fyodorovna and declared in effect: "Here's the record of my tenure as manager of your estate. From now on I am no longer your servant. I request that you discharge me and give me the following wages."

Marya Fyodorovna was perplexed. Realizing that she still needed my father, she tried again to reach a compromise, to arrange affairs in such a way that he would remain in her employ and her wishes would be satisfied. But Father knew too well how meaningless were the promises of this capricious lady of the manor. He stood his ground and demanded to be discharged. The pomeshchitsa persisted. His anger rising, Father reiterated his final decision to leave her and, deaf to further objections, left the room. Marya Bedryaga became enraged and decided to take revenge on this rebellious servant.

The following morning everyone in Father's household was still asleep. Suddenly he was awakened by someone shouting, "Get up! See what's going on outside!" Alarmed, Father went into the entrance hall. The house was surrounded by peasants. The whole family was under guard. Knowing Marya Fyodorovna's character, and seeing that she had resorted to force, he didn't doubt that she would stand firm.

He was in a difficult position. Where could he find help? In her domain? Impossible. And how could he escape? Guards blocked all exits. Fortunately these were peasants who were devoted to Father and hated the pomeshchitsa. They helped him escape. Through kitchen gardens and orchards he made his way to Zayarskaya Pisaryevka and found refuge at the home of his old friend Grigory Fyodorovich Tatarchukov.

At large, Father appealed to the appropriate authorities to free his family and compel the party who was guilty of using flagrant force to answer for her action. This was the beginning of a case that caused quite a stir throughout the province and was the source of endless worry for Father. But it caused Bedryaga no little concern, too. Later, she herself admitted that all her days had been spoiled by the expectation of unpleasant documents arriving and the need to make a formal reply to them.

What a strange case this was! On the one side was an individual possessing two thousand souls, wealth, and connections, an individual who personified arrogance and despotism and was dead certain of winning her case. On the other side was a man lacking social status and the advantages that go with it, a man relying solely on his innocence, and so poor that often he didn't have the money to buy the legal paper needed to register a suit or petition. To win the case after a lengthy struggle under such disparate circumstances required the full knowledge of the law my father possessed as well as his skill in composing legal documents.

Justice, always ready in those days to favor the powerful, wavered indecisively. The judges themselves wondered why the case didn't go according to the wishes of the wealthy and eminent lady of the manor. But they couldn't do anything, and let it drag on endlessly. When Father died, I often heard officials of the civil court say that every petition received from the plaintiff had produced a sensation among them. They would gather in a circle and read the petitions aloud, captivated by the dialectical skill and clarity of exposition. Nevertheless, Father died waiting in vain for the case to end.

Many years later, when I was in St. Petersburg, the property confiscated from Father by Bedryaga and placed in court custody was returned to my mother. All the trunks were returned, but only some rags and stacks of Father's papers were in them. The rest had disappeared without a trace.

At the beginning of the case, at Father's insistence, Marya Fyodorovna was asked on what basis she was detaining his family and their possessions. The response was worthy of Madame Bedryaga: the plaintiff, she wrote in reply, working as her manager, had ruined her estate, and the things she was now withholding had been purchased with her money. Naturally, she wasn't asked for proof. They took her word for it. At the beginning of the case Father's complaint was ignored. Then he appealed to the governor, and in the end he succeeded, at least, in having his family returned to him.

United with his wife and children, my father settled in a Little Russian hamlet, Dantsyevka, about twenty versts from Boguchar, where his case was being tried.

Again, the painful question arose: how would we live? My parents were left without the most basic necessities, as if they had lost everything in a fire. Father could have found work easily, but he was too involved with his case. It dragged on and assumed grandiose proportions. Carried away, as usual, he demanded the return of his possessions and compensation for his losses as well as legal action against the pomeshchitsa for taking the law into her own hands. At the very beginning of the case Grigory Fyodorovich Tatarchukov helped him, and later on he often rendered favors, big and small.

Thus did several months go by. Then my father was offered a job. He was asked to go to one of the Don villages and put some business affairs in order. Substantial compensation was offered. He agreed, left the family in Dantsyevka, and set out.

Always ready with falsehood and slander, Marya Fyodorovna heard about it and raised an alarm. Through the Boguchar court, she got in touch with the chief of the Don village to which Father was traveling. She informed him that my father was under investigation and therefore was not allowed to leave the area where he resided. He must be detained, she said, and put in jail.

Without looking into the case, the village authorities carried out the Boguchar request to the letter. And so my poor father, summoned to the station to perform an honest and useful service, ended up in prison again.

When I returned home from Voronezh, here is the situation in which I found my family. Mother had changed drastically. She had aged and gotten frightfully thin. Her separation from Father, from whom she hadn't had any news for a long time, killed all her pleasure in my homecoming. She and the other children occupied two tiny but tidy attic rooms in the cottage of a well-to-do Little Russian. For the past few months kindhearted Gavrilych had been keeping Mother and the children there at his own expense.

But if, as the saying goes, when it rains it pours, the same ought to apply to happy occasions. My arrival turned out to be a happy harbinger of the latter. Still, the morning of that day passed sadly for my mother. It was marked by a trivial event, but one that affected her sorely.

While doing household chores, Mother suddenly noticed that her gold wedding ring was missing from her finger. Evidently it had slipped off her wasted hand while she was cleaning the rooms and carrying firewood, and, engrossed in sad thoughts, she failed to notice the loss. Unlucky people are superstitious. Mother considered the loss of her wedding ring a bad omen and became despondent. In her grief she rummaged through her household possessions and searched every corner. The ring was nowhere to be found.

Only the shed remained to be searched, and it was loaded with straw. Mother had been there earlier to fetch some kindling for the stove. But the prospect of finding in the haystacks such a tiny thing as a gold ring, so close in color to straw, was an impossible hope.

Nevertheless, mother headed for the shed. On the way she convinced herself that if the ring turned up, it would mean that Father was alive and homeward bound. If the ring could not be found, it could only mean that Father was dead.

Nervously, she crossed the threshhold, and for a long time hesitated to raise her eyes and look around. Finally, with sinking heart, she glanced in the corner from which she had taken kindling hay earlier. A long straw stuck out through the top of the stack, and on it hung the ring! Mama cried out, crossed herself, and smothered it with kisses. She was radiant with joy, not a trace left of her sad thoughts.

Several hours passed. Twilight was falling. There was some movement at the cottage gate. Doors opened, and on the threshhold stood good, kindly Father, cheerful, some money in his pocket, and loaded down with gifts.

The next day we had a sumptuous feast to celebrate Father's return and mine as well. It had been so long since any of us had eaten such borscht with mutton or the delicious jams to which Mama, in her joy, treated us. To the utter delight of us children, at dinner there was dessert prepared from prunes and raisins brought by Papa. And eagerly sharing our joy and the plentiful meal were our kind hosts: Gavrilych, his wife, and their pretty daughter, whose clear brown eyes captured my heart.

But how was my father suddenly delivered from prison into the arms of his family? And, what's more, ending up in circumstances that had changed for the better? Our entire lives are woven of chance events. Hostile chance had driven him to Bedryaga and to the Boguchar judges who threw him in jail. Lucky chance brought him together with Cossack Colonel Popov, who then rescued my father from misfortune.

Colonel Popov had a great deal of power at the Don village where Father was under arrest. He took it upon himself to investigate the case, and in the end ordered Father's release and sheltered him on his own estate. The colonel further commissioned him to put estate affairs in order and, compensating him handsomely, let him go home in peace.

At last we breathed freely. We spent the next few months peacefully, even lightheartedly. Dantsyevka wasn't a particularly pretty place, but the region was one of the most productive in Russia. The climate was warm, the cost of living then was low. Choice fruits—cherries, apples, pears, melons, and watermelons—could be bought for almost nothing.

Dantsyevka hamlet consisted of fifty cottages—white, neat, and buried in the foliage of cherry orchards. The little settlement stretched along the banks of the Boguchar River. Now, I've heard, it has grown a lot and become a prosperous village with a stone church. But in our time, the hamlet belonged to the parish of Tverdokhlebovka village. Tverdokhlebovka is very close to Boguchar, which is almost the most pitiful of Russian chief-county towns.

The residents of Dantsyevka were state-owned Little Russians, so-called military settlers.[1] Little Russian to the core, they thrived in comparison to peasants belonging to pomeshchiks. On the other hand, they lived in complete ignorance. They didn't have schools. Literate people were a rarity among them. None of the ideas of modern civilization had seeped down to them. They were exceptional for their utter simplicity and exemplary behavior. Thieves and drunkards were known only through hearsay. Quarrels and fights? If they did occur, people were too embarrassed to talk about them.

Unfortunately, when a person becomes more civilized, he acquires new characteristics. But he loses those he possessed before and becomes infected with defects of which he previously had no concept. The law of human development does not follow a set plan to attain a certain result. Rather, it follows an inevitable course by virtue of which all innate traits within an individual must in their own time manifest themselves and reach a certain level. This occurs whether these traits then vanish forever or blend harmoniously for greater development and perfection.

We lived well and got along nicely among the simple-hearted Dantsyevka residents. For a short time they treated us as new arrivals, but they gladly accepted us into their midst and were very warm to my parents. And our kind landlord, Gavrilych, endowed with a host of common sense, was able to appreciate my father's cast of mind.

After he had rested up, Father began to think about my future. He was very eager for me to continue my education. I fully shared his desire and showed him Grabovsky's letter. As Father was familiar with the laws and administrative procedures in our region, he understood, of course, the shaky foundation on which my teachers hoped to construct the edifice of my future education. He also understood the danger to them should their nobly intentioned pretext come to light. And Father flatly refused to accept their proposal.

But my achievements at the county school inspired in him unfounded hopes that an exception would be made for me, and that one way or another I would undoubtedly enter high school. He was so carried away by this fantastic dream that he forgot that he lacked the funds to keep me in Voronezh. He was dazzled by a mirage and rushed toward it, having forgotten, as usual, how costly his awakenings to reality had always been. Be that as it may, once again my family equipped me with necessities, found someone who was driving to Voronezh, and sent me on my way.

12

◆•◆•◆•◆

Waiting in Voronezh

When I arrived in Voronezh I appeared at the old apartment I had lived in when I attended the county school. I had no money for rent and handed the landlord a letter from my father. Father asked him to take me in and promised to pay very soon for my bed and board. Kalina Davidovich Kleshcharev frowned but, kind and trusting, agreed meanwhile to give me a nook for a bed and let me dine with him.

As was to be expected, I was not admitted to the high school. I was too shy to meet the director as a supplicant, and besides, I was told, in clothes like mine I would make a terrible impression. Also, it was the custom not to appear empty-handed. And where would I find the means of securing a gift?

So from day to day I postponed my visit to him. And then, too, I found out that one of my well-wishers, without my knowledge, had seen the director on my behalf but had failed to sway him. I became utterly despondent.

I watched the boys, my former schoolmates, now high school students, as they proudly marched off to school with their new books under their arms. They seemed to be so favored by fate in my eyes that they assumed the proportions of higher beings. And the small yellow building on Dvoryanskaya Street, which housed the school, appeared to be a palace with its doors shut tightly against me alone.

I stayed home in my corner, leafing through school notebooks and, as before, devouring everything in print that I could manage to obtain. I didn't want for books because a new friend I had made supplied me with them. He was Mikhail Grigoryevich Akhtyrsky, a music teacher and my landlord's son-in-law.

A gaunt little fellow with a yellow complexion, he had had a rather wild youth but settled down after marrying. His homely appearance conveyed the wrong impression about his intelligence and education. Neither was run-of-the-mill. Besides, in Voronezh, he had an excellent reputation as a music teacher and was a fine violinist and pianist.

Since he was the owner of several trunks of books, I was particularly drawn to him, especially because I was allowed to rummage freely through those trunks. He took a great interest in me and, whenever he had free moments, helped me wile away the hours I spent waiting for some miraculous turn in my fate.

Often he would peer into my corner, sit down on my bed, and, smoking his ubiquitous pipe, chat with me for a long time.

His wife, my landlord Kleshcharev's daughter, Natalya Kalinichna, while rather ordinary-looking, had a fine mind and a passion for books. She read a great deal, mainly novels. Most likely her sophistication and intellectual maturity could be attributed to all this reading. Suffice it to say that she was able to gain a secure hold on the affections of a restless man—Akhtyrsky—on whom she had a wholesome influence to the very end.

Almost always serious, Natalya held herself aloof, even somewhat squeamishly, from women of her circle, preferring the company of her husband. Anyone else reading as many novels as she did might have become pretty muddled, but she tasted their poisons with impunity. All of which is further proof that the main role in our moral and intellectual development is played by the stock with which nature has endowed us. The influence of external conditions is secondary and subordinate to our natural abilities and inclinations.

Days, weeks, months went by with my situation unchanged. I was at the mercy of whim and chance. I hadn't received letters from Father in a long time. I knew only that he had moved from

Dantsyevka to Ostrogozhsk, abandoning the Boguchar district altogether. Evidently my landlord was finding it difficult to keep me any longer without payment. My clothes were worn out and my boots were unfit to wear. Finally I had to say farewell to my sweet dreams of high school and set out for home. But how could I travel for many days without money, shoes, and a fur coat?

Akhtyrsky came to my rescue. He provided me with a sheepskin coat, felt boots, and a round fur cap, and gave me five rubles and fifty kopeks. In return I left him my bed to sell or dispose of as he pleased.

Thus equipped, I was ready to set out boldly on my journey. I had only to find a cart going my way, but that, too, was found quickly. A peasant was driving to Ostrogozhsk. For two rubles and fifty kopeks he agreed to take me with him.

13

◆•◆•◆•◆

Ostrogozhsk
I Go Out into the World

The year was 1816. Ostrogozhsk, formerly a part of Slobodsko-Ukraine province, now belonged to Voronezh province. Sprawling Ostrogozhsk county was populated almost entirely by Little Russians transferred there in the seventeenth century, during the reign of Tsar Aleksei Mikhailovich, to protect southern borders from invading Tatars. Only a small number of Russians had nestled here and there along the Sosna River to form several small settlements.

About ten thousand people lived in the town of Ostrogozhsk. These, too, were Little Russians, except for the merchantry, who constituted a large segment of the Russian population.

At that time Ostrogozhsk was a remarkable town. In the steppe wilderness, far from the capital, it exhibited a vitality that would be hard to find in far bigger and better-located centers in the Russian Empire. Both its economic and intellectual levels were immeasurably higher not only than those of most towns in the county, but even of many towns in the province.

A manufacturing industry flourished there. Its merchants traded in sheep, salt beef, and tallow, and turned over huge capital. In outlying villages the military settlers—for example, the Golovchenkos and Larionovs—were also engaged in trade and had a turnover in capital of half a million rubles. Most of the wealthy pomeshchiks spent part of the year in town, where they had second residences. Like the Ostrogozhsk nobility, they were concerned about the honor of their class. Therefore their activity was notable for its dignity, little known in those days of corrupt serfdom.

Bribery among them was simply unheard of. Those serving during elections were true and impartial servants of society. At the head of the aristocracy stood people noted for their noble birth and their efforts to improve conditions for the peasants. Some examples were the Dolzhikovs, Safonovs, Stankeviches, and Tomilins. It's clear that the humane aspirations and enlightened views of the pomeshchiks created an environment in which rural peasants lived better than anywhere else.

Fulfilling their obligations to their masters for the use of their land, the peasants were not driven to exhaustion. The pomeshchiks treated their peasants humanely. And the peasantry, well-fed and satisfied with their lot, willingly bore their burden, thereby contributing to the prosperity of their masters. In all likelihood, it was this well-balanced, mutually beneficial relationship between the two basic classes of society that accounted for the county's economic prosperity.

It is hard to point to the source of the wide-ranging circle of intellectual interests in which moved the most educated Ostrogozhsk residents, who for good reason were called Voronezh Athenians. They inhabited spheres, as it were, hardly accessible to the provincial hinterland in which fate had cast them. They were occupied with matters pertaining to literature, politics, and society.

They wrangled not about personal interests but about principles. In the principles they voiced, their aspirations for freedom came through, as well as a conscious protest against the yoke of the powerful bureaucracy of that time.

Many people—even merchants and meshchane—owned collections of serious books such as *The Justinian Code*, Delelom's *The Constitution of England*, Montesquieu's *Persian Letters* and his *The Spirit of Laws* in Yazykov's translation, *Crime and Punishments* by Beccaria, and the works of Voltaire, in Russian, which today you can't find in a single book shop. Even the newspaper *Moscow News*, almost unknown at the time in the province, was read diligently. In social circles they talked about science and the arts and discussed domestic and foreign policy. Some were so carried away by the liberal ideas in the air, they even expressed admiration for representative forms of government.

Although reputed to be the most cultured town in the region, it was not in the good graces of province authorities, who considered it a thorn in their sides. Nowhere but in Ostrogozhsk did the rapacity of province authorities meet such persistent protest. All encounters with these authorities inevitably ended, of course, in victory for the predators, which is to say that more or less huge bribes found their way into their pockets. But this heavily damaged their moral standing, something that later returned to haunt them.

Not long afterward, when province government was restructured, the entire region was hit hard. Five provinces were placed under the command of one governor-general. Former Minister of Police A. D. Balashov was appointed to the post. The provinces placed under his command were Voronezh, Riazan, Tambov, Tula, and Orlov. The headquarters of the central administration were in Riazan.

It is hard to determine for what purpose this administrative arrangement was designed. Perhaps solely to give a dignitary a respectable post far from the imperial court. In the history of our administration, the name Balashov appears among many names and public figures of the year 1812. Maybe this Balashov had rendered some sort of service and was entitled to the honor shown him. I am not prepared to say, but I remember only too well the memory he left behind. He ruled no worse than any Turkish pasha. Maybe he didn't personally accept bribes and was unaware of the chicanery of his subordinates, but his office and agents indulged in bribery with insatiable greed.

Even prior to this reorganization of government, the counties paid a substantial tribute to Voronezh, but now they had to satisfy the central administration in Riazan as well.

The Balashov yoke lay lightest on officials. And, I daresay, it wouldn't have hurt to have applied some pressure on them so they would put less on others. The burden fell mostly on the inhabitants of the towns. New taxes were imposed constantly, supposedly "to adorn the villages and towns." Sometimes something was done for this purpose, but only for show, and usually in time for the arrival of an important personage.

No one cared what lay concealed behind this magnificent facade. For example, news would arrive that on such-and-such date a notable would be passing along a certain road where a bridge was on the verge of collapse. The entire village was mobilized to repair it. On the surface it appeared that they did a great job of raising the sagging bridge. The visiting dignitary passed over it and praised it. And immediately after he had thus honored the bridge, it collapsed.

After the War of 1812 our administrators displayed a mania for imitating German customs. Only superficially, of course. So, for example, copying the Germans, they began to plant trees along our post high-roads. But those who drove along cart-roads were left, as before, to sink into the mud, break their necks, and wreck their carriages. Abandoned lots in towns were enclosed with beautiful fences and marked with numbers to give the impression that houses were being built. No one was constructing anything there, nor was there any reason to.

Balashov occasionally toured his domain—excuse me, provinces. In St. Petersburg this must have been perceived as evidence of his diligent and useful service. How the provinces under his authority viewed this is another question. Upon arrival in a town he was auditing, his first task was to instill as much fear as possible. The town head was a special target. He had to answer for the lack of sidewalks, roadways, stone arcades, trees along the streets. In brief, everything that the governor-general admired abroad.

Balashov's aesthetic sense was offended by lopsided hovels with windowpanes of paper as well as rush and straw roofs on wooden structures. He didn't bother to look for the reasons for such phenomena, but with the cold eye of a bureaucrat, he targeted the police as the authority responsible for applying measures to eliminate these deficiencies. That the town lacked the funds, that its inhabitants were on the verge of starvation—these were the sort of trifles beneath his notice. Upon his departure, Balashov would give the police strict orders to correct everything before his next visit, that is, sidewalks must be constructed, marketplaces, and so on. The mayor would scratch his head, the town bailiff would shout at the policemen, and the policemen would dash from house to house pressuring the inhabitants to get busy beautifying the town. After several weeks went by, everything would quiet down, and nothing would have changed. These days, this sort of thing isn't possible, but in all the provinces where Balashov and his infamous chancery ruled, they are well remembered.

My picture of Ostrogozhsk society is incomplete without a description of the clergy. When I lived there the clergy was truly at the pinnacle of their calling. There were eight stone churches and a cathedral of beautiful architecture that boasted fine examples of the work of well-known members of the Russian Academy of Sciences.

Parish clergy enjoyed decent earnings that allowed them to comport themselves with dignity. Among the priests, several were particularly outstanding: Simeon Stsepinsky, Mikhail Podzorsky, Pyotr Lebedinsky. The first two far surpassed the usual level of our clergy and would have been held in high repute in any educated community. Both were gifted speakers. Their sermons, especially Podzorsky's, attracted huge audiences.

There was nothing crude or amateurish about the way these two priests conducted religious ceremonies and worship. Also, both were very attractive. Stsepinsky cut a noble, even grand figure. His face, with its prominent Roman nose, was alive with intelligence, and his manner was gracious. I have never met a member of the clergy who could produce a more favorable impression. He was innately intelligent, broadly educated, and well read. He kept abreast of science and literature, as did Podzorsky.

Stsepinsky had graduated from St. Petersburg Theological Seminary. He knew Alexander I's advisor, Speransky, and could have reached the highest theological ranks had he agreed to take monastic vows, as others had tried to persuade him to do. But he had returned to his homeland, drawn by his powerful love for it. Or perhaps some other youthful yearning was responsible for his decision.

In Ostrogozhsk, Stsepinsky quickly rose to the top when he was appointed dean of the diocese. Honors and decorations were showered upon him. He had a gold pectoral cross and other symbols of high priestly office, including a crosier, which was a rare distinction among the secular clergy. Later he received the Order of Saint Anna. It appeared that people understood and appreciated him, but he later paid dearly for these initial successes.

Antony, the Bishop of Voronezh, whom I mentioned earlier, had a brother, Nikolai, also a priest, but the most unworthy of all who bore this title. He wasn't a swindler or evil man, but he drank heavily and behaved obscenely. Antony took it into his head to kick out Stsepinsky so he could appoint his brother, the most dissolute of mortals, dean of the Ostrogozhsk diocese. In those days such was the unbridled and arbitrary power that an archbishop could wield with impunity.

The town was truly shocked, and protested, but demonstrations in support of Stsepinsky were of no avail. For several years dissolute Nikolai Sokolov stayed on as dean, upsetting his parishioners and bringing shame upon himself. Many anecdotes about him circulated. They described escapades that would be considered indecent among the secular. One episode, involving a peasant woman, created a sensation. For his unsolicited attentions, she removed her shoe and whacked the reverend father's face.

Father Nikolai didn't carouse alone. He had a companion, a mentor of sorts, in the sexton Andryushka. When Father Nikolai got drunk, Andryushka managed his charge without fuss. If the reverend father put up a fight, Andryushka coolly subdued him with a couple of blows.

But how could a relatively cultivated community tolerate this dissolute rake among its decorous and staid clergy? Unfortunately, what often happens to us is that we get all worked up over something for a while, make a fuss, and in the end become accustomed to it and live with it. We felt sorry for Simeon Stsepinsky, and even dared to intercede on his behalf. We played various mean tricks on Father Nikolai, but in the end we grew tired of feeling sorry for Simeon. We calmed down and, now and then, as the opportunity presented itself, mocked the unworthy priest.

The humiliation inflicted upon Stsepinsky cut deeply and had a disastrous affect on his health. Fifteen years later—when I was living in St. Petersburg—everything that he had lost, and more, was restored. Antony died, and his brother Nikolai was dismissed as dean of the diocese. Stsepinsky was reinstated, but his strength and health could not be restored, and he died five years later at the age of fifty.

Outwardly Ostrogozhsk presented a more pleasing appearance than most county towns, although it wasn't particularly picturesque. Located on a gentle rise of the Tikhnaya Sosna River bank, it was surrounded by densely reeded marshland. I don't know what it's like now, but at that time the vegetation was put to good use. For want of forest, the rushes went for fuel and roofing.

The small town, with two outlying villages, Lushkovska and Peski, sprawled over a broad area. It was criss-crossed by straight roads lined with neat wooden and some stone houses. The latter belonged to the more wealthy, and their pretensions to elegance were displayed in more or less successful architectural embellishments. At least, that's how it had looked before the fire in 1822 destroyed two-thirds of the town.

In my time Ostrogozhsk certainly was an inviting place. But alas, only during our fine winter and summer seasons. In autumn and spring this tidy, lively little town drowned in mud. Its unpaved roads became impassable. Pedestrians floundered in the mire and carts stalled. There was a lot of talk about paving them. To promote this, a correspondence was initiated with the province administration. Although the *duma* [province council] approved the necessary funds, the correspondence stretched out for years, and all trace of the money soon vanished. By then the town had burned down and the pavement issue sank into oblivion. To this day there is no pavement. And now Ostrogozhsk certainly is not inclined to deal with it. Ostrogozhsk has become very poor, its intellectual level has dropped, and it no longer differs from our most ordinary county towns.

My homecoming in Ostrogozhsk was not a happy occasion. After having my cherished dreams of further education shattered, I arrived to find my family devastated and despondent. Father was depressed because the deal he had counted on did not materialize, and, left without earnings, his family had become impoverished.

On top of that he bore a deep wound—his passion for Yuliya Tatarchukova. This romantic passion was a source of indescribable torment for him. Even my mother hadn't the heart to censure it. She pitied him, and with rare selflessness tried to console him.

Still another overwhelming burden was the litigation with pomeshchitsa Bedryaga. It required constant attention, intensive labor, research on the law, and endless writing of documents. From its sudden traumatic onset, the case evolved into a chronic headache, devouring his time and toil. Meanwhile, the family's need had grown. In my absence it had gained a new member—my sister Nadezhda.

My father lost heart. From time to time he managed to earn something when commissioned to draw up a petition to the court or prepare some document. The paltry compensation he received was instantly consumed by one or another basic need.

My father's failures and unfulfilled passion for Yuliya Tatarchukova made him increasingly irritable, and at times the painful yearning and frustration building up within him was vented cruelly on his family. It's quite possible that the main reason for his inability to settle down and apply himself to anything was due to the alarming state of his spirits. His despondency blunted his insight and affected his relations with people.

I don't know what would have become of our family, how we could have survived this terrible period, if not for our mother's courage and her magnanimity toward her despondent husband. Seeing him losing his strength, she took upon her shoulders the share of responsibilities in a family that normally was his, that is, earning a living.

All who knew my mother had great trust in her. She made use of this by setting herself up in a business where a middleman was needed. She became a broker for the purchase and sale of second-hand goods. Her absolute honesty was well known in town, and people willingly entrusted such dealings to her. For a long time her earnings as a broker were the principal source, if not the only source, of income.

I was stunned by the sight of our poverty. It was evident everywhere in our home: the cramped quarters, the wretched clothing, and in the unflagging toil of my mother, who spent her days roaming the town with goods and her nights mending the children's tatters in the dim glimmer of the lamp.

I wanted so badly to help her. But what could I do? Run errands for her, chop firewood, and fetch water for the kitchen? I did all these things conscientiously, but it did nothing to improve her personal lot or our welfare.

People suggested to Father that he seek an appointment for me somewhere as a village clerk. I certainly was ready to take such a position, but Father wouldn't agree to it. He feared, and not without good reason, that it would be intellectually stifling and forever end my dreams for the future, which, despite the circumstances, he stubbornly continued to believe in.

Finally, something simply incredible rescued us: I, a fourteen-year-old boy, whose formal education consisted solely of the county school curriculum, was offered a job as a teacher. True, my reading had become more focused and more serious and significantly broadened the scope of my knowledge. Nevertheless, this knowledge, without the wholesome benefit of the rigors of an academic setting, and without verification by official tests, hardly gave me the ethical and substantive right to enter the teaching profession, especially since there was no shortage of more experienced teachers with solid legal credentials.

My success in this instance can only be explained by a certain posture prevalent in Ostrogozhsk society: a strong spirit of opposition. That spirit, inspiring distrust in government institutions, drove them so far as to shun official teachers.

In Ostrogozhsk, as in other such towns, there was a county school. It was a comparatively good one—"good" being a faculty without a single drunkard or ignoramus. The instruction was incredibly poor. Engrossed in a daily struggle to support themselves and their families, the staff had no time to develop a well-balanced curriculum. They didn't go beyond the most basic requirements of their profession, and, frankly, you couldn't reproach them for that.

How strange that the well-to-do among Ostrogozhsk inhabitants, generally sensitive to society's needs—and in other instances willing to confront them—remained indifferent to the problems of public education. The way I see it, the nobility, as the chief zealots of the town's welfare, were so class-conscious that they shunned the county public school.

After all, the county school was a place where their progeny might come into contact with the children of merchants and the urban lower-middle class. And even of serfs! Having the means to educate their sons at home until they were old enough to enter a more privileged educational institution of higher learning, and able to secure tutors from the capital, they spurned the county school and its teachers.

As a result, of course, the teachers did not improve and lost standing even with the merchants and well-off meshchane. So these groups, in turn, preferred to look for teachers outside the regular system. And that is how several of them came to choose me to tutor their offspring.

In the circle in which my father moved, it had been some time since I had been looked upon as a child. The thoughtful expression on my face made me appear older than my years. Living among strangers had schooled me well and taught me self-control. But ambition began to cast its spell upon me. A bold desire possessed me, absolutely absurd for one in my situation: it was the urge to lead others and subject their will to mine. As far as knowledge was concerned, I actually was as good as any county-school teacher, and the talk in town about me further exaggerated "my erudition."

Probably for all those reasons the wealthy merchant Rostovtsev took to the idea of hiring me to teach his two sons, one a ten-year-old and the other a year younger than I. I had to take them through the same curriculum offered by the county school. Rostovtsev's children turned out to be good, conscientious students and were already fairly literate. My lessons with them went smoothly and successfully.

More than once, kindly Rostovtsev expressed his satisfaction, which, for me, finally took a tangible and most desirable form in the shape of a twenty-five-ruble note. This on the eve of Easter. I could hardly believe it! Returning home to my family with this treasure in my pocket, I literally flew. From time to time I fingered the money in my pocket and, I must confess, I imagined myself a hero, the savior of my family, who would restore normalcy to our household. But alas! How my pride fell when I crossed our threshold and saw how much was lacking there. As usual, my dreams could not withstand a clash with harsh reality. However, this time reality had its bright side. My earnings helped us greet Easter in keeping with traditional customs, which are so meaningful to Little Russians that they are deeply distressed when deprived of the opportunity to follow them.

Everyone in our region, even the poorest, goes to the limit to spend this "holiday of holidays" as joyfully and lavishly as possible. At least for one week they cast aside the needs and cares that oppress them the rest of the year. And so for our Easter holiday, my mother had the ingredients to bake us an Easter loaf—*kulich*—as fine as anyone else's. She baked it with the purest, finest wheaten flour and spiced it to Father's taste. We bought two pounds of sugar and an eighth of a pound of tea. And my sisters and brothers were dressed in new clothes.

This was the bright side of the harsh reality I confronted, so, no, it wasn't hard for me to console myself! My family's festive holiday mood during Easter impressed me profoundly. For the first time it awakened an awareness of my own strength, and suddenly I was no longer a child.

By virtue of circumstances, my childhood, a carefree one even under wretched conditions, now lay behind me forever. I was standing on the frontier of a new life, where I would face much hardship, but where, I can now say with gratitude, I also had my own share of success.

14

◆•◆•◆•◆

My Friends and Activities in Ostrogozhsk

Two years passed, during which I acquired a reputation as a good teacher. I had many pupils, and a whole school of children of both sexes that assembled at the home of burgomaster Pupykin, the merchant.

The chief, and probably only, merit of my instruction lay in my approach to learning. I did not force the children to mechanically learn lessons by heart but above all tried to instill in them a desire for knowledge, an interest in learning. Other than this I had no carefully thought-out system, nor did I employ any particular pedagogical approach in use at the time. Many of the pupils were the same age as I, but I succeeded in getting along very well with them, and so, at least, my work went smoothly.

Of course, my earnings could not fully support the family, but they at least saved us from extreme want. People looked upon me now as an adult, although I had just turned sixteen. I was not simply another ant in the anthill. People sought my acquaintance. I was warmly received by the intellectual crowd. Nor was I snubbed by such influential individuals as merchant Vasily Alekseyevich Dolzhikov, leader of the nobility Vasily Tikhonovich Lisanevich, nobleman Vladimir Ivanovich Astafeyev, merchant Dimitry Fyodorovich Panov, school inspector Fyodor Fyodorovich Ferronsky, Archpriest Stsepinsky, and Cathedral Priest Mikhail Podzorsky.

None of these people are still in this world, but the memory of them lives on in my heart. I am indebted to them for their warm interest in me, their humane disregard of my social standing as a nonentity, and the indulgence displayed for my youthful, often intemperate, aspirations. Finally, I am indebted to them for their generous support and sobering influence, which helped me stay the course in my struggle with fate and kept me from sinking into an abyss of fruitless introspection and from losing faith in goodness, in people, and in my own self.

I lived in their environment. Their society was mine. Now, in my declining years, mentally passing through the long journey I have completed, I recall with amazement and gratitude how much I owe them. They were the first to extend a hand and help me rise to that step on the social ladder where I could, with impunity, consider myself a man.

Few of these friends and benefactors could boast of positive changes in their own lives, either in their outside activities or inner worlds. Nature, having endowed them generously with intelligence and sensitivity, neglected to place them in an environment befitting their inclinations. Their honest characters could not accept bureaucratic wrongdoing and serfdom, two poisons of their society. While inwardly seething in protest, they were fully conscious of their utter helplessness in changing the existing order. Their inner conflicts fomented the development of certain quirks and peculiarities. These were completely at odds with their true character and often worthy of Dickens's pen or Hogarth's brush.

Take, for example, Astafeyev. He came from an old and noble family and belonged to the aristocrats of the county. After receiving a higher education in St. Petersburg, where he had connections, he entered government service there. All these factors added up to the promise of a brilliant career. Only twenty-four years old, he was already a collegiate assessor (the civil service equivalent of major in the army).[1]

Suddenly, for no obvious reason, he abandoned his post and connections and stole away to his remote, provincial hometown. There he was received with wide-open arms and elected leader of the gentry. Handsome and witty, with social connections, he was a bright star against the dreary background of this provincial backwater and began to break the hearts of young ladies in the district. One of them—alas! the most homely—fell madly in love with him. She exhausted all efforts to win his love. Appealing as a last resort to the magnanimity of the conqueror, she told him of her passion for him.

The lady possessed a considerable fortune. Astafeyev had already gone through his. Moved by her avowal, and even more by the girl's dowry, but not wanting to deceive her, he straightaway told her: "I do not object to becoming your husband, but love you I cannot. Decide for yourself if it is worth your while marrying me." The lady decided it was. They were wed, and the marriage didn't turn out so badly, after all. Astafeyev was not an affectionate husband, but he did not have the heart to behave cruelly toward this selfless, devoted being. He was nevertheless free and easy with his wife's dowry.

It wasn't long before provincial life turned out to be too confining for his expansive nature. Like government service, community service gave him little satisfaction. He hated vagueness and ambiguity, and pretense disgusted him. All too often he encountered such conduct when performing his duties as leader of the gentry and when meeting with province officials. Incapable of dissembling his feelings, he preferred to distance himself from these affairs. Overwhelmed by depression, he took to carousing. Very soon he went through his wife's fortune as he had done earlier with his own.

My friendship with him began much later, when he was already close to fifty and living as a childless, lonely man. He worked as a solicitor in lawsuits and earned enough to live comfortably. Despite his wild youth, his appearance and manners retained traces of the varnish of high society. He was gentle, gracious, very well read, and well spoken, despite a husky voice resulting from past and present drinking bouts. He knew many anecdotes about eminent figures who lived during the reign of Catherine the Great, and recounted them with great wit. Vladimir

Ivanovich Astafeyev spent his free time making the rounds of the district, going from one pomeshchik or farmer to another. Everywhere he received a warm welcome.

Periodically, this kind, intelligent, highly cultured man would suddenly relapse into degradation—fits of drinking. These spells always occurred at a certain time and followed a predictable course. When the attack came on, Vladimir Ivanovich would lock himself inside, receive almost no one, and cling to the bottle day and night. But the predictable period passed, and Astafeyev, as if he had served an involuntary sentence, emerged with his usual image, presenting the person he always was: honest, generous, a bit proud, and extremely amiable.

During these cruel and disabling attacks, he maintained the habits of a well-bred person. On those occasions, he usually stayed in bed in a very respectable setting. As always, his room was in elegant order. Symmetrically arranged knick-knacks—little boxes, snuff boxes, statuettes—adorned his bedside table. On another table lay books, papers, and writing accessories without a speck of dust anywhere.

There was nothing repulsive about him. He never drank himself into a complete stupor and didn't lose his well-bred manners. It seemed as if drunken Astafeyev was only an extension of sober Astafeyev. He became livelier, wittier, talkative, reasoned profoundly, philosophized, and all the while drummed his fingers.

In town everyone knew about his unfortunate weakness but willingly forgave him. Actually, in no way did it diminish his worth. It did not impair his skillfulness or knowledge of the world or people, his delicate tact, his sound and impartial judgment. These were treasures that, with his unlimited kindness, everyone could freely take advantage of no less than they could his purse—and they did. Poor fellow. An eccentric, yes, but a fine one!

Another person very close to me was the school inspector, Fyodor Fyodorovich Ferronsky. This was truly a man who endured much suffering. On thirty rubles a month he had to support a large family: a wife and five children—two adolescent daughters and three sons, one of whom was an idiot. His wife, intelligent and kind and at one time a beauty, had been suffering for the past ten years from an incurable disease that left her bedridden. With the exception of the one child not responsible for his actions, the whole family was a fine one and well educated, too. The eldest son, Nikandr, was a teacher in the lower class, or division, of the school and received only one and a half rubles per month.

I don't know how they all managed to exist, especially toward the end of each month, when their earnings were exhausted. Their home was bare as a bone. Not a thing in the house—neither bread nor money. And the sick wife needed a bowl of bouillion, a cup of tea, and medicine. Ferronsky's old woman was a pity to see. Kind people helped him as best they could, but most of them were very poor as well.

In desperation the old man finally resorted to borrowing from the state till—always, of course, with the strict intention of returning the loan at the first opportunity. But the opportunity never turned up, and the poor old fellow was threatened many times with a court suit. Each time he was rescued from misfortune by the honorary superintendent, Safonov, who, before an audit, would replace from his own pocket the shortfall. From time to time private lessons would come the way of father or son, and then they breathed a little easier.

The school under Inspector Ferronsky's jurisdiction was in a terrible state, as were all state educational institutions until 1833, when Tsar Nicholas I granted them new teaching staffs and put Uvarov in charge of the Ministry of Education.[2]

Earlier I spoke about the deficiencies of Ostrogozhsk county schools and the reasons for their decline. Superintendent Ferronsky was not to blame for these conditions in his school. On the contrary, he was the one who suffered most. He was one of the finest people I have ever known. He possessed such a sober, enlightened mind and such lucid views on life and society. And, too, he had a noble heart, the likes of which one would like to see more of today, in our progressive times, in administrators of primary schools and institutions of higher education.

Both Ferronskys were very good to me. The son and I were

the same age. He was of average intelligence but possessed a unique talent and could have been a very fine actor. He was most attractive, and had a sonorous singing voice and a rare gift for mimicry. His dream was a career on the stage, but he lacked the energy to pull himself out of the rut into which fate had pushed him. To the end of his life he subsisted on his earnings as a teacher.

Poor as they were, the Ferronsky family radiated so much warmth and love that there was more than enough for their own family and for others as well, even those more destitute. I was warmly received in their home, treated kindly and supplied with books.

And all this went on at the same time that I, so to say, stood in the son's way and took away his bread by gaining attention with my pedagogical successes. Had the senior Ferronsky wanted to, it would have cost him nothing to ruin me, and he had a convenient opportunity to do it. But I'll go into that later.

There was another friendly family—the Dolzhikovs. I remember the head of it as the most remarkable person in our region. Everything about him was striking, including his appearance. Looking at him, one would never know he was a Russian merchant. The typical Russian merchant possessed characteristics that usually hit you in the eye.

Here's how he looked the first time I saw him on an Ostrogozhsk street. This majestic old man, a cascade of gray hair round his handsome face with its delicate profile, didn't walk. He marched, literally marched—erect, strong as a mighty oak grown in the rich Little Russian soil.

To this day I remember how my heart began to pound, as if one of the heroes of my ideal world in which I had been spinning in a daze had suddenly appeared before my very eyes. Utterly enchanted by this astonishing spectacle, I followed him with my eyes until he disappeared around the corner. And for the rest of that day I could not recover from my mesmerized state.

Vasily Alekseyevich Dolzhikov had studied at Kharkov College, where he acquired a knowledge of Latin and other subjects.[3] But I do not know where he got that noble touch, that remarkable tact, those grand manners, and the visage of a sage as he calmly and deliberately pursued his mission in life. Encountering someone like this, how can one say that superior characteristics are innate in this or that class or caste?

More than anyone else, he nurtured me and tamed my impulsive nature. Rarely did I miss a visit with him. I bared my soul to him with ease. Respected by all, this old man, way beyond me in age, experience, and civic achievements, was always patient and listened sympathetically to my impetuous and often provocative prattle.

Vasily Alekseyevich Dolzhikov was a liberal and a progressive, although at that time neither he nor anyone else used these terms. He hated slavery and longed for radical changes in our system of government. He sympathized with the liberal movement in Europe, mourned unsuccessful insurrections of Italian patriots, and joyously welcomed the first strikes toward freedom in Greece.

I was as enthusiastic as he about these movements and events but lacked his understanding of the real issues. After one of my discussions with him, inspired by the latest news from Greece, I spent the night composing the draft of an appeal to rebellious Greeks in the name of their heroic leader, Ypsilanti.[4] The next morning I read the appeal to Vasily Alekseyevich. With the ingenuousness of a youth, he was carried away by my dream and, in turn, suggested various additions and alterations in my draft.

Our discussions in the setting of Dolzhikov's country garden were a most enjoyable experience! Vasily Alekseyevich had designed the garden and planted it himself, lovingly tending every tree and bush. The garden was a short distance from Ostrogozhsk. Spring and summer evenings we went there together, sprawled on the grass beneath a young oak or apple tree—and where, oh where, our dreams didn't take us! As usual, I became absorbed in a maze of intricate abstractions; and he tactfully maneuvered me back to sober reality and historical truth. After a while, dear Vasily Alekseyevich would remember that a sixteen-year-old youth with an insatiable appetite would never refuse to season food for the soul with earthly fruits, and for the return trip he would supply me with a variety of produce from his garden, depending on the season.

At one time Dolzhikov had been mayor of Ostrogozhsk and had done many good works for the community. He was particularly concerned with improving the lives of the poorest inhabitants. Anyone needing assistance or protection could always turn to him for help.

But among his own merchant class he had many enemies. Also, his advocacy of town interests brought him into open opposition with provincial authorities. Eventually these two evil camps united to destroy him. They succeeded in hauling Dolzhikov to court with slander and intrigue. He had to resign as mayor but did not give up the fight. And when he despaired of Voronezh justice and the Riazan judges who had presided in his case, he brought his case to Moscow.

The Dolzhikov family was a picture of domestic happiness one rarely sees. You would almost believe that Vasily Alekseyevich's wife, Praskovya Mikhailovna, was created especially for him. Her loving heart went hand in hand with a keen, amazingly judicious mind. Restrained, a bit on the cold side, even stately in manner, at first glance she gave the impression of being difficult to approach. Actually, she didn't make herself easily accessible. She was particular in her choice of close friends as well as of acquaintances. Once accepted into her home, however, you received a cordial and sincere welcome. Conversation with her was not only pleasant but instructive. Studded with flashes of humor and original ideas, it was a delightful experience.

Praskovya Mikhailovna was in full charge of home and family matters but never abused her authority. In keeping house, she did everything quietly, calmly, and, of course, meticulously—without haste, fuss, constant reprimands, or exhortations. Nor could one detect undertones of discontent or grumbling. She did not own household serfs, although she could have secured them by registering them under someone else's name, as did other wealthy merchants.[5]

She raised her daughters in keeping with family traditions and responsibilities. They weren't fluent in French, but with their intelligent mother's assistance and guidance they matured nicely, especially the eldest daughter, who read a great deal and most sensibly, too. The second daughter loved music, and they provided her with the means to develop her taste. The youngest daughter, in my time, was still a child.

Of Dolzhikov's five sons, two were already adults. The eldest, Aleksandr, managed business operations on the estate and ran the brewery, which supplied beer to the entire province. The younger of the two, Mikhail, worked away from home, trading and traveling around to government offices and making frequent trips to Voronezh, Riazan, and Moscow. He, too, was passionately fond of music and enjoyed a reputation as a fine violinist. With Mikhail I had a closer friendship. He was livelier and more communicative than Aleksandr, who was completely absorbed in his business affairs.

After lengthy judicial ordeals, Dolzhikov triumphed over the combined machinations of enemies and biased judges. He was acquitted of all charges: of exceeding his authority and of arbitrary behavior. And, to the immense satisfaction of Ostrogozhsk citizens, he was restored with honor to the position of mayor.

But that victorious day turned out to be fatal for him when, overflowing with emotion, he delivered a speech outlining his plans for the future of Ostrogozhsk. He spoke enthusiastically about its needs and enumerated the remedies, insisting on earmarking decent premises for a school, the immediate construction of pavement, and so on. He became overheated and did not notice that he was standing in a draft the entire time. Returning home, he felt ill, took to his bed, and died of nerve-fever on the seventh day. He was only sixty years old.

Living among such affectionate and hospitable people, I was further spurred to educate myself. But this I could only accomplish by reading, which I now pursued in a more meaningful, organized fashion. I read and systematically copied down excerpts, and wrote my own critiques of them.

My friends and benefactors supplied me with books. Stsepinsky, Podzorsky, Dolzhikov, and Panov owned lots of books—almost all serious works. By this time novels had lost their appeal for me. I had had my fill of them, and my mind was searching for more substantial nourishment. And indeed I found it, for example, in these works: *Contemplation of Nature* by Swiss naturalist and philosopher Charles Bonnet; *Metaphysics and Logic* by Christian Baumeister; *Corpus Juris Civilis,* a code of laws (the foundation of Roman law) composed by Justinian I, emperor of the Byzantine Empire; *The Spirit of Laws* by Montesquieu; and other works of this nature.

One book that especially captured my interest was *A History of My Time* by Frederick the Great, King of Prussia, who, for a time, became my favorite hero.

In world history I drew knowledge from Tredyakovsky's translation of *The Song of Roland,* and from the works of John Miller, Scottish philosopher and historian. Of Russian history, I knew very little. Other than the textbook used in secondary schools, I had no sources.

But not all the books that came my way were within the reach of my poorly disciplined mind. Such was the case, by the way, with Galich's *History of Philosophical Systems,* published in 1818. I received it from Ferronsky and pounced on it avidly, believing it would reveal to me at once the deep recesses of human wisdom. But alas! To grasp this book's philosophical postulates was beyond even the capacity of people who were better educated than I. The author's pithiness and expository style created formidable obstacles. It was not surprising that I hit a stone wall in many of its passages and, like one possessed, knocked in vain on the door of a cathedral closed to me.

Especially at such times, the ugly, unvarnished unjustness of my social status would hit me in the face. It had locked me out of high school and continued to close off future paths toward knowledge, toward the light. But meanwhile, my rebellious mind did not cease to evoke the seductive mirage of the university.

How dared I believe in the inevitable fulfillment of my

dreams, especially after my experience with high school, when its doors were closed to me? I don't know. But deep down in my heart lived a spark of hope, a yearning to enter the inaccessible university, a spark that in the end would never die out. But this spark rarely flared brightly enough to make me fully conscious of it. It smoldered somewhere. Mostly I was visited by moments of deep despair.

No, no one and nothing can convey the moral struggle a strong and courageous sixteen-year-old went through to consider suicide and find relief in the idea itself. A shaft of light, it made an indelible impression and raised my spirits. I realized that letting myself wallow in despair would solve nothing. "No," I told myself, "this self-pity won't do! So what if I'm not my own master; so what if I'm nothing in the eyes of society and its laws! Still, I have one right that no one can take away from me! The right to die. If worse comes to worst, I shall not fail to use it. Until then, boldly onward!"

For some reason, I preferred to die by the gun. I acquired a pistol, powder, and two bullets, and from that instant on I felt better. A new sense of daring took root in me. Death had taken me under its wing, and nothing more could frighten me.

Having placed myself beyond the indignities to which people could subject me, I became proud and independent. Now, when I think about my frame of mind at that time, I can smile, but I retain a bitter awareness of lost illusions.

How I felt then was fully expressed in two sayings with which I hastened to adorn my portrait. Here's how the sayings got into the picture.

At my mother's request I was sitting for a portrait. Zikran, an amateur painter, had been hired. He fiddled with it a long while, having a hard time getting the eyes just right. He'd curse and tell me and my eyes to go to the devil. Finally he announced that the portrait was ready. At the time people found it a good likeness. But, unfortunately, it disappeared, most likely destroyed in the fire several years later that consumed a good deal of Ostrogozhsk. Zikran painted me holding my diary, its pages open. One page was adorned with the motto "Live with honor or die." And on the facing page—"Wisdom is patience." Poor, self-confident youth! He grew up, matured, and life, of course, took him down a peg. But his premature independence left traces of fierce obstinacy, which, if it helped him get what he wanted, was often a stumbling block on his path.

Under the influence of these lofty ideals, I dreamed up an apologia of suicide in the form of an essay titled "The Voice of a Suicide on Judgment Day." I was very attached to my mother. So, in this mental scenario, I dedicated to her the result of my deep reflections.

In my fantasy, she stood there, tormented, hands outstretched toward me, pleading that I spare myself for her sake. But I explained to her the reasons for my decision, and she blessed me for my terrifying deed. "You are right, poor child!" Sobbing, she exclaimed: "Go in peace. People sheltered you for a moment, only to destroy you later. Go with God! He is more merciful than people. He will forgive you for seeking the light and the truth from Him alone. Go! I myself shall sew your shroud and wash it with my tears. In utter secrecy, I shall prepare your grave, and no one will defile your remains!"

I searched for the light in Galich's philosophical writings but failed to find it. Pure reason could not answer my soul-searching question. So I rushed headlong to the other extreme: I began to seek the light in mysticism.

Around that time, between 1818 and 1820, mysticism cropped up in our backwater and found many followers. Some of my friends were attracted to it as well. They certainly tried hard to "enlighten" me, supplying me with books on the subject.

You would think that these books would have made a strong impression on me, because, in addition to having a fiery imagination, I was very impressionable and tended to be attracted to the supernatural.

Actually, it turned out quite differently. The apparitions conjured by these books slipped right by me, their phosphorescent glow not quite grazing me. In truth, during the most insecure period of my childhood and youth, I loved everything eerie and secretive, but it did nothing more than titillate my imagination. Reading through such works, I remained cool and even seemed to take a critical attitude toward swallowing fantasy whole. In Ostrogozhsk, I reacted the same way.

I set to reading mystical books with enthusiasm. From cover to cover I read *The Key to Nature's Secrets* by Eckartshausen, and he didn't unlock anything for me. I doubt that anyone else could have, since nature's secrets are too securely locked away. And the key the author offered for discovery was like a simple rusty nail, incapable of opening anything.

Some other books I read were *The Adventures of a Soul at Death* and *My Life*, both by Jung-Stillung.[6] I was bored with the first book, but the second was of greater interest. Like me, Jung-Stillung was poor. He nevertheless succeeded in becoming a scholar and achieving fame. Still, I distrusted him. I felt he was a charlatan who misled people by convincing them that he had seen something no one else had, and that he knew something no one else knew. I ended my research on mysticism with mystic A. F. Labzin's the monthly periodical *Messenger of Zion*, but I didn't manage to get through more than three issues.

After all this groping in the dark, how clear and convincing the simple, real truths of Gospel teachings seemed to me. I don't mean that I had already recognized the wealth of wisdom hidden in them. No, in this regard, I didn't question my convictions at all. My faith was purely that of a child. At first, I believed only because I had learned this at my mother's knee. And later, at the time I'm describing, Christ's life and teaching turned out to have a special, personal meaning. This really was a sheet anchor. It helped me cope with the bitterness I felt at times about people and my cruel fate.

Whenever I gazed at the Savior's image in one of the side chapels of our cathedral, I heard his gentle call: "Come unto me, ye toilers and burdened, and you will find repose." I thought, so what if people are evil and unjust? I have in the Intercessor a true refuge where I can be sheltered from any kind of malice and persecution. He, most gracious and all-knowing, will not drive me away. And then, if the burden is beyond my strength, I shall willfully appear before Him!

On the other hand, I performed religious ceremonial rituals half-heartedly. Probably the reason for this lay in the example of people in my circle. All these Astafeyevs, Dolzhikovs, and Panovs, infected by the free thinking of Voltaire and the Encyclopedists, scorned church rituals. Although in my presence my friends never touched upon the subject of their own or my religious beliefs, they could not conceal their indifference to the formal practice of such beliefs.

However, a spontaneous urge would often draw me into church, especially when the choirboys were singing or when the stately Simeon Stsepinsky conducted divine services. Also I recall the uplifting sensation I experienced on Holy Thursday during a reading of the Twelfth Gospel by a simple, uneducated priest in the Ilin church. He read without any dramatic exclamations but with such feeling and sympathy that, unwittingly, he communicated the source of his inspiration.

15

◆•◆•◆•◆

My Friends in the Military; General Yuzefovich; The Death of My Father

Changes occurred in our life at home, an indirect effect of Grigory Fyodorovich Tatarchukov's death. The year before he died, his young wife had moved to Moscow with her little daughter. Besides his widow and the child, his heirs included two sons from his first marriage. Of two other daughters, whom I mentioned earlier, one died in childhood while her father was still alive; the other, who had married Belyakov, received her share of the inheritance earlier.

The sons of the deceased hated their stepmother and, unlike their father, were greedy. They would go to any length to deprive stepmother Yuliya of her inheritance and unscrupulously took advantage of her inexperience. The young widow and her small daughter were facing utter ruin, when she decided to turn for protection to a knowledgeable and honest man who could extricate her from the traps Tatarchukov's sons had set for her. But where could she find such a man? And there he was, close at hand, in the person of my father. But knowing his passion for her, for a long time she hesitated to turn to him for help. Finally Yuliya put aside her punctiliousness and wrote my father a letter, begging him to take from her a power of attorney and hasten to Boguchar to save her and her daughter's inheritance. Father's chivalrous soul was instantly aroused, and he seized the opportunity to do a service for the woman he loved. Forthwith, he set out for the field of battle and so ably and skillfully handled the task that Yuliya quickly received everything she was entitled to.

But Father's concern for her didn't end there. In the inheritance proceedings, the village had been divided up. It was necessary to transfer the peasants given to the widow from the village and move them to a new place. For this, a new settlement had to be established. Consequently, Father's separation from the family dragged on, and without the family he never did well. His worship of the charming widow provided plenty of nourishment for his fantasy but gave nothing to his heart. He needed support and consolation. Away from home, he was deprived of an inexhaustible source in the sympathetic heart of a magnanimous wife.

Father couldn't bear the loneliness, even though this solitary existence was devoted to his concern for the welfare of his beloved. So he hastened to summon the family to the Boguchar district, where he was staying. Without delay, Mother set out on the journey, and, with the younger children, settled in the newly created village. To please the pomeshchitsa, who was of German origin, the village was named "Ruetal."* The name proved to be a very fitting choice, for the village was located in a beautiful, peaceful place.

Father didn't want to take me away from my teaching position, so I remained alone in Ostrogozhsk. Meanwhile, an event occurred in our town that brought into our community a group of people with new social views and provided me with a source of fresh impressions. Napoleon's star had faded. The curtain on the bloody drama that had disrupted Europe's peace came down on the Island of St. Helena. After a long series of victories our armies returned home from France to savor a much-deserved rest. They were stationed in various provinces and towns of the Russian Empire. Ostrogozhsk's turn came, too.

One fine day in the spring of 1818, its dreamy streets sprang to life, brilliant with colorful flags and uniforms, ringing with the clatter of horses and the thump of military music. Everyone—townspeople, farmers, and peasants from surrounding areas—streamed into Ostrogozhsk to enjoy a spectacle the likes of which

*Ruetal is derived from the German word *ruhig* (peaceful).

they had never witnessed and to welcome the special guests. The people willingly provided shelter, and the cream of the community threw open their doors to officers on leave.

The First Dragoon Division was billeted in Ostrogozhsk and the surrounding area. The division consisted of four regiments: the Moscow regiment and its staff, the Riga regiment, the Novorossisk regiment, and the Kinburn, which arrived later. New life began to hum and new interests awakened.

The officers of these regiments constituted a group of people who were in their own way quite remarkable. This was especially true of the officers of the Moscow regiment, in whose staff command the elite of regimental society was concentrated.

Participants in world events, these officers were not figures engaged in fruitless debates, but men who, within the limits imposed by their stern, practical duty, had acquired a special strength of character and determination in their views and aspirations. They stood in sharp contrast to the progressive people in our provincial community, who, for lack of real, sobering activity, inhabited a fantasy world and wasted their strength in petty, fruitless protest.

The contact the officers had had with Western European civilization, their personal acquaintance with a more successful social system worked out by thinkers of the end of the last century, and, finally, the struggle for the grand principles of freedom and the Fatherland all left their mark of deep humanity on them. In this respect they were completely at one with the representatives of our local intelligentsia. It's no wonder, then, that a lasting relationship developed between them. Nor was I rejected by these officers. On the contrary, I was received with outstretched arms and warm concern. In me they saw a victim of the order of things that they hated. Under the influence of this hatred, they looked at me, as it were, through magnifying spectacles, exaggerating my talents and, at the same time, the tragedy of my fate. Hence, their attitude toward the poor, unfortunate lad reflected their interest and respect. People two or three times my age and ever so superior to me in knowledge and experience associated with me as an equal. I was a constant participant in their discussions, evening gatherings, and diversions. They took me along to parades, I went hunting with them, and I even accompanied one of my closest friends on sentry rounds when he was on duty.

All these activities were most pleasing to me and very flattering, too. Still, they did not lull my anxiety about the future. I lived the double life of a carefree youth and a despairing one. Frivolously, I indulged in short-lived pleasures. But, with early maturity born of bitter experience, I did not lose sight of what awaited me beyond this relatively bright phase. And my frustrated pride goaded me to dream with renewed fervor about further achievements and more enduring ones. This only served to exacerbate my impatience with my oppressive yoke. While my castles in the air grew higher and higher, my thoughts of suicide grew stronger and stronger. My castles were destined to collapse, and I would perish beneath the ruins.

Be that as it may, my growing intimacy with these people served as a new stimulus to my development and significantly widened my intellectual horizons. They, by the way, introduced me to the latest works of Russian literature. Until then my knowledge of it was limited to Lomonosov, Derzhavin, and Kheraskov with his *Rossiada* and *Vladimir.*[1] As a child I was introduced to Lomonosov's work by wandering blind minstrels. Roving from farmstead to farmstead for alms, they sang "Make My Breath Sing Praise to the Lord" and other spiritual poems of this author. But of contemporary belles lettres, I knew nothing. And suddenly, what a host of new impressions! Returning from salons where the officers gathered, I walked around in a daze.

Readings were not the least of salon activities, and often they went on for most of the evening. Some of the officers recited entire dramas superbly. Here, for the first time, I heard Ozerov's *Oedipus in Athens,* and was introduced to the works of Batyuskov and Zhukovsky, which had just been published. We were intoxicated by the music of their poetry and memorized whole works: for example, "My Penates," "The Dying Tasso," "At the Castle Ruins in Sweden," or excerpts from "A Bard in the Camp of Russian Warriors," and so on. Many brought notebooks in which they jotted aphorisms or excerpts from readings that caught their interest.[2]

Around this time an individual appeared fleetingly in my life who, a little later, with several others, had a decisive influence on my fate. But he became one of the main victims in the dark tragedy that played out when Nicholas I ascended the throne.

That fleeting encounter took place at the annual Ostrogozhsk fair. Books had been brought to the site along with other wares. I was strolling around the fair with one of my friends, and I couldn't resist dropping into a shop selling wares that were most tempting to me. At the counter stood a young officer who had come in before us. Glancing at him, I was captivated by the soft radiance of his clear, dark eyes and his gentle, thoughtful face. He asked for Montesquieu's *Spirit of Laws,* paid for it, and gave instructions for delivery to his lodgings. "I and my cavalry troop are not billeted in the city," he remarked to the merchant, "we're stationed rather far away. I came here for a short time, no more than a few hours. May I ask you to deliver the books without delay? I'm staying at . . ." He gave an address. "Have the messenger ask for Lieutenant Ryleyev."[3]

At that time his name meant nothing to me, but the elegant image of the young officer left an indelible impression. I didn't meet him again in those parts. Besides, he soon left, married, and retired from the service. I met him again in St. Petersburg under completely different circumstances.

Our officer circle was soon augmented by a group of other young people who had just become officers. It can hardly be said that they introduced something new and original into the group. Fresh out of the cadet corps, where, at the time, studies not strictly related to military skills were not highly regarded, they were no match for their older, more worldly comrades. However, they performed their duties conscientiously, but spent their free time in rather wild drinking sprees.

Good lads, they befriended me and invited me along on their binges. That's when the absence of guidance from my father or anyone else might have had a disastrous affect on my ways. Fortunately, I was physically repelled by excesses of any kind. At these binges I, too, wet my lips at the punch bowl and drank up a goblet of another frothy Don concoction. But this I did like a boy fond of sweets who still hadn't outgrown his love of them. Intoxication was repugnant to me as well, stemming from my ideal conception of the dignity of a person and from pride. My pride was the scourge of my youth, but at the same time it was a bridle that kept me from falling.

The two types I've described, the heroes of 1812 and the good lads fresh from the cadet corps, were not the only types stationed in Ostrogozhsk. Among them was a third type, veteran campaigners of the old school and hardened disciplinarians. They were not only ferocious in battle but, alas, in peacetime, too, battering their defenseless subordinates. The treatment of their soldiers was, to say the least, cruel. Barbaric! Fortunately we had few such disciplinarian father-commander figures. There were two I'll never forget: Trofim Isyevich Makarov, commander of the Life-Guards cavalry of the Moscow Dragoon Regiment, and Captain Potemkin, commander of the reserve cavalry of the same regiment.

Makarov left the most indelible impression. An enormous man, a face furrowed with wrinkles, a frown beneath thick, overhanging brows; his appearance alone was enough to make his subordinates tremble. They say that his outstanding trait was bravery, but a singular kind of bravery under battle conditions; he never got carried away in the heat of battle, made no impulsive moves, and remained cool and calculating. According to the testimony of his comrades, he was usually the first to charge in an attack but never for an instant lost his composure, which is why his blows always hit the target. Though only a staff-captain, he had already been awarded the Order of St. Anna and the Order of St. Vladimir.

When dealing with soldiers who had committed petty offenses, he behaved cold-bloodedly, without a trace of indignation or an angry outburst. He punished them with blows, using birch rods, the flat side of a sword, or even his fists. Discipline gained nothing from this; even without such practices, discipline was strictly observed in our armed forces.

One wonders where Makarov's orderly and cavalry Sergeant-Major Vasilyev got the physical strength—to say nothing of moral strength—to endure the torture that they, as the people closest to the captain, were subjected to almost daily.

And yet, for all this, strange as it may seem, Trofim Isyevich was certainly not an evil person. When need be, he could display sincere warmth and humanity. Take, for example, the way he treated me with such kindness, even overindulgence. From this and from looking at him, one would be hard pressed to suggest that he was a brute.

Whenever he ran into me his face would brighten and he'd pat me affectionately on the shoulder. He invited me to his home, took me hunting, loaned me a horse to ride. But in the treatment of his soldiers he was hidebound, clung to old traditions, and sincerely believed that the rod was absolutely necessary to maintain military discipline. What contributed in no small measure to this approach was his lack of the most basic education. I don't know what his calling had been or whether he had studied anywhere, but I do know that he could barely sign his name.

The other one that sticks in my memory is Captain Potemkin, a positively malicious man who made no exceptions for anyone. Cruelty, which for Makarov was likely a result of ignorance and a poor understanding of his responsibilities, for Potemkin was deeply rooted in his nature. He gave free reign to this cruel streak with a kind of sensual gratification. He appeared to thoroughly enjoy himself when his orders for punishment were executed and unfortunate soldiers were beaten and brutally flogged half to death.

Meanwhile, Potemkin belonged to so-called elite society and stood immeasurably above Makarov in intelligence and education. The rest of the officers in the regiment viewed the methods of these two captains with indignation and deliberately avoided their company. But neither the contempt of their colleagues nor the admonitions of their superior—the good, chivalrous, kindhearted

Colonel Geismar—had any effect on them. Nothing could be done to curb their savagery, since they acted within the limits of the law.

My position in the circle of staff officers grew ever stronger. In fact, the chief commander of the First Dragoon Division, which was stationed in Ostrogozhsk, took notice of me. To fully appreciate how much this circumstance elevated me in the estimation of my fellow townsmen, one must keep in mind the prestige the rank of major-general conferred on its bearer in those times.

During the reign of Nicholas I and in the last years of Tsar Alexander I, a general was regarded as a very special person. He enjoyed a position of unparalleled importance in our social life and in government administration. There wasn't an appointment to a high post or position in government where preference would not be given to the bearer of thick silver or gold epaulettes. These decorative shoulder pads were acknowledged as the best guarantee of intelligence, knowledge, and ability, even in fields requiring specialized training. Sure of the magic power of their epaulettes, their bearers placed themselves beyond reproach. They were imbued with a conviction of their infallibility and boldly cut Gordian knots.

Initially trained in the spirit of strict military discipline, later they became its guardians in the ranks of the army. And even when governing a peaceful civilian community, they introduced the very same policy of unconditional obedience. In so doing they were merely promoting the views of the administration, which, it seemed, had set itself the goal of disciplining the nation; that is, the government wanted to create an environment wherein no individual would deviate in thought or action from a given policy. As a result of this barracks-like mentality, every general, in whatever branch of the administration, first and foremost took care to instill in his subordinates as much fear as possible. That's why these generals looked sullen and cross, spoke sharply, and, for the slightest reason—and even without any—upbraided one and all.

But Major-General Yuzefovich hardly resembled those tongue-lashing types. For a general to lack such distinctive characteristics was unthinkable then. There was good reason to include Dimitry Mikhailovich among the champions of freedom for Russia and Europe. From his encounter with the West, he brought back quite a few humane ideas and a measure of restraint in dealing with his subordinates that was scarcely known to his peers. When the allied armies had entered France, he was appointed governor-general of Nantes, and he left behind a fine memory of his tenure. Though he was capable of bending to circumstances and, as a result of his intelligence and education, of bridling innate tendencies, there remained in him a despotic streak. Rarely displayed, it came through in his personal relations and in the performance of his duties. When he took a liking to someone, he showered the person with tokens of his attention; but when some petty thing or slight misunderstanding arose, his manner would change to one of careless indifference.

Of all his traits, ambition was the most outstanding. At the beginning of his career it was subtle and restrained, but toward the end, it raged in him to the point where it caused his moral downfall.

When I knew him he was about forty-five, but not more. His height, intelligence, lively expression, rapid speech, and imperious bearing made him an imposing figure. Gracing his neck was a decoration that he was never seen without, the Order of St. George. Other such decorations, a First Degree Anna and the Prussian Eagle, he wore on solemn occasions only, at parades and public prayers.

Broadly educated, he loved literature, kept an eye out for the latest literary works, subscribed to all the Russian periodicals and newspapers (even the awful *Kazan News*) and all reissued books—though these were hardly outstanding works. In his free time, evenings, at gatherings of close friends, he loved to read aloud from works of the latest poets, such as Derzhavin, Merzlyakov, Batyushkov, and Zhukovsky.[4] He was interested in every new idea, enjoyed every well-constructed verse, apt expression, and turn of speech.

Dimitry Mikhailovich tried his hand at writing but seems

never to have published anything except for an article, which he translated from the French. It appeared in a Kharkov publication of that time, the *Ukrainian Herald.* He prepared the article as a keepsake for a sweet young girl, Zveryeva, who lived with her mother on an estate near Kharkov.

Occasionally Dimitry Mikhailovich visited them there and stayed a while. He respected the old woman and was in love with the daughter, whom he wanted to marry. But he couldn't because he already had a wife. It was strange somehow that he had married very early and now was trying in vain to get rid of her. They say she hadn't had any sort of education and was very stupid. But no one knew her because she had been living somewhere in a distant village.

In Ostrogozhsk, General Yuzefovich lived with his sister, Anna Mikhailovna, and her daughter, a girl of about ten. Another niece of the general, Marya Vladimirovna, lived with him for a time. She was the daughter of his brother, a hypochondriac, who preferred to live alone in the country.

I don't know how rumors about me reached the general, but one fine day I was invited to his home to discuss the possibility of his employing me to tutor his nieces. Dimitry Mikhailovich entered the room, threw me a piercing glance, mumbled a few words, and vanished, leaving the interview to his sister. Anna Mikhailovna and I had a lengthy and thorough discussion. With subtle feminine tact she outflanked me and drew from me everything she wanted to know.

In the end they found me suitable, and without delay I began to give Russian language and history lessons to the two girls. Although I was only sixteen, my youth was not an obstacle. The decision they made to employ me reflected the bias against public school teachers in our region at that time. As a last resort even an intelligent, educated man like Yuzefovich, himself a government official, preferred a half-educated lad to government teachers.

At any rate, I became a teacher in General Dimitry Mikhailovich Yuzefovich's home, and gained a strong foothold there. My pupils grew fond of my lessons, the general developed great faith in me, and, what is most remarkable, he became interested in me. My earnings were small, but in addition Dimitry Mikhailovich clothed me and rented a nice little flat for me nearby.

Little by little I became his man. To my teaching duties he added others, related to his library. It was quite extensive, but in disorder. I did an inventory and rummaged tirelessly through his books. Dimitry Mikhailovich received newspapers and periodicals and jotted notes on the pages. My job was to copy these notes into a special notebook and add my comments. For what purpose, I do not know. During the period that I was in Dimitry Mikhailovich's good graces, more than once he invested me with some unique powers. For example, one day he summoned me to his study and handed me a thick notebook of beautiful vellum paper.

"Take down," he said, "everything that I say and command, and jot your comments next to it. Don't be afraid to be frank if they aren't always favorable. From now on you will be my personal librarian and editor."

On another occasion he gave me the beginning of an essay titled "On the Glory and Greatness of Russia," and ordered me to continue it. Even for those times, the piece was remarkable for its rare eloquence; judging from numerous corrections and stylistic alterations in the unfinished text, its author had taken great pains with it.

But at that time, I didn't want to or couldn't see this. And, after expressing the impossibility of my contribution measuring up to his, I obeyed my patron's will to continue his article and zealously set to work in the wake of his bombast and high-flown rhetoric.

And indeed, I was not up to the task. I was inclined to idealize everything that captured my heart or imagination, and so I had placed Dimitry Mikhailovich on a pedestal. I viewed him as a great historical figure and felt it would be impertinent to identify his shortcomings or tread in his footsteps, even though he had asked me to.

Actually, everything was a lot simpler. In the general's essay, in which he presumed Russia's glory and greatness, for want of a clear understanding of his topic he got lost in a maze of pompous sentences, and he gave me the job of getting him out. Naively accepting his challenge in good faith, I, in turn, spread my wings, which failed to support me. Obviously I wasn't up to the role assigned to me. Still, this episode did not spoil our relationship at this early stage. For a long time afterward he was kindly disposed toward me and showered me with signs of his attention.

Relations with the general's sister were far simpler and warmer. Anna Mikhailovna was young then, about twenty-seven or twenty-eight. You wouldn't exactly call her a beauty, but there were such attractive things about her, like the intelligent and kindly expression on her pleasing face and a sincere simplicity of manner, that you couldn't help but be open with Anna Mikhailovna.

The general's sister was educated in St. Petersburg, at Catherine Institute, and she recalled very vividly the time she spent there. Often she told me about student life at the institute, their habits and customs, studies, pastimes, and the teachers. She spoke enthusiastically about their favorite teacher, I. I. Martynov, who taught Russian literature. Later he became director of a department in the Ministry of Public Education and was well known in academia for his translation of Greek classics.

Carried away by her goodwill toward me, sometimes Anna Mikhailovna drew a parallel between Martynov's popularity with Catherine Institute students and my popularity with my Ostrogozhsk pupils. Whether in jest or in serious spirit, she predicted a brilliant career for me. It never occurred to either of us that fate, indeed, was priming me for a certain measure of success within the walls of the same institution where Martynov taught, and in the same subject, too.

I was really very happy with my pupils. Anna Mikhailovna's daughter was bright and gifted, as were most of my other pupils. An awfully homely girl, she took such a liking to my lessons that she had to be restrained from working too hard. As if it were now, I can feel the intent look of those quick little eyes. Head tilted to the side, lips pursed, she listened to my explanations. Her cousin, Marya Vladimirovna, whom everyone called Mashenka, lagged far behind in ability and diligence. She was nevertheless a charming girl. Even in later years I saw few women with such a fresh face of striking beauty. She was barely emerging from childhood and presented a winsome mixture of childish naiveté and the first glimmer of feminine dignity. If the comparison of a young girl with a blooming rose wasn't already hackneyed, it should have been created for Mashenka. It sprang to mind at the sight of her darling milky-white cheeks tinged with pale pink, which, at the slightest emotion, flared into a bright flush and spread over her entire face, neck, and arms. What added to her charm was a shadow of pensiveness lurking in her eyes and in the corners of the subtle arc of the mouth. Often I had occasion to notice her lips quivering and eyelashes weighted with tears. This pensiveness, combined with the wholesome glow of her dear, childlike face, was both touching and thought-provoking.

You couldn't say that Mashenka didn't have a reason to be pensive. Her parents lived in the country and gave little thought to her education. Her childhood was spent with a hypochondriac father and a kind and intelligent mother who suffered from consumption. Finally, her uncle took her in and, for the first time, saw to her education. But he didn't have time to keep an eye on her and handed her over to his sister, Anna Mikhailovna. Although in all other respects a worthy woman, she failed to measure up to herself in this situation. She was a very devoted mother, but nature had denied her daughter the most ordinary good looks. This was the source of Anna Mikhailovna's irritation with the beautiful Mashenka. She envied her and, to avoid unfavorable comparisons with her own child, kept her niece at a distance. Thus, poor Mashenka, even in her uncle's home, was lonely.

Timely or not, I now appeared on the scene. At first Mashenka avoided me and threw me unfriendly glances from beneath her long eyelashes. To her I was a teacher, a distasteful creature who, she believed, was bound to introduce a new element of boredom and coercion into her already dreary life.

On my part, I took up my lessons with her eagerly. Never before had I had a pupil like this. Only a year younger than I, with her radiant beauty and slumbering mind, it seemed to me—with my mind filled with fantasy from novels—that she was the sleeping beauty whom I had been called to awaken. Carried away by my imagination, I made up my mind to stir Mashenka's mind and heart. Alas! The first remained a dream and the second gave me momentary, but little, satisfaction. Mashenka quickly became convinced that I was not a boring teacher but a lively, attractive youth, who, with all his airs of importance and exacting requirements, was capable of displaying sympathy for her and easing her academic burden as much as possible. The stern and reserved expression of a little woman gave way to childish trust.

She confided to me her small secrets and worries. And I, depending on the circumstances, would sometimes console her gently and other times lecture her with the pomposity of a mentor. But, little by little, our feeling for each other became more ardent and urgent than the fraternal goodwill with which we continued to deceive ourselves.

Anna Mikhailovna never was present at our lessons. Left to our own devices, in our inexperience, I don't know how far we would have gone and what might have been the outcome of this dangerous game spiced with passionate glances and affectionate handclasps. But meanwhile, the time had come for the general's departure from Ostrogozhsk. Dimitry Mikhailovich did not want to subject Mashenka to the unstable nature of his nomadic army life any longer. He enrolled her in Kharkov Institute to complete her education.

Our parting was sad. We knew we would never see each other again. Our last lesson found us in tears, bitterly bemoaning our fate. Toward the end we couldn't contain ourselves. We hugged each other and exchanged our first and last kiss. Mashenka departed, and I sent after her a long farewell elegy in prose, which, as a mentor, I tried to lard with lofty maxims and homilies.

With this, the first romantic episode in my life ended. Others will dismiss it as trivial. Very well, but in the absence of happier interludes in my working and deprived youth, this was a bright ray of light whose memory warms me to this day.

Soon afterward, a new event further strengthened my relationship with General Yuzefovich. Father had finished the case in which he represented Yuliya Tatarchukova. He parted with his client as soon as she no longer needed him. However, his romantic passion for the young widow kept growing until it reached proportions that seriously began to disturb her peace. Having secured for the widow her rightful inheritance, having feathered her nest, Yuliya's ceaseless admirer envisioned settling down in the Arcadia he had created—if only to enjoy endless contemplation of his goddess. The young woman did not agree with his plans. They quarreled. They parted, this time for good—she, enraged by his audacious designs, and he, taking with him a deep wound of rejection.

In the meantime, General Yuzefovich had long wanted to employ my father to manage his own affairs. The general hastened to take advantage of the opportunity and offered him the job of handling a lawsuit involving his estate in Poltava province in Piryatin *povet,* as Little Russian districts were called then. Thus, Father faced another separation from the family. He had to go to the site of the litigation; that is, to the general's estate, Sotnikovka. Father didn't like to take on jobs involving litigation, especially those of dubious character, as later was the case with the job now being offered. The general was squabbling with peasants for land that, it seems, was taken from them illegally. At that time Father didn't know anything about this, and needing to earn money, he again agreed to plunge into a maelstrom of litigation that he hated so much. He went to Sotnikovka. In my father's absence, Dimitry Mikhailovich assumed responsibility for our family's welfare. Indeed, he arranged things for Mother so that, for the time being, she was free of want.

The general went even further than that. Several months later, acceding to Father's wish to see someone from his family, he dispatched me to Sotnikovka. With rare concern for my welfare, Dimitry Mikhailovich equipped me for the journey, took on all my travel expenses, and, cognizant of my youth and inexperience, assigned a venerable noncommissioned officer to accompany me to ensure my safety. I found Father overwhelmed by his tasks and in very low spirits. Added to the pain of his unrequited love and the tedium of loneliness was an oppressive dissatisfaction with himself for taking on responsibility for litigation whose justification he had begun to doubt.

My visit with him raised his spirits considerably. But when I departed, I didn't suspect that I had seen him for the last time. And Mother, for only a short time thereafter, continued to enjoy a relatively worry-free existence under Yuzefovich's wing. Two months after my trip to Poltava province, we received the news of Father's death. He died in Piryatin after a five-day illness. To the very end fate dogged this poor, suffering man. He died dispirited by an awareness of the fruitlessness of his labors. The hands of strangers at his deathbed closed his eyes. His beloved family was not present to ease the pain of his last moments. Poor, poor Father! His talents, the nobility of his feelings, the honesty of his deeds—what good did they do him? All these things were distorted in Father, crushed by the environment and circumstances. Can he be blamed for not overcoming his fate, for letting his passions run away from him at times? No, let people look for heroes where they please, but not in the Russian serf, for whom every asset in his character was a curse, a new reason for his downfall. And my father, to his last breath, retained so much respect for his trampled human dignity that despite the ignominy of his position, he did not disgrace himself with any dirty business or a single dishonest thought.

16

◆•◆•◆•◆

Farewell, Ostrogozhsk

The news of my father's death reached us through General Yuzefovich. He tried as hard as he could to soften this new blow to our poor mother. The general himself joined us in our grief. He said that in my father's death he had lost an indispensable assistant. He promised, as before, to take care of the family.

A strange incident preceded his death. Among the complicated and muddled phenomena we encounter in life, some generate superstition in simple-hearted people. That was the case with my mother. Not long before Father died, she had a dream in which, for the rest of her life, she never ceased to see prophetic meaning. And indeed, it did coincide surprisingly with subsequent events in her life.

Mother had dreamt that Father, she, and I were going somewhere in a wagon. The locale was unfamiliar. I was sitting next to her. Father, on the coachman's seat, was driving the horse. Suddenly the sky lit up, and above us we heard a deafening crack of thunder. Instantaneously Father vanished. The frightened horse panicked and threatened to overturn the wagon. Mother was terrified, but I grabbed the reins and exclaimed: "Don't be afraid, I'll drive. We'll make it there." Two days after that dream, news of Father's death arrived. And I really did have to take the reins into my inexperienced hands to manage our family's little world and lead them further on the journey of life.

The year 1820 had arrived. General Dimitry Mikhailovich

Yuzefovich was assigned to command the First Horseguards Division instead of the Dragoon Division. The Horseguards Division was stationed in Elets, and Dimitry Mikhailovich had to proceed there without delay. He invited me to go with him. My affection for the general and his sister, and the financial advantage to my family, of whom I was now the sole breadwinner, compelled me to agree. As for Mother, painful as this new separation was for her, she recognized the soundness of my decision and did not oppose it. After all, I wasn't going to the end of the earth!

But it wasn't so easy to leave my Ostrogozhsk friends. I never suspected that they considered me such an important person. The circle in which I mixed and, especially, the parents of my pupils were very upset. They heaped reproaches on me. And the general got his share—behind his back, of course—for "kidnapping" me. But I was openly censured for betraying the town that had so cordially embraced me. Bewildered and distressed, I was ready to take back my word that I had given to the general. But, in true military style, he took charge of the situation. Quick as a flash he roused the entire household and, giving me no time to change my mind, led me away with him.

And so I found myself in Elets. The general was allotted spacious quarters—the entire home of Zheludkov, one of the wealthiest merchants in the town. At that time Elets was reputed to be one of the finest county towns. It was very nicely built up. There were quite a few stone structures and as many as twenty-two churches. It could boast a stone roadway, then an almost unheard-of luxury. To the eye, Elets was clearly far more attractive than my beloved Ostrogozhsk, but it could scarcely compare to its atmosphere and way of life.

Elets was exclusively a commercial town; it conducted an extensive trade in flour. There were very few members of the gentry. The local aristocracy consisted of merchants, whose only goal was to reap profits. Accordingly, the competition between them was confined to boasting to each other, trickery, and swindling. The government bureaucracy competed with the merchants in striving for profits and in the art of self-enrichment. Without exception the bureaucrats took bribes and robbed public coffers. The leading spirit there, as befitting such conditions, was the number-one official in the town, the mayor. A retired colonel and a deadbeat, he fleeced people unmercifully and enjoyed appropriate respect among people like himself. The way the townspeople lived was generally very backward. It was dirty, in a primitive sense, and crude: there was no place in their daily life for social or family virtues. The women, following the example of their grandmothers, still disfigured themselves with powder and rouge.

Piety did not go beyond the construction of homemade icon-cases and the observance of fasts, not excluding, however, gluttony with rich *sterlets* [a small species of sturgeon] and pies. When passing a church or in the presence of the deceased, they made sweeping signs of the cross over their foreheads and bellies; but catching sight of a priest, they spat vigorously to ward off evil forces.

At any rate, at least among the merchants, all the above did not exclude their own special ways of displaying their good natures and traditional Slavic hospitality. These were certainly redeeming features in the character of this ignorant community, steeped in age-old prejudices. Nevertheless, the hospitality offered by the merchantry was also unique, in keeping with their usual way of conducting themselves. For example, a wealthy merchant would invite guests to his home, treat them to an excellent dinner, and then order a servant to lock the gate. A guest could not leave and, like it or not, must drink until he passed out. Not to treat or be treated in this fashion was considered bad manners and taken as a bitter insult.

However, here too, as everywhere, there were exceptions to the rule. Several merchant families stood out as not being involved in this general decadence and petty tyranny. These exceptions had not been mellowed by education, for it wasn't available in this trading enclave. Their ways were shaped by their own innate, more refined tastes and inclinations. To this group, incidentally, belonged the families of a very wealthy, respected citizen—Kononov—and of our host, Zheludkov. There was a certain restraint in their manner, and in their households they strove for orderliness and comfort. In the countryside both owned dachas with luxuriant parks and greenhouses. Sumptuous dinners were given there for General Yuzefovich, and I was invited to attend with the general's family.

At such events, of course, there were no drinking bouts or other excesses; everything was managed with decorum, "in a stately manner." However, in other homes, where such refinement was not the norm, an exception was made for us. Guests and hosts alike felt somewhat intimidated by the general, who comported himself with an air of grandeur. When he was present the host never ordered that the gate be locked. The real party began with the general's departure.

My responsibilities in General Yuzefovich's home increased. I continued to tutor Anna Mikhailovna's daughter, as well as three nephews who joined the general's household in Elets. They were Mashenka's brothers. As I mentioned earlier, their father had been suffering from hypochondria. In the meantime, he had completely lost his mind and died shortly thereafter. Two of the boys didn't present any special problems. My lessons with them went very well. But the third boy, Ksenofont, lazy and unruly, at times even wild, caused me no little concern. Nothing worked for him, neither strictness nor kindness. Probably a more experienced teacher could have handled him, but I, a mere boy myself, hardly knew what to do with him.

For some time this poor Ksenofont was the only thorn in an otherwise rosy situation. In general, my life in Elets breaks down into two phases. The best of my memories belong to the first phase. Like all good things, it was the shortest and sweetest period. I can say I was almost happy for a time. Gone was the pain of my departure from Ostrogozhsk—the farewell with Mashenka and others dear to me. And gone, too, the grief that I felt when my friends had expressed indignation over my leaving. Also, my mother and the younger children were, to a certain extent, provided for.

Now I stood closer than before to the object of my worship.

At that time Dimitry Mikhailovich was the hero of my dreams. To me he was the personification of valor. Without reservation I had faith in him and trusted him. How wonderfully kind he was to me then! With the move to Elets, I lived in his home and was treated like a member of the family. The atmosphere of contentment, warmth, and elegance was conducive to my moral and physical development. Dimitry Mikhailovich constantly drew me into conversation and, it seemed, sympathized with my wildest dreams. No wonder that I flourished, grew bolder and brasher. My spirits soared. But not for long, of course. And I paid bitterly for those moments of happy oblivion. My morale was shattered again; this time by the very same hand that had raised it.

I've mentioned several times my craving for authorship. Here in Elets, my vanity was flattered to the point that my desire to write raged with a new intensity. I even started to write a novel in the style of *La Nouvelle Heloïse* by J.-J. Rousseau. Shortly before that, I had happened to read this work, poorly translated by someone named Potemkin. Also, I went through *Emile,* translated by one Elizabeth Del'salle.

Both books made a big impression on me. Without giving it much thought, I undertook to imitate the first of these two works. Alternately I wrote and tore up what I had written. I filled up a lot of paper and scrapped just as much. Obviously, the work didn't go well, but I kept going and sometimes stayed up all night with this nonsense, which, I am happy to say, has remained unfinished.

In this instance, too, it was that very same Dimitry Mikhailovich who encouraged me. Admittedly, he still hadn't read a single line of what I had written, but he always knew what was going well for me. In his free time, at evening tea, he liked to question me about what I was doing, what I was writing, even what I was thinking about. And he always looked with approval on all my ventures.

And unexpectedly, everything changed! It happened one day when, bursting with excitement, I confided my plans to him. Head down, the general listened. Suddenly his lips curled into a smirk and, instead of his usual compliment, a biting comment escaped his lips. He said it was useless, that I was giving myself airs, for which I possessed neither moral or corporeal rights. Everything suddenly went black. What was this—a nasty joke or the bitter truth? I was deeply hurt, but not for long. The sharp pain from this unexpected blow gave way to agonizing doubts. In my eyes, the infallible general was, of course, right. I lacked both legal rights and talent. My cherished aspirations and dreams were merely a play of vanity. All right, then, I told myself—from this moment on no one will have any grounds to reproach me in this regard. I gathered up my books and papers, rushed into the kitchen, and, with one heave, tossed the whole lot into the blazing stove, to the amazement of the French cook.

For the time being this action seemed to have drained all my energy. Morally and physically exhausted, I sank into apathy. But the general wasted no time trying to pull me out of it. That same evening at tea he continued to taunt me with incomprehensible persistence. Holding my tongue, I became more and more aware of my status as a non-person. But Dimitry Mikhailovich grew more cruel and more venomous. That's when I hardened myself and remarked rather sharply: "From now on you can stop reproaching me for my foolhardy aspirations and pursuits. I burned all my books and writings." The general found my words insolent and my deed stupid. He dismissed me from the room.

Alone in my room, I felt utterly miserable. My descent from the clouds, where I had hovered all this time, was too rapid. It stunned me and opened old wounds. A little while later, my pride awakened and helped me gain control of myself and my situation. But at first, I could think of nothing but the sad collision with Dimitry Mikhailovich. The exalted love I felt for him flared in my heart with all the strength of the last outburst of a dying fire. I forgot my humiliation and anger and yearned only for reconciliation with my idol. The first time I saw him the next day, I expressed something in this vein to him. He listened coldly and dismissed me from his presence. Disappointed and disheartened, I left the room.

A wall had sprung up between us. The general no longer spent time with me and looked upon me solely as the teacher of his niece and nephews. I kept to myself and to the performance of my duties. We were evidently both disillusioned and each returned to his own sphere. Neither I nor anyone else in our circle could account for what had transpired. It's still hard to explain his behavior, unless it can be attributed to the early symptoms of a cruel disease, which actually developed in him before long. But this is only conjecture, and perhaps Dimitry Mikhailovich's coolness toward me was justified by some weighty reasons unknown to me.

On the other hand, Anna Mikhailovna didn't change at all. She remained sincere and friendly, even, I might say, displayed a new warmth toward me. And our relationship stayed that way to the end of my stay in the Yuzefovich home. Especially dear was the sympathy she showed when my feelings were all mixed up, the very first instant after the estrangement between the general and me. I so wanted to believe in myself, in the correctness and legitimacy of my intentions, and to hold on to the trust in the person whose opinion, only yesterday, was gospel for me.

Gradually I settled down. My natural inclinations took their own course, and, aided by pride, the all-powerful lever within me, I returned to that moral and intellectual track from which I had been derailed. New books on my shelf replaced those I had burned. Again I accumulated a pile of papers covered with writing. Once more fantasy spun mirages of future successes, and I settled into my former double life.

No, I thought to myself, I will not surrender faintheartedly. If a whole legion of generals were to take up arms against me, I should prevail, or . . . if I could not live with honor, I would die. Now it seemed that the motto beneath my portrait was inscribed like blazing letters in my brain.

All this swirled through my mind like a whirlwind but never went further than the pages of my diary. The experience I had just survived made me cautious. But, evidently, fate hadn't wanted to embitter me. It soon sent me a new friend, with whom I have close ties to this day. From Moscow had come still another of the general's many nephews. This was the eldest son of the general's deceased brother. He had just graduated from the Moscow University boarding school for children of the nobility.

Shortly before his father died, the young man had arrived in Elets and stayed with the intention of enlisting in one of his uncle's regiments. He was only a few years older than I, but was educated and had the mark of fine breeding imposed by a certain social status. A singular bluntness came through in his character—in his features and the way he expressed himself—which clashed with other traits. But nothing could have been more erroneous than to interpret this as haughtiness and arrogance.

Mikhailo Vladimirovich was the personification of generosity and simplicity. The affectation of arrogance was nothing more than youthful bravado. He was full of it, impatient and bursting to perform a good deed that would instantly catapult him from young adulthood to the stature of a mature man.

But where would he find such an opportunity? Pending its appearance, Mikhailo Vladimirovich was impatient to distinguish himself, at least, by fighting a duel. Sometimes his zeal in this respect had its comic side. Once he almost did cross swords. This is how it came about.

Mikhailo Vladimirovich was very devoted to his uncle. He was proud, justifiably, of the general's intellect, character, his rank and military prowess. Suddenly rumors reached the young man that some officer, at one time, somewhere, had spoken disrespectfully about the general. Mikhailo Vladimirovich immediately exploded in anger and issued a bold challenge to the officer. But alas! It never occurred to anyone to attack the honor of the respected general. The rumors turned out to be a fabrication or else a stupid joke to tease the young Yuzefovich. Thus the *causus belli* vanished by itself. He had to lay aside his weapons. And for lack of an opportunity to stand up for his uncle, he consoled himself with the thought that he had made an impression and firmly established his reputation in the community of officers, which he certainly had.

For us it was friendship almost at first sight. And as time passed, it grew stronger. What joined us was a commonality of tastes and a similar cast of mind. Afflicted with idealism, we had been searching in vain in the world around us and in ourselves for fulfillment of our immoderate demands. Now it seemed to us that we had found in each other the desired common ground. We were equally captivated by heroes of the ancient world and the new world and, with the boldness and inexperience of youth, aspired to become like them.

The discord between my inner world and my external circumstances stirred young Yuzefovich's sympathy for me. His vivid imagination filled in the rest. No less similar was our passion for literature. How many pleasant, wonderful hours we passed together, reading and discussing various books. Among them were *Emile* and *La Nouvelle Heloïse,* which I had acquired somewhere to replace those I had burned following my estrangement from the general.

No one disturbed us during our studies or friendly chats. As I've already said, the general stopped bothering with me. Anyway, he really didn't have the time. Often he was away reviewing the regiments of his division; the rest of the time he spent working on a project. He had been working on it back in Ostrogozhsk and was now planning to present it soon to the tsar. Thus, young Yuzefovich and I were left to our own devices and our friendship.

Pride is certainly a cruel trait! It can give you pleasure, and it can cause you grief. My pride was involved in our friendship. My friend's endless kindness and tolerance saved our relationship. I was very poor, and that was at the bottom of the pride problem. The meager compensation I received for my teaching duties went to my mother. It was barely enough to feed her and the four small children. But I, having room and board in the general's home, didn't experience extreme want. At the beginning of my stay, my poverty didn't show, but gradually it came through in my clothing. Finally, my wardrobe ended up in a pitiful state. My outerwear was still in one piece, thanks to what was left to me when my father died. So, in the presence of others, I appeared decently attired, but my underclothes were full of holes. I was on the verge of arming myself with a needle and somehow darning or mending my pitiful semblances of shirts. But very soon it was evident that they were beyond repair, and I gave up. I ignored the problem; fretting about it wouldn't help, so it wasn't worth thinking about. But someone else did.

That someone else was Mikhailo Vladimirovich Yuzefovich. Somehow he had found out about my poverty and took it into his head to offer assistance. His father had been an elegant dresser and, when he died, had left a pile of clothing and underwear, all in good condition. My friend picked out an assortment of articles and asked me to use them, as he had more than enough already. Since we were such close friends, it would seem the simplest thing to do, but I took it into my head to take offense. The notion that I might receive a gift and be unable to reciprocate hurt my pride. One doesn't have true friendship, I thought, when one person is dependent on another; I would be dependent on the person from whom I accepted a favor.

I bore my poverty with complete indifference and didn't feel I had to apologize for it. Point-blank and somewhat resentfully, I rejected the gift. Fortunately, Yuzefovich took it extremely well. He understood my position and regretfully accepted my refusal without ill will.

Our relationship didn't suffer in the least. We resumed our heart-to-heart chats, continued to confide in each other our views on life and man, to read new literary works in the abundant supply of magazines to which the general subscribed, and to be carried away by the beauty of the solicitor's daughter, a shining star amidst the ladies of Elets.

Incidentally, about the solicitor, her father—this was a cunning operator. He spent more time on private business than government business and by hook or by crook amassed an incredible fortune. Two sons were educated in Moscow at the university boarding school. They were schoolmates of young Yuzefovich and had arrived in Elets with him. One was a simple, dull-witted fellow, the other a chatterbox and dandy who affected salon manners.

The wife of the solicitor and mother of the lovely lady who captivated Yuzefovich and me was a shrewd wench with provincial ways. Despite her fading beauty, the general did not disdain her and usually spent his free time with her alone, chatting. The husband looked the other way at the conduct of his dear other half, figuring that he would have much to gain from her friendship with the general. He calculated correctly. Dimitry Mikhailovich made it up to him. For the pleasant hours with the solicitor's wife, he awarded the husband the Order of St. Anna, Third Degree. And to this day, I cannot, without revulsion, recall the cuckold's delight and his hymns of praise and gratitude to the "eminent dignitary."

In General Yuzefovich's home was one more person with whom I was friendly. Aleksei Ivanovich LaConte was a young man, very handsome, cultured, with gentle, elegant manners. He occupied a strange position in the household and appeared to be an enigmatic figure. He had previously served as a volunteer in the military and had participated in the campaign against the French but was discharged without rank for lack of certain documents. Most likely he was someone's love child. French in name, as well as in his exquisite courtesy and refined manner, he spoke Russian and wrote it as well. At that time Russian was spoken here but not many people wrote it. His voice was most pleasing. Often he charmed us, singing popular romances that he rendered with taste and expression to the accompaniment of a guitar.

In LaConte's handsome face there was always a touch of sadness, and this in particular attracted me to him. The uncertainty of his position and the general's patronage evidently weighed upon him. But either he did not want to make his way to freedom or he didn't know how to go about it.

The talk was that some kind of secret existed in the relationship of these three people: the general, his sister Anna Mikhailovna, and LaConte. There was even a rumor that Dimitry Mikhailovich, impulsive and wild in his youth, at one time had taken a fancy to his own sister but now had her in mind for LaConte. And for that purpose he had taken the young man into his home. In this maze of rumors, gossip, and, perhaps, slander, it wasn't easy to figure it out. People everywhere are always greedy for scandal, and provincials even more so. Besides, the Yuzefoviches occupied such a visible place in the community in which they mixed that they served as the object of lively gossip and speculation. During my stay in the Yuzefovich household, no one ever betrayed their secret in my presence—if a secret really did exist—and I did not suspect that I was living amidst such stormy passions.

I must give Dimitry Mikhailovich credit for not allowing his sudden coolness toward me to affect his concern for my mother's welfare. He understood how painful the separation from her son was for the recent widow and gave her the opportunity to visit him. He sent for her to come to Elets and provided expenses for the journey. And she managed to save some of the money to renew my wardrobe. When she departed for home, I could consider myself a rich man: I had four new shirts.

Of the many individuals I had occasion to encounter during this time, the figure of Leparsky, then a colonel, is vividly engraved in my memory. Who today doesn't know the name of this noble personage? Called upon to guard the exiled Decembrists* in Siberia, he managed to act humanely and do many good things in the exercise of his difficult and delicate assignment without neglecting his obligations in the least. If the government, in appointing him to this post, had the magnanimous intention of easing the lot of these unfortunates, it fully achieved its aim.

Although no longer a young man when he lived in Elets, he was hale and hearty. Under General Yuzefovich he commanded the Novgorod-Seversky cavalry chasseurs. It is difficult to imagine a more likable person. He was a good-natured man. It was written all over him. You could see it in the tall, strapping figure; it shone on his broad face with its gray mustache; it could be heard in the soft, measured speech, its sincerity inspiring trust. Even then, he was known for his ability to maintain his position of authority while displaying gentle and fatherly concern for subordinates. In return they were faithful to him, body and soul.

*The Decembrists were members of revolutionary societies that conspired to overthrow Nicholas I in December of 1825.

Meanwhile, General Yuzefovich's project was completed and sent to St. Petersburg, and then the author himself was summoned there for personal discussions. The project proposed the distribution of Chuguyev's residents to three counties in Voronezh province: Ostrogozhsk, Starobel, and Biryuch. Vague, sinister rumors had circulated about this even when Yuzefovich was stationed in Ostrogozhsk. In fact, he was putting the project together there. The peaceful inhabitants of this gracious region were terribly upset by these rumors. Somehow they knew about Arakcheyevan regimes in the military settlements and, principally, had heard plenty about the terror in Chuguyev.[1] What could have prompted the general to propose such an unpopular and cruel measure? Ambition, perhaps, which increasingly raged in him, and in the end clouded his mind and heart.

At any rate, Yuzefovich's project was received favorably in St. Petersburg, and he was charged to implement it. Chuguyev was to serve as the center and model for the new settlements proposed in the project. The general received an order instructing him to place Chuguyev under his command first. Directly from St. Petersburg, without stopping in Elets, he proceeded to his new post and instructed his family to start on the journey to Chuguyev without delay.

At the end of April, exactly one year after our move to Elets, we set out for Chuguyev. We traveled slowly, stopping frequently, and, incidentally, stayed for three days in Ostrogozhsk. I saw my mother again and visited my friends, whose anger by this time had subsided. They welcomed me with open arms.

Next we stopped in Kharkhov province at the home of pomeshchitsa Zveryeva, a venerable old woman, to whose daughter—as I mentioned earlier—our passionate general was not indifferent. And, finally, not far from Chuguyev, we spent several days in the village of Saltova, the estate of the wealthy Khorvat family.

Neither Khorvat nor his wife was still of this world, and their only daughter possessed the family's enormous fortune. She was a charming young girl. Her living arrangement was unique. Residing with her in this splendid home were an old governess and an elderly priest who had been a friend of her parents and was now teaching her Scripture. Our stay in Saltova left me with a pleasant memory.

The luxury and elegance there, of even the most minute details, were in keeping with the beauty of our hostess. Everything in and near her soothed the eyes. Hers were so full of sincerity and warmth that my first glance at her, and our exchange of a few words, made me feel as if I had been sprayed with the Elixir of Life. My heart, or, more truthfully, my imagination, was ignited like gunpowder. I was enraptured and, as they say, let myself go. I daresay I was in form. I talked incessantly, and they willingly listened. Our dear hostess encouraged me, first with a glance and then with a smile. And each morning, she bestowed upon me a fresh bouquet of roses that she herself had gathered on an early stroll in the garden. Anna Mikhailovna teased me about it, but I could not contain my excitement.

Those wonderful days passed quickly, and we arrived in Chuguyev in the middle of May. How dreary it seemed to us, fresh from our delightful experience in Saltova. The mark of relentless Arakcheyevan discipline and a gloomy, despondent mood lay heavily upon Chuguyev. Everything here was topsy-turvy. Confusion everywhere. Reorganization and the construction of new buildings. New streets were laid out, old ones altered, uneven ground leveled off, to say nothing of what was done to hills and knolls. An entire hill was razed to the ground, locking in a settlement on one side. And all this had just begun or was half done. Only a small wooden palace stood fully ready, in case the tsar should visit. Meanwhile, the general settled into it.

The palace was situated on picturesque heights, the other side of which bordered a settlement. From the palace site, terraces sloped down to the limpid, silent Don, and a park was being laid out. Judging from the extraordinary works already produced under the supervision of a skillful engineer and a gardener, the park promised to be magnificent.

But hovering above all this was the shadow of memories of the terrible cruelties perpetrated here by Arakcheyev not long before General Yuzefovich's appointment. The main population of Chuguyev consisted of Cossacks. When the news had reached them about the plan to turn them into military settlers, disturbances had broken out. As everyone knows, Arakcheyev didn't treat such things lightly; in this instance he was a brutal executioner. More than twenty men had been killed running the gauntlet, while countless others were beaten half to death. Like a nightmare, terror had gripped the unfortunate Chuguyevans in its clutches.

After the delightful Saltova interlude, it seemed as if I'd landed in a hell on Earth. The reappearance of my old ailment, homesickness, which had lain dormant in Elets, didn't help. The three-day stopover in Ostrogozhsk had revived it, and now it awakened with full force.

At first I managed to find some consolation in the kindness of my good friends Anna Mikhailovna, LaConte, and, especially, Mikhailo Vladimirovich Yuzefovich. Also, I made new, pleasant acquaintances. Of these, I'll mention a few. One was the general's adjutant, Andrei Fyodoseyevich Raevsky, who joined the general's staff in Chuguyev. A well-educated young man, he was the author of poems published in the *Europe-Herald.* Also, he translated Archduke Karl's works on military strategy. At that time the archduke and General Zhomini were very popular among military men.

Soon another official of the general's special staff arrived here from St. Petersburg at his request. Flavitsky, too, was a very amiable and cultured man. Often we met in the evening and had lively discussions, mostly about literature. As for the general, I saw him only at dinner and teatime. He was very busy and rarely home. I continued to tutor his niece and nephews.

But gradually, both my teaching duties and the kindly concern of my friends ceased to keep up my spirits. A severe depression consumed me and finally laid me low. I became terribly ill, and if I didn't die, it was only due to the care Mikhailo Vladimirovich gave me. But even after recovering physically, I could not pull out of my lassitude. I longed to return home, to my family, to my own people. Chuguyev's air seemed poisoned to me, and I felt that nothing but a return to my native region would save me.

I decided to ask the general to release me from my obligations, which were now beyond my strength. He became angry, and at first wouldn't even hear of my leaving. But later he softened and agreed to let me go—and not empty-handed, either. Greatly relieved, I began to prepare for my journey.

Meanwhile, some strange symptoms began to appear in Dimitry Mikhailovich's behavior. Those who had only known him in Chuguyev thought they were innate characteristics of his nature. But people closer to him, and those who had known him earlier, noticed with alarm the sudden change. His manner turned cold and stern, and more and more often he was subject to angry, unprovoked outbursts. His behavior grew erratic and his verbal communication incoherent. For a long time all this was attributed to overwork and too many worries. Strange and incongruous things slipped through in division orders printed on the printing press he had brought from St. Petersburg. They stood out for their excessively florid style and often were inappropriate to the matter at hand. I can remember such an order of his, issued around that time. It involved a minor infraction of discipline by one of the younger officers. "Lieutenant (so-and-so)," said the order, "lapsed into sin." The rest was some sort of preaching or sermonizing, ending with a touching exhortation "not to sin henceforth." Everyone was amazed, but no one foresaw the approaching catastrophe.

I departed in the middle of June 1821. Despite my burning desire to return home, it was terribly painful for me to part with my dear friends Anna Mikhailovna and the young Mikhailo Vladimirovich Yuzefovich. With the first of my two friends, it was farewell forever; with the second, we met and renewed our friendship twenty-five years later. By then he was already assistant director of the Kiev school district, and I had become a professor in St. Petersburg and, as they say, an influential figure in the Ministry of Education.

17

◆•◆•◆•◆

Home Again in Ostrogozhsk

Mother wasn't expecting me, so it was an especially joyous occasion for her. As usual, I found her in difficult straits. My modest earnings, which were sent to her, had always been quickly exhausted, and, until the next pay packet would arrive, she had to eke out a living from her own labor.

Now I had returned home with three hundred rubles in my pocket, which promised to ease her financial burden. This made our reunion an even happier one. The money also gave me the opportunity to rest and get my bearings before searching for employment.

My Ostrogozhsk friends also gave me a warm reception. But army personnel had been reduced here, so my friends in the military had been transferred elsewhere. The Moscow Dragoon Regiment, which I had gotten to know so well, had been moved to another town, and the Kargonol Regiment was assigned to replace it. General Zagrazhsky commanded the division, and I didn't know anyone on his staff. Nevertheless, my friends among the townspeople were the same ones I had known before.

After recovering from my journey, I had to think about what I was going to do with my life and how I would feed my family. But how could I think of doing anything but the monotonous job I did before—teaching? So I took it up again. Fortunately, neither pupils nor parents had forgotten me, and now, when I returned, they easily forgave me for having left. Very few of my former pupils had moved away, and they were more than replaced by new ones. Soon I had so many pupils that I started a school in my home. I worked diligently. Mother was untiring in the help she gave me. And with our modest needs, we could consider ourselves contented. That is, if new troubles didn't come our way.

I had, of course, a lot of support from the town authorities, but my position was insecure. The problem was that I, strictly speaking, had absolutely no right to teach, and less so to run a school. If I had gotten away with it up to now, it was only because of the readiness in our society to skirt the law at every opportunity. But any moment another force could appear that was hostile to my supporters and with one jolt could overturn the bit of prosperity I had achieved. My very success could only hasten this, which is exactly what happened.

I had nothing to fear from two of my best friends, whom I described earlier. They were county School Inspector Ferronsky and his son Nikandr, a teacher in the lower division of the county school. But there were some among the public school teachers who viewed my intrusion into their field with less tolerance. One of them took a very dim view of me! He was irked by my competition and galled by my success. Secretly, he had long been angry with me, and he seized the first opportunity to pursue me openly.

It happened on the day that the county school held its annual assembly. This year the customary speech given on these occasions was delivered by my rival. The topic he chose was different methods of teaching. Developing his subject, suddenly he burst into vicious philippics against self-anointed teachers. "God knows," he ranted, "where the tramps come from who insolently intrude into the ranks of official teachers and only pull the wool over the eyes of good people." And so on, with such transparent hints that the identity of the individual being denounced was no longer a secret to anyone. Obviously, the orator wanted to scare me and lower the public's opinion of me.

But the speech produced a completely different impression than he had expected. The audience considered it indecent and felt sorry for me as the victim of jealousy. I was deeply distressed, not so much by the insult inflicted upon me as by the realization of the bitter truth that had served as the pretext for it. Indeed, I thought, what was I if not a tramp or impostor in a society where he, my rival, was a legitimate representative of intellectual interests? No, it was not he who was to blame, but my cruel fate! This I felt very deeply and I tried to explain it to those who expressed their regret to me about the incident.

But, obsessed as I was with this notion, I could not, under attack, acknowledge defeat without a struggle. I had to fight for myself as well as for my loved ones. Despite all the sympathy the Ostrogozhsk community shared for my plight, I felt that this event could have dire consequences. In keeping with customary procedure, a copy of the teacher's speech was sent to the superintendent's office. There it was treated as information to be turned over to the authorities, which could result in legal action. And that could mean big trouble, and not for me alone.

For all I knew, even the old man Ferronsky might have to pay for being so bighearted toward me. We had to prevent a double misfortune. My well-wishers advised me to journey to Voronezh and personally discuss the matter with Pyotr Grigorevich Butkov, who had recently been appointed superintendent of schools there. Vasily Tikhonovich Lisanevich, our respected marshal of the nobility, the most influential of my supporters, insisted on this. He knew Butkov in St. Petersburg and was on friendly terms with him. He sent me off to Superintendent Butkov, along with a letter of recommendation lavishly praising my work.

Complimentary rumors about the new superintendent made the rounds. Talk was that he was intelligent and well educated, and had many connections in the capital. Although this raised my spirits, I was nervous when I appeared before him.

Butkov cast a fleeting glance at me while reading the marshal's letter. My modest appearance, I suppose, didn't raise any suspicions in him, and Lisanevich's intercession did its job. Pyotr Grigorevich was very warm to me, and sympathetically plied me with questions about my circumstances, about where I had studied and how I was teaching others now. When the interview ended he said:

"Officially, I can't give you written permission to teach. But, please, don't worry and continue to teach as before. Very soon I'll be reviewing the schools under my jurisdiction. I'll be in Ostrogozhsk. Then, I'll personally arrange matters in your case so that you won't be bothered in the future. I myself will write to my friend Lisanevich. I wish you Godspeed. And pass on to Ferronsky everything I've told you."

About two months later, Butkov indeed did come to Ostrogozhsk. He was met with a unanimous appeal on my behalf. Moreover, an official document was presented to him certifying the general respect of the townspeople for my character and conduct. "Such-and-such person," went the document, "has shown himself in all respects to be a person of honesty and nobility, deserving of attention and praise; and by his observance of the holy commandments of a Christian and citizen is worthy of universal trust. Attested to: December 11, 1821." Signatures followed.

To this day I treasure the document with deep gratitude for the good people who supported me when I was in trouble and guided me out of it with honor.

Lisanevich and Ferronsky were the most active of all the people appealing on my behalf. But, then again, Superintendent Lisanevich didn't cause any problems. Ferronsky, as school inspector, received a public order stating that henceforth no obstacles were to be placed in the way of my teaching at my school. The dear old man was truly delighted with the turn of events.

I cannot say, of course, that all this was very lawful, but it certainly wasn't a crime either. In this case, transgression from the letter of the law did not harm society but merely eliminated a particular wrong.

Many years later fate again brought Pyotr Grigorevich and me together. And where do you think? Within the walls of the Academy of Sciences, where both of us were members, and even sat side by side. He was very old then, and did not recognize me at first as the poor youth who had appeared before him at one time as a petitioner. I reminded him of his good deed, and we struck up a very close friendship that lasted until his death.

I don't know if people were kinder in those days or if fate, wanting to counterbalance the evil responsible for my social status, more often steered me toward the good people than the others—of whom, at least in my youth, I had my share. For example, that same individual who at the beginning of our acquaintance had caused me so much trouble very quickly showed himself in a completely different light. Not stupid and generally decent, but proud and intolerant, he sincerely considered me a self-styled charlatan, harmful to society. When convinced that he was wrong, he willingly confessed his mistake and held out his hand to me. He even became my ardent supporter and no longer tried to harm me in word or deed. Thus, I was rid of the only enemy I had in Ostrogozhsk.

True, I was rid of my enemy and had emerged triumphant from an embarrassing position—but for how long? I was tormented by the thought that the law was still against me, and any day I could become a victim of unforeseen, hostile circumstances. And my profession, over whose insecurity I grieved, did it really satisfy me? I labored conscientiously to provide for myself and my family, but, you see, this was only my duty, and not the goal and mission of my entire life. The urge to change course and, finally, to stand on solid ground grew increasingly irresistible. At times, my craving for freedom and knowledge and for expanding the range of my activities possessed me to the point of physical pain. Then my heart would sink with longing, and my head would spin, trying to find an escape route to the world. But I did not doubt that there was a way out, and, strange as it may seem, the greater my impatience, the more hopeful I became. And for what? I had no idea, but kept expecting that something would surely happen and steer me onto my true path. In brief, as the saying goes, I believed in my star with fierce determination. Well, I thought to myself, if Napoleon, when studying in military school, had told anyone that he expected someday to be an emperor, he would have been sent straight off to an insane asylum. "I'm no Napoleon," I told myself. "But then, too, my claims are surely more modest. I'm not dreaming about a crown, but only a seat at the university. Beneath the rays of my star, only this dream shines down upon me, and on this alone all my designs must focus."

But two yokes weighed heavily upon me at this time, one heavier than the other: the burden of my serf status and my poverty. How could I cast them off? How, first, could I attain the freedom I yearned for so desperately? Belief in my star was not enough. I told myself: you must act! Go out into the world, whither your star is calling you. And so a wild idea occurred to me. Cut off the evil at its roots! And this I would accomplish with the help of the one who held my fate in his hands. In short, I decided to write to my master, Count Sheremetev, and ask him to grant me my freedom so I could complete my education, the germ of which he could see in the letter itself.

I can't say that I seriously believed anything would come of it. It seems to me that I took action only to salve my conscience. I realized that I was launching my ship on the boundless sea of chance and pinning my hopes on luck. My weak grounds for success consisted of hearsay about my master's goodness, and I counted on his youth. After all, I consoled myself, if he's young, he still hasn't grown callous. He had had an excellent education under the supervision of such a good-hearted person as Tsarina Mariya Fyodorovna.

He had studied the humanities and history. Surely, I thought, he must have absorbed from them the lessons they conveyed about nobility and magnanimity, and, surely, as the heir of a prominent family, he was well aware of his important position. Well, I told myself, with a background like that, how could he not be broad-minded and sympathize with a person who was seeking a route to freedom in order to educate himself? Besides, what financial loss would he suffer from the release of one insignificant boy out of 150,000 people in his power?

Finally, I asked the count for permission to see him personally so I could lay before him my case in greater detail.

But, as I learned later, Count Sheremetev was a very narrow-minded person. All that I might realistically have expected from him was quite beyond his comprehension. He was unreachable, incapable of common decency. Yet people who are educated and in his position sometimes are able to go beyond common decency and develop more enduring qualities of the mind and heart. Although taught much and taught well, he learned nothing. People said that he was good. Actually, he was neither good nor evil; he was a nothing and completely dominated by his servants as well as his comrades, officers of the Horseguards Regiment in which he served. Shamelessly, his servants fleeced him. So did his friends, but with the appearance of decorum; they squandered and lost easy money and made him pay their debts.

The count was extremely apathetic and even incapable of enjoying his wealth. Of his personal extravagance, only one such instance is known. He was on intimate terms with the dancer Istomina, and the story goes that she cost him more than three hundred thousand rubles. But that was a paltry sum compared to what people around him made away with. Finally, his enormous fortune tottered. When rumors about it reached his lofty patroness, she convinced him to entrust the management of his financial affairs to some honest, intelligent administrator. They found such an individual in the person of Kunitsyn, a former professor at Tsarskoe Selo Lycée who later became the director of the Department of Foreign Religions. The choice turned out to be a good one. The count's new trustee paid off a significant part of the debts amassed on his property and stemmed the reckless stream of expenses. Unfortunately, Kunitsyn died before he could finish the fine job he had begun. However, the main job had been done, and the count's property was saved.

Two months passed without a reply to my letter. Then a decision arrived, conveyed to me by the administrative office of his Alekseyevka lands on January 17, 1821. I was stunned by the count's devastating, blunt rejection of my appeal: "Not worthy of attention." That, then, was all my letter had achieved.

And so evidently my fate had been sealed forever. How could one help but surrender to despair? Since I hadn't really expected anything else for my efforts, my failure disappointed me but did not put an end to my hopes. In the proud awareness of my human worth, I did not believe that I was fated forever to remain in the power of another person who was intellectually and morally worthless. An inner voice whispered that this could not be the last word on my fate, meaning that the time had not yet come to resort to the last means of escaping from it. Now all my energy was devoted to heeding my second motto: "Patience is wisdom." I will hold out until absolutely nothing remains of my hopes or faith . . .

Stimulated by these thoughts, I lived in a constant state of excitement, in a kind of daze. Images haunted me day and night of a university—undoubtedly St. Petersburg—in the form of a temple, radiant with light, inhabited by peace and truth.

But nothing in my appearance gave away my secret torments and ambitious wishes. Outwardly I remained a humble teacher, seeming to have reconciled myself to my duties. Only my diary was my confidant. Leafing through its pages now, how many traces of hidden tears I find in it; but also, what an abundance of vitality, of faith in the inevitable triumph of goodness and truth! My belief in these ideals suffered from the discouraging encounters I'd experienced. But with the passage of time, that very experience revived my belief. Moreover, it took a different form, a purer one. No longer did it apply to earthly needs, but to those eternal, immutable laws of truth and goodness, whose source lies beyond the mundane.

My routine continued as usual. My school thrived and, as before, enjoyed the favor of Ostrogozhsk's citizens. The friends I visited most were Ferronsky and the Dolzhikovs, as well as Stsepinsky and Lisanevich. With them I was my own person, in the full sense of the word. And whenever Astafeyev came to town, he was as warm and supportive as the others. His presence always added new excitement to our circle. Around this time it had grown by one member who played a major role in it. He was the recently appointed mayor of Ostrogozhsk, Gavrilo Ivanovich Chekmaryev. He had once served in the military and participated in campaigns, as evidenced by the deep scar on his face from a saber. But long before Napoleon's invasion of Russia in 1812, he had retired with the rank of major.

Gavrilo Ivanovich had had a genteel upbringing. He was quite proud of his old noble lineage, and only a shattered fortune compelled him to condescend to accept the modest post of mayor in a county town. Moreover, he endured a misfortune that was far worse in the illness of a dearly beloved wife. The Chekmaryevs had two children. The elder, seven-year-old Vanya, quickly took his place among my pupils.

Gavrilo Ivanovich was a remarkable individual. Almost beyond belief. For, while serving as mayor in what was certainly a wealthy town, he never took a bribe. In all that time he received a meager salary of three hundred rubles a year and some infinitesimal income from his ruined Tambov estate. And so if that very same incomparable Ostrogozhsk community hadn't come to his aid, he would have had a hard time making ends meet. Valuing his devoted service, the community took it upon itself, without resorting to official formalities, to supplement his state salary. Thus did the townspeople show themselves worthy of their mayor. They lived in close friendship and mutually supported each other.

I, too, received warm support from Chekmaryev. Initially invited to his home as a teacher, before long I was embraced by the family. The mayor and his wife and children treated me as kin. I lived a few steps from their home, and I don't know which was more of a home to me, theirs or my own.

The following events occurred before Chekmaryev's appointment to Ostrogozhsk. Grigory Nikolayevich Glinka was the mayor. He, too, was a retired soldier, but this fellow had a nasty nature. Taking advantage of the influential position of his two well-known brothers, Sergei and Fyodor, he treated ordinary townspeople of modest means contemptuously, giving free rein to both his tongue and hands. He besieged them mercilessly with demands for bribes. And in the end he burned down most of the city. Here's how it happened.

Aiming to extract a sizable bribe from the owner of a pitiful hovel, first he forced him to billet the regimental bakery in his shack. The tiny structure—wooden, of course, with a thatched roof—stood in the center of town. But bakery stoves required continuous and intense stoking. The law specifically forbid placement of bakeries in densely populated sections of town. But what did laws mean to our crafty mayor!

It was summertime, and a drought parched the region. The stoves in the house ran without rest. The poor owner had no peace, expecting the stoves to blow up any minute, creating a disaster for him and his neighbors. Tearfully, he pleaded with the mayor to transfer the bakery from his house to a safer place. I daresay the mayor did agree, but only on condition that the poor homeowner grease his palm with a sum well beyond his means.

As the days passed, the stove glowed ever brighter and finally burst, setting the bakery afire. It was midsummer, a sultry but windy day. The blaze rapidly enveloped neighboring structures and, like a stream, flowed through the streets of the town. Our firefighting apparatus was limited to four damaged pumps. The inhabitants could do nothing to stop the fire, which, in the end, destroyed over three hundred homes on the finest streets. A good third of Ostrogozhsk was turned into a pile of ruins, from which, at least as far as I could tell, it could not recover. Fortunately for me, the house where I lived survived, though we were plenty frightened and did not come through it without some loss.

The mayor's crime was too obvious to cover up. But he probably had some powerful protectors, because he didn't pay for his deed in any way. He was simply transferred, as a mayor no less, to another town, called Bobrov. To replace him at that time, we were given Chekmaryev. We gained, but not the inhabitants of Bobrov, whose lot it was to suffer for another's troubles. It reminds me of one of Krylov's fables about a pike who committed an offense and was sentenced by the judges to be drowned in a river.

At that time, the letters I received from my Chuguyev friends were a great consolation. Their letters were so intelligent and warm, full of such interest in me, that the days I received them were like holidays. Still, these letters had another meaning. They were a link connecting me to the milieu from which I had been torn but to which all my thoughts turned. Soon, however, this link, too, was broken. My friends had suffered a terrible blow, one that put an end to my relationship with them.

At the end of June I had received a very sad letter from Anna Mikhailovna. She told me that her brother, Dimitry Mikhailovich Yuzefovich, had become insane. "Alas!" she wrote, "the one on whom the fate of all of us depended, particularly the fate of the orphans—Lyula and me—has completely lost his mind, and for us is as good as dead . . . Somehow I had gotten used to my sorrows," she continued, "but this misfortune has utterly numbed me. All I am able to do is ask everyone: what should I, a poor orphan, do now?" The letter went on about some details. The tsar had retained for Dimitry Mikhailovich the rank of division commander with full pay and dining allowance. The whole family went to Kiev and from there planned to journey to Carlsbad for the cure. LaConte had written me about that.

The general's strange behavior, which I had witnessed as well, had been perceived by those closest to him as irritability brought on by overwork. In reality his strange actions were ominous precursors of insanity. And now it was attributed to the general's excessive ambition and to the inner conflict that had developed in him.

It is unlikely that the Arakcheyevan systems of military settlements really appealed to his heart. But his desire, at any cost, to distinguish himself compelled him to forgo his convictions and ignore the admonitions of his enlightened mind and noble heart. From this came his vacillation, his dissatisfaction with himself and the people of his circle. And, in the end, catastrophe. But couldn't all this be explained in a much simpler way, that is, as an inherited defect, of which his own brother had earlier become a victim? Be that as it may, in Dimitry Mikhailovich Yuzefovich a highly gifted individual had perished, an individual deserving a more detailed and objective evaluation. As far as my personal relationship with him is concerned, I can remember him only with gratitude. He didn't suffer for long and died without making it to Carlsbad.

Anna Mikhailovna wrote me another two or three letters from the late general's Poltava estate, Sotnikovka. Young Yuzefovich and LaConte wrote me about two letters, and then I heard nothing more from them. I know nothing about them. But wherever they may be, alive or dead, I will always remember them as some of the finest people I have known, as the best friends I have ever had.

18

◆•◆•◆•◆

The Dawn of a New Day

The year 1821 was gone, and the end of 1822 was drawing closer. I had passed my eighteenth birthday. There was no change in my situation, neither was there a hint of one on the horizon. In the meantime a historic political event, scarcely noticed by the general public, brought me closer to my goal.

In Russia in the 1820s, Bible societies were introduced almost everywhere. Their purpose was to spread the Holy Scripture, principally the Gospel.[1] At that time, the entire New Testament and the Psalter of the Old Testament were translated into Russian and published together with a Slavonic text.

In our country the introduction of Bible societies coincided with, or rather was prompted by, a political pact—the so-called Holy Alliance—which saw in the societies a useful weapon for the implementation of its agenda. This alliance, formed in Europe after Napoleon's defeat, consisted of the sovereigns of Prussia, Austria, and Russia. Their aim, they stated, was to secure the welfare of their nations. And this would be achieved with their declared intention to rule in the spirit of Christian brotherhood. Actually, the alliance had a different, secret purpose.[2]

Created by the Austrian statesman Metternich, the alliance planned to counteract ideas inspired by the French Revolution, that is, to paralyze the people's movements in their struggles for freedom from feudal tyranny and to establish the great principle that the people do not exist for rulers, but rulers exist for the people. Using any available means, the alliance turned for help to religion, too, or, rather, that segment of it that suited their purpose: the preaching of meekness and obedience. Skirting the concept of fraternal equality that constitutes the essence of Christ's teachings, the alliance unscrupulously adhered to the letter of well-known truths. These, when taken separately, can always be distorted to suit one's purpose. This is how obscurants throughout history have acted. They used religion to dull the mind, their aim being to crush initiative and obliterate thought. Let's not forget how the popes acted and how, to this very day, French clerics and ultramontanists are acting.[3] And how can we possibly forget the era of the Runichs and Magnitskys?[4] Tsar Alexander I was a man of good intentions and lofty ideas, but he was not a profound thinker and lacked the courage of his convictions. Such people always are sincerely inclined toward good and are ready to do good deeds, as long as fortune smiles upon them. But if difficulties arise on their path—which is inevitable—and they lose their way, they become discouraged and rue the grand and fine intentions they earlier possessed.

Their position demands great deeds, but to accomplish them character is needed, and this is what the tsar lacked. Such individuals, transfixed in mediocrity, are fit for ordinary endeavors but unsuited for responsible positions.

The kind of radical change that occurred in Alexander Pavlovich [the tsar] is common knowledge. This change followed the first failures of his liberal inclinations. As soon as he realized that Russia's crude ways, its ignorance and muddled administration, could not be changed so quickly, despite his well-meaning but improvident plans, his heart cooled toward Russia. He spurned reforms that earlier he had recognized as necessary and good. His need to pursue a systematic, firm policy that would not encounter obstacles or suffer early failures prompted him to turn away from reforms. When he joined the Holy Alliance, he naively believed that one had only to proclaim great Christian truths for people to become good and love truth and peace, to create harmony between them and respect for the law, and to stop civil servants from robbing both government and people.

He was, of course, more honest than Metternich; he didn't consciously turn religion into a weapon of political intrigue. However, owing to a strange self-delusion, he saw in religion a personal ally that would make it easier for him to rule because religion would instill in the people the desire to conform to a moral code of conduct. For this reason he looked favorably upon the Bible societies springing up everywhere in Russia. And he encouraged their activity under the guidance of their chief founder, Prince Aleksandr Nikolayevich Golitsyn.

But manipulative stratagem aside, one can't deny that the basic idea of Bible societies was appealing in itself. Their efforts to raise the moral level of people indirectly led to the spread of literacy among them. They were responsible for the interest in and active support of Bible societies among all social classes. In Russia, new branches kept opening. They were called "fellowship societies," whose administrative center, headed by Prince Golitsyn, was in St. Petersburg.

It goes without saying that an enlightened community like Ostrogozhsk certainly did not want to lag behind. The prime movers in getting a society started in our region were the wealthy gentry. Prosperous citizens willingly joined them, and the organization was on its way. The sum needed for the opening of the new society was collected quickly, and the formal opening took place at the end of 1822. Vladimir Astafeyev was elected chairman, and the secretary was none other than I!

This was a great honor. Neither my station, age, nor position offered evidence of my fitness for the post. There were many among the members of the society more worthy than me. And these were people of high rank, too, who would willingly have undertaken these responsibilities and would have been flattered to have been chosen. The position of secretary did not carry any financial advantages. But to the members of the fellowship the post was a prestigious one, and for the person chosen for the role it seemed important in terms of provincial ambition.

This esteem seemed to me and my close friends the most important aspect of my election to the office. No one suspected that its significance still lay ahead, and this was but the first step in that direction.

I set about my duties with enthusiasm. The job couldn't have been more in line with my frame of mind at that time. The concept of morality lay at the foundation of all my ideals. To work in its behalf seemed to me the highest good. My head was still filled with Plutarch's heroes, but my heart saw nothing but light in the Gospel's truths and comforting promises. I was carried away by my imagination, and reality went down the drain. In my eyes the activity of the fellowship society assumed the proportions of a civic deed. And I, allowed to play a part in it, drove myself to a point approaching asceticism to justify the trust shown in me. My enthusiasm for the work, actually a very modest amount, came as no surprise to anyone. In our provincial naiveté, all of us saw nothing beyond the aims and intentions that inspired us. For lack of real work, we gratified ourselves with illusory feats.

We certainly didn't spare expenses, and, by the way, ordered a large quantity of publications of the central Bible society. With the funds at hand we paid one ruble per copy of the Gospel and fifty kopeks for each Psalter. The money came from membership dues. Then we distributed the books around the parishes, offering copies to anyone wanting them. Those who did and could pay for them, paid. Others received them free.

While I was occupied with these new duties and my teaching job, more than a year passed. But then a day arrived that I shall never forget: February 9, 1824. It was the day of the first general meeting of our fellowship society. We wanted to make it a grand affair. Many of the gentry from the district came. Respected townspeople and all the leading officials gathered in the meeting room. I addressed the assemblage with a report I had compiled for this day about the activities and financial status of the fellowship. In conclusion, I delivered a speech I had composed. I spoke about the lofty significance of religious truths that the Gospel had given us, about their salutary influence on the morals of individuals and society. In this vein, I touched upon the benefits that could be achieved by the joint efforts of enlightened citizens through their widespread distribution of books of Holy Scripture.

Thinking about it now, it seems that the sincere enthusiasm and youthful ardor with which I delivered the speech was the main reason for its remarkable reception. This won over the hearts of the audience, most of whom, moreover, were well disposed toward me.

At the end of my speech there was a burst of applause, and I was given a real ovation. The assemblage unanimously resolved to present my speech to the president of the Bible society of Russia—the minister of ecclesiastical affairs and education, Prince Golitsyn—and to petition for permission to print it.

I don't know if my friends, in coming to this agreement, enter-

Triumphal Arch, the entrance to a Golitsyn estate. Prince A. N. Golitsyn had appealed, unsuccessfully, to Nikitenko's master, Count Sheremetev, to free the youth.

tained some sort of hope for my future. But for me, it was a ray of hope. Deep down I had a feeling that an extraordinary resolution of my fate was close at hand. "It's now or never," I thought. "If this chance passes without a trace, then it's all over for me." I was so excited I lost sleep as well as my appetite. I wandered around like a shadow. I couldn't sit still.

This lasted almost a month. Then Astafeyev received a letter from Prince Golitsyn. The prince wrote that "with great pleasure" he had read the speech that had been sent to him. "The speech is evidence of its author's erudition and talent and the nobility of his thoughts." In addition, the prince asked that the following information be delivered to him: "the name of the author of the speech, his profession, age," and "does he have a family?" The society hastened to give satisfactory replies to all the prince's questions.

For a grandee possessing the means to do good, it is not hard to show sympathy for the condition of the poor peasant who comes his way and to help him in passing. But to extend a helping hand to an oppressed man with the firm intention of extricating him forever from the abyss of undeserved disgrace requires a staunch, kind heart and strength of character. Prince Aleksandr Nikolayevich Golitsyn was a truly good and noble person.

He felt that my case was worthy of attention, and he did not disdain to take it on amidst a mass of more important administrative and personal concerns. It was necessary to get to work on it without delay and to exert every effort on my behalf. In this case a fleeting magnanimous impulse wouldn't have accomplished anything. But the prince was not the kind of person whose interest easily wanes and ends with a few sympathetic words to the petitioner. Having received the requested information, he personally appealed to Count Sheremetev. In flattering terms he spoke about my gifts and insisted on the need to allow them the development they deserved so they could be used to promote the common good. At the same time the prince wrote again to Astafeyev, informing him that he had personally contacted the count about my case.

Discussions, negotiations, depositions went on until April,

and at the end of the month I was summoned to St. Petersburg! The count's office in Alekseyevka was supposed to supply the money for the journey. The amount hadn't been determined yet. It was left to me to present my requirements.

At the count's office, I was advised to take advantage of the right granted to me to determine the sum I would need for the trip. "Stretch your estimate a bit," they suggested, so my departure would not cause my mother undue hardship. Strange folk! They couldn't get it through their thick heads that we were seeking freedom and nothing more than that. The count's favors were still an exercise of power, and therefore no different than any other use of his power. But such was the corruptive effect of slavery: for a long time we did not consider it sinful to fleece the landowners and the state.

The news that I had been summoned to St. Petersburg raced through Ostrogozhsk with the speed of lightning. It stirred the town into a frenzy of activity, as if a major social event was anticipated. My close friends were excited, and even people who had only heard about me reacted as if this were happening to their own child and held out promise for my complete success. When I prepared for the journey to Elets, it didn't occur to anyone to detain me or reproach me for frivolity. On the contrary, everyone goaded me to lose no time, to take advantage of the opportunity and depart as soon as possible.

And how did I feel? It is difficult to convey in words the varied emotions that suddenly rushed through me. Here it was, the long-hoped-for opportunity! A gathering wave was about to raise me aloft and carry me away to a yearned-for but mysterious world. Before me the expanse of a wide horizon opened up. It was as if I had grown up and felt a kind of proud joy. But in the next breath, an alarming question arose: well, and then what?

In his relationship to me, the count had already showed his small-mindedness. Would he be touched by the interest others had shown? And, finally, would my patron, the prince, have the stamina to win freedom for me in the face of all the obstacles that confronted him?

At times I was cruelly beleaguered by these and similar doubts. True, with my youthful flippancy, I hastened to dispatch them. Allaying my fears, I told myself that the main thing was to get to St. Petersburg, where futures of every possible kind are worked out. My star was shining there now and for good reason was signaling me to come. But then my joy and doubts, all my fears and hopes, were overwhelmed by thoughts of the farewell ahead—a parting with everything dear and close to me that was the joy and meaning of my life. In those moments of cruel anguish I paid for the egotistical joy that in other moments raised me to the skies. I remember how, at one of the farewell parties in my honor, at the Ferronskys', I literally broke down under the pressure of all these feelings. My closest friends had gathered there. They spoke enthusiastically about the changes awaiting me and about the promise of a brilliant future, as if this were in store for me in St. Petersburg. I listened in silence to their kindhearted speeches. I broke into a cold sweat, then suddenly burst into tears. I sobbed so hard I could scarcely breathe. Everyone stopped talking, but no one tried to cheer me up. Instinctively they understood what I must have felt in those moments when the twilight of an unretrievable past was about to conceal from me forever everything dear that I had known until now. And ahead, the dawn of an unknown future was barely beginning to glimmer.

What also depressed me was the thought of my poor mother and my helpless little brothers and sisters. I was their only support. This gave me no peace. There were moments when it seemed to me that, by leaving, I was violating all the commandments concerning a son's duties and love.

In desperation, I turned this way and that, not knowing what to do. Finally, I decided to confide my doubts and fears to Father Simeon Stsepinsky. He listened patiently and said, with the solemnity so in keeping with his stately figure: "Dear Aleksandr, your feelings are understandable and praiseworthy, but you should not turn back from the path to which fate is calling you. Go, and do not look back. All great undertakings are fraught with sacrifice and emotional distress. God will watch over your mother, as He did when you were little and couldn't care for her, and she took care of you. To think now of doing something else, other than following your inner voice to go forward, would be both a mistake and a crime."

These words put an end to my vacillation but not to my grief.

While preparations were being made for my departure, the society commissioned me to gather information around the district about how its affairs were going. Then, together with the society's written report, I was to present this information personally to Prince Golitsyn.

Thus, before my departure, I had occasion again to travel around the places that I loved so much and to take with me to the far North vivid memories of the fertile South. It was toward the end of April [1824]. Clear, peaceful, fragrant days. Greedily I took in the delightful places along, or close to, the banks of two rivers, the quiet Don and the Kalitva. I listened attentively to the talk of the good-natured Little Russians, who received me everywhere with their customary hospitality and affection. I knew that, if not forever, I was leaving them for a long, long time. Especially memorable was the reception at the home of the wealthy landowner Lazarev-Stanishchev, who treated me wonderfully well. And the other reception was at the modest refuge of a Kalitva priest, young and well educated. My conversation with him provided me with substantial spiritual nourishment.

I returned to Ostrogozhsk refreshed by the trip that my Ostrogozhsk friends had designed for me. Now I could approach the big change ahead of me with better self-control.

My last week in Ostrogozhsk dissolved in a whirl of farewells, parting injunctions, and best wishes. The day of departure arrived. From early morning until I left, the house was a lively spectacle. It couldn't hold everyone coming to shake my hand for the last time. They crowded into every corner. And when it was time for me to leave, and I went outside to get into the cart, I couldn't make my way through the crowd. The horse was ordered to go at a walking pace. And I, surrounded by family, in the center of the colorful and noisy mass, followed slowly behind the wagon. It barely crawled and had to keep stopping at one dwelling after another as the heads of households emerged with bags and parcels for my journey. All this they piled into the wagon: roasted poultry—chickens, geese, turkeys; whole hams; pies of every possible size and variety of stuffing; an assortment of jams in jars; drinks in bottles; and so on. Someone slipped a whole bottle of sweet *mors* [fruit drink from cranberries] between the cushions.

Soon we reached the town gate, beyond which began a stretch of the high-road. I was in a daze and don't remember how I wound up in the wagon or how we passed the first few versts. I was totally unconscious of everything except the ringing in my ears of the last voice crying out to me, leaving an unbearable pain in my heart. It was the wail of my mother, her hands convulsively clutching the wooden cross with which she had blessed me at the last moment.

From the sublime to the ridiculous is but a single step. The wheels jangled, the coachman diligently urged the horses on. Suddenly we hit a pothole. The wagon rolled into it and emerged safely, but the jolt threw me off the seat. I found myself lying on the floor of the wagon beneath a mass of provisions. The bottle cleverly hidden among the pillows flew out and showered me with a stream of red-colored sweet mors. I had to dry myself and clean up the mess. These petty cares brought me around again.

I looked outside. My beloved Ostrogozhsk had already disappeared from sight. I told myself that nothing would ever dislodge it from my memory. I vowed that the kindness I had met there would always guide me in my future relations. Whatever snares might await me, I would not lose faith in the human heart, in its ability to love and manifest greatness. My Ostrogozhskins instilled this belief in me, and it would never, never leave me.

19

◆•◆•◆•◆

St. Petersburg
My Struggle for Freedom

I left Ostrogozhsk in early May of 1824, and arrived in St. Petersburg on May 24th. I traveled in a cart drawn by hired horses, so-called *dolgiis,* rather than by stagecoach. The first day I only got as far as Voronezh, where I had to stop anyway to pick up a copy of my certificate of graduation from the county school. I figured on spending three or four hours in Voronezh, but stayed several days. When I finally departed, my former teachers, Morozov, Grabovsky, and School Inspector Sokolovsky, arranged as memorable a send-off as my Ostrogozhsk friends had given me.

These good-natured, kindly souls considered my career already secured and unselfishly enjoyed my success, something they hadn't known in their own lives. But, alas! Here, with success smiling upon me for the first time, I was exposed to the dark side of the human heart. Bylinsky, director of Voronezh High School, had once denied me permission to cross the threshold of his building. But now, having learned that "the minister himself" had invited me to St. Petersburg, he hastened to see me "to present his compliments" and asked that I "not forget him amidst the honors and pleasures awaiting me in the capital." Actually, I was grateful to him for these words: it gave me an opportunity to intercede successfully on behalf of that kindly old man, my friend Ferronsky.

As I journeyed farther to the north, beyond Elets, I began to see unfamiliar places. Their novelty was striking, although I can't say always pleasing. After departing from nearly every station where I bedded for the night, I pulled my overcoat more snugly around me. With each day the landscape grew bleaker, and so did my hopes. The feeling of loneliness amidst this alien landscape increased with the growing contrast of this gloomy, bare picture with our merry month of May to the south. My terrible fatigue only added to my misery. The roads everywhere were absolutely the worst, and the log highway from Moscow to St. Petersburg could literally shake the life out of you.

Thus did I enter St. Petersburg, far from the conquering hero envisioned by my provincial friends and by those who, with an eye to the future, had hastened to curry favor with me.

The day was waning. I went directly to the home of Count Sheremetev on the Fontanka. Living quarters with his office functionaries awaited me. I say "functionaries" because their tasks, position, and wages in the count's office matched those of government functionaries. I was housed in a nice, clean room with two chief clerks. Generally, I was given a courteous, even cordial reception, although their curiosity was evident. They already knew about me from correspondence between Prince Golitsyn and the young count and were interested in seeing how the whole business turned out.

The next day I rested and then appeared at the office for an introduction to the staff's main managers, or, as they were called, expediters. There were two: Mamontov, in charge of the financial department, and Dubov, in charge of other administrative branches of the count's properties. The nature of their subsequent relationships with me became clear immediately.

On one hand, the sincere simplicity with which Mamontov met me inspired trust and the feeling that he might help me should the need arise. On the other hand, Dubov, having showered me with sugary compliments, quickly exposed himself as my enemy. He informed me that I could not appear before Prince Golitsyn, who had summoned me here, without first receiving permission from Count Sheremetev.

Never before in the struggle I had undertaken against absolute submission to another's will—inherent in the unnatural and immoral order of things in our society—had the exercise of that will confronted me so importunely and palpably as in that relatively petty situation. Mamontov took it upon himself to help me get permission.

But while I waited, like a beetle or ant crawling through mounds of garbage toward the light, a change occurred on high government levels that threatened disaster to my slim chances for success.

Rumors circulated in the city about intrigues, as a result of which Prince Golitsyn had apparently lost favor with the tsar.[1] They said he was no longer a minister, that he had been demoted to the position of director of the postal service. Thus, the public's view of him had fallen considerably.

For a long time I tried not to believe the ominous rumors. At the count's office they assured me that the sign on the prince's home on the Fontanka—"Minister of Education and Ecclesiastical Affairs"—had been replaced by a new sign, which said: "Director of the Postal Service." I wanted to see this with my own eyes, and I did.

Barely had I left the office and stepped onto the bank of the Neva River, when the golden letters of the freshly painted sign, evidently just hung out, pierced my eyes like needles. My God! Only a starving man who has had a piece of bread torn from his hands just as he had lifted it to his mouth could understand the despair and impotent rage that seized me. What more was in store for me?

A faint ripple on the surface of the water dazzled me seductively. With an incredible effort, I tore my eyes from it and dejectedly returned to my nook. I spent a terrible, sleepless night, tossing as if in a fever. Only the next morning did I gain sufficient control of myself to come to this conclusion: I would not resort to decisive measures until I heard from Prince Golitsyn himself whether he was able and willing to continue his involvement with me.

For a long time Mamontov tried, without success, to secure from Count Sheremetev permission for me to appear before

Prince Golitsyn. Finally he won permission by referring to the commission entrusted to me by the Ostrogozhsk Bible society.

"Let him go there!" the count muttered to Mamontov. Then, pausing, he added with a sneer: "The prince can't be bothered with him now!"

The count measured others by his own standards; he did not assume that anyone, and especially a disgraced courtier, could have feelings more humane than his own. But he miscalculated, and to a significant degree I owe my salvation to this mistake. Willingly or reluctantly, permission was granted, and I hurried to take advantage of it.

Prince Golitsyn, accompanied by his court, was spending the summer in Tsarskoe Selo. By this time the original rumors about his disgrace had quieted down. Now they were saying that, although circumstances had compelled him to give up his ministerial post, he continued to enjoy the favor of the highest-ranking members of the imperial family, and of Empress Mariya Fyodorovna in particular.

On June 8, 1824, I departed at dawn for Tsarskoe Selo. Despite recent reassuring rumors about the prince's personal affairs, I was troubled. The sight of the grandiose imperial residence surrounded by a maze of paths lined with lindens and oaks overwhelmed me, a mere provincial. And I felt miserably weak and lonely. Pale, skinny, clothed by an Ostrogozhsk tailor, I looked like an impoverished seminarian, certainly not like a brave young man fighting for his personal honor and independence.

The prince was staying in one of the summer houses on the palace grounds. The first guard I encountered showed me the way. Timidly I entered his excellency's reception room. There sat a gray-haired old man—the prince's valet. He received me so warmly, and so willingly did he go to the prince to report my arrival, that instantly I felt a sense of relief. Two minutes later, I was in the prince's study.

Like all true provincials, I visualized a great noble, a minister, in the splendor and grandeur of his high station, with all the attributes of overpowering superiority. And suddenly, before me stood just another old man in a simple gray frock coat. The prince had a more refined face and manner, yet with a no less respectable and good-natured air than the first old man, his valet. The prince cast a searching glance, then, smiling warmly, invited me into the interior of the room.

"I'm very glad to meet you," he said softly. "I hope my abrupt summons didn't alarm you. You see, I felt that a person with your gifts doesn't belong in the backwoods, and I wanted to open the way for you to expand your activities. The question is, how, indeed, do we go about it? You're so young. You still need more education."

"I dream only of this, Your Excellency," I replied excitedly, "to receive a serious education! My studies ended when I graduated from the county school."

"But tell me," he began again, "how could you, still so young and without any means at all, acquire so much knowledge and the ability to produce such literary language?"

"I read everything I could get my hands on, and copied out passages . . ."

Encouraged by Prince Golitsyn's interest in me, I poured out my heart to him. I forgot the great noble, the dignitary, and saw only an intelligent, kind, knowledgeable person, who was listening to me with obvious sympathy and was ready to extend a helping hand.

When I ended my confession, he said, "In all this I see the hand of God. You must follow the way it is pointing. Our century is full of troubles and unrest, and all of us must contribute as much as we can for a successful outcome. For that we need talented and well-educated people. You must join them, but not before your ideas and knowledge have fully matured. There is no question but that you must go through the university course of study."

"But in my situation, how can I do that without preparation for it? . . ."

"Well, we'll take care of all that. I shall write to Count Sheremetev to grant you your freedom and also provide you with the means to complete your education. In the meantime, I'll introduce you to another person who also takes a lively interest in you. Pray and hope!"

He wrote down a few lines and gave the note to me. Then he summoned the genial valet and instructed him to escort me to *Gospodin* [Mr.] Popov, who lived nearby on the palace grounds.

Popov gave me a gracious reception, spoke a lot about his excellency's liking for me and about his own feelings. But for all that, what a difference in the way these two people received me! Instead of the sincere simplicity with which the prince received me, now I experienced Popov's affected civility. There was a certain aloofness, a coolness about him. Even his friendly assurances rang, if not a false note, an indifferent one. Nowhere on his immobile face did I detect a hint of the graceful gentleness, the heartfelt warmth, that came through in the prince's every word and gesture.

Most unpleasant of all were his eyes, so dull and lifeless. Almost always averting them, Popov looked down; when his eyes fastened their gaze on you, they repelled even the faintest inclination toward openness. I don't know if Popov's manner truly reflected his character, but our meeting certainly left me somewhat dejected.

My meeting with the prince nevertheless left me feeling as if I had been sprinkled with the Elixir of Life. I felt greatly relieved. Now, with jaunty gait and head erect, I ambled through the park, where my earlier walk had put me in such a dejected mood. Now I could enjoy the soft bloom on the trees, the clusters of lilac bushes bursting with flowers, the smooth surface of the lake with swans gliding along it majestically, and the multicolored carpet of flowerbeds in front of the palace.

The return trip to St. Petersburg also seemed shorter and pleasanter. I saw everything through the prism of revived hopes. It was a clear, bright day. I traveled along a highway as smooth as a tablecloth. Plowed fields covered with a faint green haze rushed past neat little houses of settlers and stands of weeping willows and birches. In the air, steeped in the fragrance of young foliage, there was something invigorating to body and soul. Despite my distaste for the bleak northern landscape, I surrendered myself wholly to this wondrous day, one of those rare days that St. Petersburg presents us with.

I was already picturing myself with one foot in the door of the university. But soon fate demonstrated that it didn't intend to spoil me with easy success. Prince Golitsyn kept his promise and wrote a letter to Count Sheremetev. In it he informed him of my visit and earnestly requested that he grant me my freedom. The letter went unanswered. The count, a young lieutenant in the Horseguards, did not deign to extend common courtesy to a venerable man who was old enough to be his father and whose distinguished record naturally entitled him to greater attention.

Again dark clouds gathered on my horizon. I don't know what I did to arouse such antipathy in one of the count's minions, Dubov, whom I mentioned earlier. He wanted to get into the count's good graces and proposed to him an easy way to get rid of me, namely, without further ado I was to be shipped back to Alekseyevka. The proposal also placed a strict ban on my leaving any place on my own, no matter where I might be sent. As a last resort, Dubov suggested that I be sent as a schoolteacher to one of the count's estates.

The day of departure was set, but all their plans were carefully concealed from me in order to throw me off guard. Fortunately, one of my friends at the count's office warned me in time. In desperation I rushed again to Prince Golitsyn. In him alone I saw my salvation.

Around this time he had moved from Tsarskoe Selo to Kamennoy Ostrov, and it was not hard for me to get there. But on the very threshhold of his house, an unexpected obstacle confronted me. When I requested an audience with Prince Golitsyn, his valet replied:

"His excellency is preparing to visit his majesty, and is not receiving anyone today."

Apparently struck by my expression of dismay, he said, "Is it really so necessary? Can't you postpone it?"

I burst out, "If I do, I'll be done for! It'll be the end of me!"

The kindly old man shook his head, shifted his feet hesitantly, but finally, with a wave of his hand, left to announce me. Before I could regain my composure, I was called to the prince's study.

"Your Excellency!" I began rapidly, shaking with excitement. "I am in terrible danger . . ." And I told him about my discovery.

The prince's face darkened. For a minute he was silent, and then he said:

"Don't worry! I give you my word that I shall do everything in my power to rescind this decision. The idea of sending you back to Alekseyevka empty-handed is, in the first place, absolutely absurd, because you deserve something better. And secondly, by summoning you to St. Petersburg, we deprived you of the employment you had in Ostrogozhsk. I shall write to the count at once. And, I hope," he added with a significant smile, "that this time I am not left without a response."

Two days later I learned that the plan to get rid of me by shipping me to Alekseyevka or somewhere else was dropped. Another proposal took its place. But this time, the count's servants viewed it as such a creditable one that everybody in the chancery was excited.

The proposal involved the matter of bringing me closer to the count; in brief, they wanted to make me the count's secretary. This brilliant idea occurred to the young count's uncle, his namesake, General V. S. Sheremetev, and the general stubbornly insisted on it. Prince Golitsyn's high opinion of me and his ardent intercession on my behalf increased my value in the eyes of the arrogant noblemen and intensified their desire not to let me out of their hands. General Sheremetev had a powerful influence on his nephew and ran his affairs as if they were his own.

The general summoned me to appear before him, using a peremptory tone to put an end to my "audacious pretensions." I was received with haughty condescension. He tried to convince me that I'd had enough education, that there was no need to continue to study, that by remaining in my present situation I would have far more to gain.

"Everything is fine in moderation," he said. "Too much education is as harmful as excess in anything else. I am ready to arrange your future," he added in conclusion, "and therefore I advise you to put a limit on your desires. The count wants to keep you here with him as his personal secretary. He needs people of ability. In time he will hold an important position, and, working with him, you can build the best future for yourself. As far as your freedom is concerned, I am the judge of that issue, and I am opposed to it. People like you are rare and it's necessary to treasure them."

Consequently, the noose grew even tighter. They needed me. Prince Golitsyn himself confirmed this. He had come here to speak personally with the young Count Sheremetev on my behalf, and the general asked the prince that I "remain, at least for a short time, as the young count's secretary."

Naturally, all this stiffened my resolve, alive or dead, to tear myself from their clutches. My friends and foes at the count's chancery worried in vain. What to them seemed an honor that could turn out to their advantage or disadvantage was for me a new humiliation. To be kept on a short leash by the narrow-minded son of a nobleman and do deals behind his back could be lucrative for me, but I certainly didn't care for that.

I wanted to live and work at my own risk. Dubov and his crowd had nothing to fear. I was not up to the role intended for me. And if circumstances should compel me to agree to take the post, vengeance would certainly be on my mind. Later Dubov was satisfied that this was the case, but meanwhile he thought differently and went out of his way to harm me. Not only did he put spies on me, but he personally kept a sharp eye on my every move.

But luckily for me, with the few exceptions of Dubov's cronies, the entire chancery, led by Mamontov, stood behind me. Thanks to this support, I was able to throw my enemies off their guard.

From all this it's obvious that the fateful question "to be or not to be" was not quickly resolved for me. If one minute the noose around my neck slackened, then in the next it tightened again.

Prince Golitsyn continued to plead on my behalf. From time to time I appeared before him to present an account of my affairs, and each time I left encouraged. But his own position had become so shaky that small-minded souls no longer felt obliged to please him. However, Empress Mariya Fyodorovna remained true to him; should the need arise, he intended to turn to her as a last resort. But until then I had to try every means I could think of.

With this in mind, I decided to make use of the letters of reference with which my dear Ostrogozhsk friends equipped me when we parted. One was from Father Simeon Stsepinsky to his seminary classmate, Councillor of State I. I. Martynov. However, my link with him was short-lived. He had forgotten his old friend Stsepinsky and expressed this without mincing words. I bowed and left, not to return again.

The second letter was from Chekmaryev. A different reception awaited me at one of Chekmaryev's relatives, Dimitry Ivanovich Yazykov, the esteemed translator of Shletserov's *Nestor* and Montesquieu's *Spirit of Laws.*[2] He worked at the Ministry of Education as head of a department. Dimitry Ivanovich enjoyed a reputation as a superb specialist in Russian history; above all, he was a person of the most noble character. At first glance, his appearance and manners were hardly engaging. What struck me was the awkwardness of this short, stocky, middle-aged man. He walked hunched over, spoke little, and rarely smiled. Yet he did not produce a negative impression. What his angular face lacked was redeemed by the good-natured expression on it, which instantly made me like him. And despite Dimitry Ivanovich's reticence, I was instinctively drawn to confide in him. He led a life of toil, a secluded existence, and therefore couldn't help me in any practical way. But in his few words there was so much sincere feeling that from then on, whenever I felt low, I always went to him for consolation, and his reserved but warm interest in me was so reassuring.

I had with me a third letter of recommendation. This was from Vladimir Ivanovich Astafeyev to a relative on his wife's side, Kondraty Fyodorovich Ryleyev. It involved some sort of mission. Now I have reason to think that Vladimir Ivanovich had contrived this mission in order to draw me close to this man with so rare a mind and heart. But at that time, I did not suspect this and presented myself to Kondraty Fyodorovich not as a supplicant but as the middleman between his Ostrogozhsk friend and him.

At that time Ryleyev managed the chancery of our American Trading Company and lived in the company building by the Siny Bridge. His apartment was on the ground floor. Its windows on the street side were protected by convex grillwork. Now the structure has been rebuilt, but for a long time it was a source of grievous memories for me, and I couldn't pass it without intense emotion—one window in particular. It looked out from the study, where, on a certain evening, I was getting to know the master of the house better. I listened to him recite a poem he had just completed, "Voynarovsky."

Also present that evening, and, like myself, listening to and admiring the recitation, was a demoted officer in the uniform of an army private—Yevgeny Abramovich Baratynsky.[3]

Never have I known anyone with such magnetic power as Ryleyev. Of average height and well built, he had an intelligent, serious face. With his very first glance he gave you a feeling of that charm to which you must inevitably succumb when you got to know him better. To give yourself over to him with all your heart, you had only to see a smile light up his face and look a little deeper into his amazing eyes. At moments of great excitement or poetic inspiration, those eyes sparkled. You were awestruck: there was so much strength and fire in them. But that is how I knew him later on. Now, however, at my first visit, for the most part I experienced the captivating effect of his humanity and goodness.

On that occasion, induced to be frank, I told him the whole sad story of my hopes and struggles. He listened with great interest and then and there outlined the plan of a campaign on my behalf.

However, the first attempt was unsuccessful. He had turned for help to Madame Danaurova, a close friend of Count Sheremetev. The punctilious lady found it awkward "to interfere in such a delicate matter."

"But, don't worry," said Ryleyev, telling me about the failure, "we'll find other ways. I've already spoken about you with my friends in intellectual circles. I repeat: don't worry! You'll see, everything will work out!"

At that meeting Kondraty Fyodorovich advised me to draw up a document outlining the main features of my past and to deliver it to him together with one of my essays. Armed with these documents, he began to win over new allies. Meanwhile, my biography produced a great sensation among the circle of Horseguards officers, comrades of the young Count Sheremetev. Ryleyev was very close friends with some of them. Conspiring on my behalf, they devised a real plot to help me and agreed to compose a joint written declaration about me for presentation to Count Sheremetev.

The most active in this operation were two officers, Aleksandr Mikhailovich Muravyev from the Horseguards and Prince Yevgeny Petrovich Obolensky from the Finland Regiment. The sudden onslaught embarrassed the count. He didn't want his friends to think badly of him, so he gave his word to accede to their demand.

What could be better? That's what I thought. Figuring that my cause had won out, my spirits soared. But days passed and nothing changed. Just the opposite. At the chancery a rumor circulated that the count, yielding to the demands of his uncle the general, was preparing a flat rejection. New fears, new despair! But my defenders were not dozing. They mustered new forces. Rumors about my situation percolated through the fashionable salons of high society. Ladies from the highest circle became interested in me. One of them, Countess Chernisheva, personally undertook to attack the count on my behalf. Having learned about his vacillation, she resorted to the following ruse.

She invited many guests to a salon at her home. Among the guests was the young Count Sheremetev. Countess Chernisheva went over to him and, smiling graciously, held out her hand and said within everyone's hearing: "Count, I heard that you recently performed a wonderful deed, before which pale all your other good deeds. A man with extraordinary gifts was found among the people on your estate who shows promise of a great future. And you granted him his freedom. I consider it the greatest pleasure to thank you for this: to give society a useful member means giving happiness to many."

Bewildered, the count bowed low and muttered in reply that he was delighted to have any occasion to please her excellency.

Actually, the count was in an awkward predicament. Not having strong feelings one way or another about anything, accustomed to following others, he suddenly found himself caught between two fires. On one side were two people: his uncle and usual guide General Sheremetev, plus Dubov, one of his favorite servants. On the other side were his friends, high-society ladies, public opinion . . . To whom should he defer?

The Horseguards officers didn't let a single encounter with the count pass without speaking to him about me. The poor young man could not take a step without hearing my name. The tables were turned; now I had become his despot.

One day, as he was leaving the palace, he ran into Muravyev and another fellow officer. To avoid hearing one more time the refrain about me, of which he was sick to death, he hastened to forestall them:

"I know, gentlemen," he said, "I know what's on your mind: always that same Nikitenko fellow!"

"Count, you're absolutely right. And the sooner you settle with him, the better!"

On September 22, 1824, a whole crowd of the count's fellow officers gathered at his home to celebrate his name day.[4] They did not fail to take advantage of this special occasion to remind him about me again. This time too, the count "gave his unconditional and solemn promise to renounce his rights to me."

Nevertheless, no orders were drawn up at the chancery, which would have heralded a quick end to my anguish. None of the chancery staff was aware of the pressure my supporters had put on the count, and therefore they continued to consider that the decision about my fate was a negative one. Fearful of Dubov's calumnies, I kept everything secret, even from Mamontov.

The whole month of September and the first week of October passed. The count's "unconditional and solemn" promise was no different than his earlier, simple one that wasn't dressed in such high-sounding phrases . . .

No, no intermittent fever could so exhaust a person as these alternating ups and downs of my spirits. I didn't expect the count to go back on his word altogether, but this despicable game promised to go on for a long time . . . and then what?

So I decided to reveal everything to Mamontov, who was well disposed toward me. I felt it would be easier for him than anyone else to wring from the count, in the wake of his promise, the document I needed with his signature. Listening to my story about how the count was attacked from all sides, he couldn't believe his ears. He had been feeling sorry for me, as if all was lost. And now, suddenly he saw me on the eve of victory and that I had turned to him to deliver the final blow. He was a very kind person but also an ambitious one. My turning to him at the last minute flattered him, and he promised to help me.

The great day arrived for me on October 23, 1824. As usual, Mamontov appeared before the count in the morning with a report, then skillfully maneuvered the conversation to a discussion about me. Barely had he pronounced my name when the count impatiently interrupted him:

"What should I do with this fellow?" he declared, exasperated. "At every step I run into his supporters. Prince Golitsyn, Countess Chernisheva, my fellow officers. Everyone demands that I free him. I was compelled to agree, but I know that General Sheremetev won't like it."

Tactfully, carefully, Mamontov began to argue that the voice of public opinion was more powerful than that of one individual, although it belonged to someone dear to him, and, therefore, it was urgent that he satisfy the public's voice with great haste. The main thing was to win over the count so that immediately, on the spot, without seeing or consulting anyone else, he would order that the manumission document be drawn up. This wasn't an easy task, but clever, kind Mamontov succeeded. In the end the count remarked:

"However, this young man needs a good dressing-down for

Liberation: Peasants discussing Alexander II's Emancipation Manifesto of February 19, 1861. Oil painting by M. M. Zaitsev.

creating such a stir. Indeed, you'd think I wasn't able to do on my own what I am now doing out of respect for others."

Mamontov lost no time obtaining the manumission order and immediately presented it to the count for his signature.

The entire chancery staff rose to their feet. All work ceased. My friends swarmed into the chamber to congratulate me and celebrate. Only Dubov remained aloof. What a pity! For I would have willingly extended a hand to him: his intrigues had failed, and I was so lucky!

I will not describe the emotions I experienced in those first minutes of profound, stunning joy . . . I can only say Glory to the Almighty and proclaim my eternal gratitude to those who helped me to be born again.

THE END

Translator's Epilogue

The newly liberated serf destroyed his diary entries for 1825. And no wonder! In December an uprising against Tsar Nicholas I failed. Among the leaders of the Decembrists were some close friends of Nikitenko, including Prince Yevgeny Obolensky, in whose home he had been living as a tutor to the prince's younger brother.

The Decembrists were members of secret revolutionary societies whose goal was a democratic form of government. Their ranks consisted of many officers in the Russian army who had served in Western Europe during the Napoleonic wars. During that time they had encountered liberal Western ideas, and upon returning to Russia they formed the revolutionary societies.

In 1888, the Russian newspaper *Russkaya Starina* published the following article by Nikitenko's daughter about her father's life during that historical year—1825.

> The young Nikitenko left the home of Count Sheremetev with renewed spirits, but without any means of sustenance—he lacked shelter and had scarcely enough in his pocket for food. Mamontov had pleaded that the newly liberated serf not leave the count's chancery empty-handed. But Mamontov could only obtain one hundred rubles, which the young man, gritting his teeth, subsisted on for the better part of the following year [1825].
>
> Meanwhile, thanks to the unfailing support of Prince Golitsyn and, thereafter, others who took an interest in his future, he was admitted to St. Petersburg University without particular dif-

ficulty. Although intellectually mature and talented, he lacked a well-grounded formal education and hardly could have coped with a routine entrance examination.

In his case an exception was made. Without taking the entrance examination he was allowed to attend first-semester lectures on condition that he pass an entrance examination to advance to the second-year program.

The group led by Ryleyev that had supported him in his struggle with Count Sheremetev did not sever its relationship with him. Its members soon became his good friends. He met especially often with Decembrists Ryleyev and Prince Obolensky. Moreover, in July of 1825, Prince Obolensky invited Nikitenko to live in his apartment as a tutor for his younger brother, who had been sent to him from Moscow to complete his education.

Here the young Nikitenko found himself in the very center of the progressive movement of the time. Heartened by the humanity of the members of this circle, where he was so warmly received, Aleksandr Vasilevich felt that he had reached a safe haven. He had not the slightest suspicion that a new threat to his future was lurking close by. It struck him on that fateful day, December 14, 1825.

His supporters and friends had compassion for his youth and inexperience, and, perhaps lacking confidence in his maturity, did not confide their secret of the political revolution they had planned.

Nevertheless, the reverberations of the disastrous undertaking couldn't help but indirectly affect Nikitenko. Would it be proven that, in word or deed, he was privy to the conspiracy? His residence in the home of one of the conspirators and frequent contact with the others placed him under suspicion, but within weeks he was cleared.

So it is understandable that a whirl of new doubts and dangers assailed the young man once again. The fate of his friends and his own future tormented him. It was with these concerns and fears, at the crossroads of despair and hope, that he found himself at the beginning of the new year—1826.

The diaries Nikitenko kept from 1826 until his death in 1877 record his rapid rise from newly liberated serf to eminence.

Ironically, while serving as a university professor and occupying high government posts, he had to struggle to gain freedom for his mother and brother. These excerpts from his diary describe his final efforts on their behalf:

> March 11, 1841
> I have been getting ready to offer payment for the freedom of my mother and brother. I wrote to Count Sheremetev but haven't heard anything from him yet. God Almighty! Here I am, a full-fledged member of society and enjoying even a certain fame and influence, and cannot bring about—what? The freedom of my mother and brother! A half-witted noble has the right to refuse me, and this is called a right! It makes my blood boil. I am impatiently awaiting Zhukovsky's arrival from Moscow. Perhaps his influence will bring results.
>
> March 23, 1841
> I went to see Zhukovsky today and asked for his assistance in my mother and brother's case. He listened to the story of my unsuccessful attempts to buy their freedom and expressed his disgust with the count's response. Vasily Andreyevich Zhukovsky promised to do everything within his power to help me. If the count demands payment for their release, I will not stop at any price to buy their freedom, no matter what I shall have to do to raise the money. My God! If only I can hold out in this struggle.
>
> April 9, 1841
> Today, at long last, an unbearable weight has been lifted from my heart: at last my mother and brother can breathe freely with me. Count Sheremetev has already signed the release documents, freeing them without payment. I received the news today. To whom am I indebted? To Zhukovsky? Or, finally, to the count's own resolution to free them? No matter, the past is forgotten and forgiven.
>
> April 14, 1841
> My mother and brother's case ended so happily only because of Zhukovsky's intercession. God bless him! I visited him today and thanked him.
>
> May 5, 1841
> What a happy day this is for me! I sent off the release documents to my mother and brother.

Notes

Foreword

1. Others include N. N. Shipov, "Istoriia moei zhizni: Razskaz byvshago krepostnago krest'ianina N. N. Shipova," *Russkaia starina* 30 (1881), 133–48, 221–40, 437–78, 665–78; M. E. Vasilieva, "Zapiski krepostnoi," *Russkaia starina* 145 (1911), 140–51, recently translated by John MacKay and published as "Notes of a Serf Woman," *Slavery and Abolition* 21 (April 2000), 146–58; and the anonymous poem-narrative *Vesti o Rossii: Povest' v stikakh krepostnogo krest'ianina, 1830–1840 gg.*, ed. T. G. Snytko (Iaroslavl: Iaroslavskoe krizhnoe izdatel'stvo, 1961).

2. Among the most revealing of these autobiographies are Olaudah Equiano, *The Interesting Narrative of the Life of Olaudah Equiano, or Gustavus Vassa, the African, Written by Himself* (London: the author, 1789, and numerous subsequent editions); Charles Ball, *Slavery in the United States: A Narrative of the Life and Adventures of Charles Ball, a Black Man* (New York: John S. Taylor, 1837); Frederick Douglass, *Narrative of the Life of Frederick Douglass, an American Slave, Written by Himself* (1845) (New York: New American Library, 1968); and Harriet A. Jacobs, *Incidents in the Life of a Slave Girl, Written by Herself* (1861), ed. Jean Fagan Yellin (Cambridge: Harvard University Press, 1987). On these and many other autobiographies, see William L. Andrews, *To Tell a Free Story: The First Century of Afro-American Autobiography, 1760–1865* (Urbana: University of Illinois Press, 1986).

3. The American figures are for 1860 and the Russian for 1858. Unless otherwise indicated, generalizations in this foreword are drawn from Peter Kolchin, *Unfree Labor: American Slavery and Russian Serfdom* (Cambridge: Harvard University Press, 1987); for the statistical contrast, see 51–57.

4. For an influential theoretical statement of the socially constructed nature of race, see Barbara J. Fields, "Ideology and Race in American History," in *Region, Race, and Reconstruction: Essays in Honor of C. Vann Woodward*, ed. J. Morgan Kousser and James M. McPherson (New York: Oxford University Press, 1982), 143–77. Interest in this question has recently spawned a burgeoning new field of "whiteness studies"; for prominent examples of this scholarship, see David R. Roediger, *The Wages of Whiteness: Race and the Making of the American Working Class* (London: Verso, 1991), and Noel Ignatiev, *How the Irish Became White* (New York: Routledge, 1995).

5. Historian Ben Eklof estimated a Russian child's chance of attending a government-sponsored school in 1857 as one in 138, but a serf's chance

would have been much slimmer; see his *Russian Peasant Schools: Officialdom, Village Culture, and Popular Pedagogy, 1861–1914* (Berkeley: University of California Press, 1986), 35. In 1867, shortly after the abolition of serfdom, 8.7 percent of Russia's new military recruits (the vast majority of whom were peasants) were literate. Literacy rates for peasant women lagged far behind those for men; censuses conducted in eight provinces between 1863 and 1873 yielded literacy rates of 12.2 percent among male peasants and 1.5 percent among female peasants. See B. N. Mironov, "Literacy in Russia, 1797–1917: Obtaining New Historical Information Through the Application of Retrospective Prediction Methods," *Soviet Studies in History* 25 (Winter 1986–87), 89–117 (statistics 109–11). It should be noted that not all of these peasants had been serfs, and that the rate of *serf* literacy almost certainly would have been lower than the rate of overall peasant literacy. Estimates of slave literacy in the southern United States are of necessity imprecise, but evidence suggests a figure for the late antebellum years of 5 to 10 percent; see Janet Duitsman Cornelius, *"When I Can Read My Title Clear": Literacy, Slavery, and Religion in the Antebellum South* (Columbia: University of South Carolina Press, 1991).

6. The best general survey of the pre-emancipation peasant commune under serfdom is V. A. Aleksandrov, *Sel'skaia obshchina v Rossii (XVII-nachalo XIX v.)* (Moscow: Izdatel'stvo 'Nauka,' 1976). For an informative article on the commune in the immediate post-emancipation years, see Boris Mironov, "The Russian Peasant Commune After the Reforms of the 1860s," *Slavic Review* 44 (Fall 1985), 438–67. For a fascinating case study that emphasizes divisions and rivalries among serfs on a large absentee-owned estate, see Steven L. Hoch, *Serfdom and Social Control in Russia: Petrovskoe, a Village in Tambov* (Chicago: University of Chicago Press, 1986).

7. For two pioneering articles on the unusual world of lowcountry slaves, see Philip D. Morgan, "Work and Culture: The Task System and the World of Lowcountry Blacks, 1700 to 1880," *William and Mary Quarterly* 39 (October 1982), 563–99, and "The Ownership of Property by Slaves in the Mid-Nineteenth-Century Low Country," *Journal of Southern History* 49 (August 1983), 399–420. More recent works on the internal economy include Ira D. Berlin and Philip D. Morgan, "Labor and the Shaping of Slave Life in the Americas," in *Cultivation and Culture: Labor and the Shaping of Slave Life in the Americas,* ed. Ira Berlin and Philip D. Morgan (Charlottesville: University Press of Virginia, 1993), 1–45; John Campbell, "As 'A Kind of Freeman'?: Slaves' Market-Related Activities in the South Carolina Up Country, 1800–1860," ibid., 243–74; Roderick A. McDonald, "Independent Economic Production by Slaves on Antebellum Louisiana Sugar Plantations," ibid., 275–99; and Larry E. Hudson, Jr., *To Have and To Hold: Slave Work and Family Life in Antebellum South Carolina* (Athens: University of Georgia Press, 1997).

8. Washington remembered little of slavery since he was born in 1858 or 1859 and was only six or seven years old at the time of emancipation; see *Up from Slavery,* reprinted in *Three Negro Classics,* intro. John Hope Franklin (New York: Avon, 1965), 23–205. Douglass, like Nikitenko, acquired his

freedom at age twenty. *Narrative of the Life of Frederick Douglass* appeared in 1845, seven years after the author's escape from slavery.

9. Douglass wrote two subsequent versions of his autobiography. *My Bondage and My Freedom* (New York: Dover, 1969), which appeared in 1855, expanded on his earlier *Narrative; Life and Times of Frederick Douglass* (London: Collier-Macmillan Ltd., 1969), published in two editions (1881 and 1892), supplemented Douglass's account of life under slavery with information on his experiences as a Republican statesman in the Civil War and post–Civil War years. There is a large, and growing, scholarly literature devoted to Douglass. For a sample, see Dickson J. Preston, *Young Frederick Douglass: The Maryland Years* (Baltimore: Johns Hopkins University Press, 1980); Waldo E. Martin, Jr., *The Mind of Frederick Douglass* (Chapel Hill: University of North Carolina Press, 1984); and William S. McFeely, *Frederick Douglass* (New York: W. W. Norton & Co., 1991). For a collection containing selections from the three autobiographies and from Douglass's other writings as well, see Michael Meyer, ed., *Frederick Douglass: The Narrative and Selected Writings* (New York: Random House, 1984).

10. Unless otherwise indicated, page references to quotations are from this translation of Nikitenko, *Up from Serfdom,* and from the 1968 reprinting of Douglass, *Narrative of the Life of Frederick Douglass.*

11. In his expanded 1855 autobiography, Douglass offered a surprising generalization, absent from his earlier, starker version, about boyhood under slavery, which he termed "about as full of sweet content as those of the most favored and petted *white* children of the slaveholder." The slave boy, he concluded, "is, for the most part of the first eight years of his life, a spirited, joyous, uproarious, and happy boy, upon whom troubles fall only like water on a duck's back. And such a boy, so far as I can now remember, was the boy whose life in slavery I am now narrating." Douglass, *My Bondage and My Freedom,* 40, 42. Two recent studies present a less sanguine picture of slave childhood: see Wilma King, *Stolen Childhood: Slave Youth in Nineteenth Century America* (Bloomington: Indiana University Press, 1995), and Marie Jenkins Schwartz, *Born in Bondage: Growing Up Enslaved in the Antebellum South* (Cambridge: Harvard University Press, 2000).

12. Aleksandr Nikitenko, *The Diary of a Russian Censor,* abridged, edited, and translated by Helen Saltz Jacobson (Amherst: University of Massachusetts Press, 1975), 281, 305, 367.

13. John Bartlett, *Familiar Quotations,* 16th ed. (Boston: Little, Brown and Co., 1992), 761 (for King's version) and 794 (for the anonymous spiritual). For Annie Harris's slightly different version, see Charles L. Perdue, Jr., Thomas E. Barden, and Robert K. Phillips, eds., *Weevils in the Wheat: Interviews with Virginia Ex-Slaves* (Bloomington: Indiana University Press, 1980), 128.

Chapter 1: *My Roots*

1. Voronezh province—formerly Sloboda Ukraine. This vast territory, located east of Poltava and centered around present-day Kharkov, was tech-

nically within the borders of Russia. Because it was largely unpopulated and vulnerable to Tatar attacks, the tsarist government allowed several waves of Ukrainian refugees (who were fleeing the constant strife in their homeland) to settle in this region in the mid-seventeenth century and to establish autonomous, Cossack-style self-government. Orest Subtelny, *Ukraine, A History* (Toronto: Canadian Institute of Ukrainian Studies, 1988), 153.

2. Cossack: The Turkish word *Kazak* was used to describe fugitives from serfdom in the Central Asian Turkish states who preferred a nomadic life in the steppes. Later, for the same reason, when Poland ruled the western part of what is now called Ukraine, Kazak was applied to peasants fleeing from their Polish landlords. At the beginning of the sixteenth century, the Polish kings started to organize Cossack-manned military forces. When Ukraine was partitioned between Poland and Russia in the mid-seventeenth century, Russian tsars used the Cossacks to protect the borders from Tatar incursions. For more, see Subtelny, *Ukraine,* 108–122.

Serfdom: Though the process by which serfdom was established in Russia is obscure, it can be said that it was brought about by three factors—peasant indebtedness, the fiscal needs of the government, and the landlords' need for labor. Hugh Seton-Watson, *The Russian Empire, 1801–1917* (Oxford at the Clarendon Press, 1988), 21–27. On May 3, 1783, Catherine the Great extended serfdom to the Ukraine. For extracts from the decree she issued, see George Vernadsky, senior editor, *A Source Book from Early Times to 1917,* vol. 2, *Peter the Great to Nicholas I* (New Haven: Yale University Press, 1972), 460. During the time (1672–1687) that Ivan Samoilovich was hetman (commander-in-chief of the Cossacks and head of the Cossack State), when peasants were first invited by the thousands from western Ukraine and later brought in by forced migration, the hetman state also began to impose upon the so-called common people the "regular obligations of serfs." Michael Hrushevsky, *A History of the Ukraine* (New Haven: Yale University Press, 1941), 351.

Although the position of the once-free peasantry in Ukraine had deteriorated from the time of its annexation by Russia in 1654, in the middle of the eighteenth century Ukrainian peasants still enjoyed the theoretical right to give up their tenancy and move from one landlord to another. The practical exercise of this right was hindered by various restrictions. In 1763 a change of tenancy was made subject to written permission from the landlord, and freedom of movement was formally abolished in some of the Ukrainian provinces in 1765, and in the whole of the land in 1783. By a decree of December 12, 1796, issued by Paul I but presumably prepared during Catherine II's lifetime, serfdom was extended to the remaining southeastern regions, including the Caucasus and the territory of the Don. Michael T. Florinsky, *Russia, a History and Interpretation in Two Volumes* (Toronto: Macmillan, 1970), 1: 584–585.

3. In 1743 Count Pyotr Borisovich Sheremetev (1713–1788) married the wealthiest marriageable woman of the time, the daughter of Chancellor A. M. Cherkassky, Varvara Alekseyevna. The bride brought with her a dowry of twenty-six *votchinas* (ancestral estates). The serf populations in-

habiting the villages and hamlets on these lands now became the property of the new master. K. N. Shchepetov, *Krepostnoe pravo v votchinakh sheremetevykh* (Moscow: Trudy Ostankinskogo Dvortsa-Muzeya, 1947), 2: 12. Nikitenko's figure, 150,000 serfs, includes only adult male "souls." To arrive at a fairly close estimate of a total serf population (male and female) we generally double the number of men. Thus, Nikitenko's "up to 150,000" for the Sheremetev holdings translates to up to 300,000 serfs. Statistics for 1860 quote the Sheremetev family's holding of "male souls" as 146,374 in seventeen provinces of Russia. Doubling this figure we arrive at a total estimate of 292,748 serfs. Shchepetov, *Sheremetevykh,* 2: 26. Nikitenko quotes his figures as "recent statistics." He began his autobiography in 1851, and by 1877, when he died, his autobiography was unfinished. He may have made revisions from time to time, so his use of the word "recently" could refer to any year between 1851 and 1861, the year serfdom was abolished.

4. Little Russians: Ukrainian as an ethnic name was first adopted by the Romantic intellectual movement in the early nineteenth century (from the name of the seventeenth-century Cossack state "Little Russian Ukraine") and became universally used in the 1920s. Before then Ukrainians called themselves simply Russians, but among Great Russians they were known as Little Russians, beginning in the seventeenth century. S. V. Utechin, *A Concise Encyclopedia of Russia* (New York: E. P. Dutton, 1964), 574.

5. Pomeshchik—noble landowner (male); pomeshchitsa—noble landowner (female). Until the eighteenth century the terms referred to the holders of land on service tenure (military or civil service); later, they were generally applied to noble landowners. Jerome Blum, *Lord and Peasant in Russia: From the Ninth to the Nineteenth Century* (Princeton: Princeton University Press, 1961), 622 and 168–198. In 1762 Peter III issued a manifesto freeing the nobility from compulsory service. For Gary Marker's translation of the tsar's manifesto and other documents on compulsory service, see Daniel H. Kaiser and Gary Marker, *Reinterpreting Russian History: Readings, 860–1860s* (New York: Oxford University Press, 1994), 228–232.

Chapter 2: *My Parents*

1. Proskovya Ivanovna Kovaleva, whose stage name was Zhemchugova, died when her son, Count Dimitry, was three weeks old. She was a soprano and performed in major roles of eighteenth-century operatic repertoire. B. A. Vvedenskii, ed., *Entsiklopedicheskii slovar v dvukh tomakh* (Moscow: Gosudarstvennoe Nauchnoe Izdatel'stvo, 1963), 1: 367; K. N. Shchepetov, *Krepostnoe pravo v votchinakh sheremetevykh* (Moscow: Trudy Ostankinskogo Dvortsa-Muzeya, 1947), 2: 14. Count Dimitry was six years old when his father, Count Nikolai Petrovich Sheremetev, died. The count's only son was placed under guardianship in St. Petersburg. Among the guardians were Senators Alekseyev and Danaukov. Tsarina Mariya Fyodorovna, wife of Paul I, assumed the role of chief guardian. See Chapter 5.

2. Stepan Degtiaryov (1766–1813), a serf owned by the Sheremetev family, was a composer, conductor, and singer. He was the author of the first ora-

torio on a Russian national subject. Vvedenskii, *Entsiklopedicheskii,* 1: 314. Degtiaryov's compositions are performed to this day. In 1999 his work was presented in New York City by Lincoln Center at its outpost on the Upper East Side of Manhattan, the Church of St. Ignatius Loyola. Although the *New York Times* described him in a review as a "little or lesser known composer," no mention was made of his serf status. *New York Times,* March 31, 1999. He was a pupil of Sarti in St. Petersburg and became one of the most important Russian composers of his period. He composed sixty concertos, a quantity of church music, and the oratorios *Minin and Pozharsky, The Liberation of Moscow,* and *Napoleon's Flight* (unfinished). *Grove Directory of Music and Musicians,* vol. 2, 5th ed., edited by Eric Bloom (New York: St. Martin's, 1966), 645. Some of the most prosperous pomeshchiks had private orchestras, acting troupes, or harems made up of house serfs. Peter Kolchin, *Unfree Labor: American Slavery and Russian Serfdom* (Cambridge: Belknap Press of Harvard University Press, 1987), 161. Also see Shchepetov, *Sheremetevykh,* 2: 82.

Chapter 3: *Father's First Attempt to Introduce Truth Where It Wasn't Wanted*

1. The peasant village not only had to provide recruits for military service, but also had to outfit them and pay their transportation to their military post. It was left to the village commune or pomeshchik to select and send forth the number of recruits the government demanded. The quota was apportioned according to the male serf population. Jerome Blum, *Lord and Peasant in Russia: From the Ninth to the Nineteenth Century* (Princeton: Princeton University Press, 1961), 465–468.

Chapter 4: *My Early Childhood*

1. In the seventeenth century the Cossacks won independence from Poland for the central Ukraine and entered a union with Muscovy. W. E. D. Allen, *The Ukraine* (New York: Russell & Russell, 1963), 133–141.

The loss of self-government in eastern Ukraine had a negative effect on the development of national culture. Publications and the schools in Ukraine became subject to hostile Russian censorship. It was impossible to secure a permit from the censor to publish any book in the Ukrainian tongue. In 1769 a monastery at Kiev petitioned the (Russian) synod for authority to publish a Ukrainian grammar book, but permission was refused. Michael Hrushevsky, *A History of Ukraine* (New Haven: Yale University Press, 1941), 411–418.

Chapter 5: *Exile*

1. Exile to the cold North: For a detailed description of the events leading to Nikitenko's father's dismissal, imprisonment, and exile, and the confiscation of his home and its contents, see K. N. Shchepetov, *Krepostnoe pravo*

v votchinakh sheremetevykh (Moscow: Trudy Ostankinskogo Dvortsa-Muzeya, 1947), 2: 149–156. To punish "troublesome and undesirable serfs," Count Sheremetev exiled them to a cold, remote region, Churilovka, in Smolensk province.

Chapter 6: *Home from Exile*

1. Serfs as entrepreneurs: Although the majority of serfs performed agricultural labor, a significant number spent some or all of their work time in ventures that required the application of various specialized talents. Serfs engaged in a broad range of market-oriented activities, and a few became quite wealthy, occasionally even purchasing their "own" serfs in their master's name. In 1810, on the Sheremetev holdings, 165 of the family's "capitalistic" serfs on ten different estates owned a total of 400 male and 503 female serfs. A tiny number of serfs acquired enormous wealth, although legally it belonged to their owners, not to them. Peter Kolchin, *Unfree Labor: American Slavery and Russian Serfdom* (Cambridge: Belknap Press of Harvard University Press, 1987), 334–343. Cotton mills, one of the most prosperous branches of Russian industry in the first half of the nineteenth century, were founded and owned by the serfs of Count Sheremetev. In 1794, on some of the estates of Count Sheremetev, one-seventh of the entire servile population were de facto property of the other serfs. Michael T. Florinsky, *Russia, a History and Interpretation in Two Volumes* (Toronto: Macmillan, 1970), 1: 583.

Rich Serfs on Ten Sheremetev Estates Who Had Purchased Serfs from Other Pomeshchiks, 1811

		Serfs owned by rich serfs	
Estate	*Rich serfs*	*Male*	*Female*
Ivanova	30	189	249
Vasilyevskoye	28	9	32
Pavlovo	25	11	36
Voshchazhnikovo	8	11	8
Iukhot	65	104	148
Poim	1	4	5
Vorsma	3	7	5
Prudy	1	10	8
Balanda	1	2	—
Mikhailovka	3	4	6
Total	165	351	497

Legally, serfs could not buy land or serfs. With permission from their pomeshchik, and in his or her name, they could purchase land and serfs from other pomeshchiks. K. N. Shchepetov, *Krepostnoe pravo v votchinakh sheremetevykh* (Moscow: Trudy Ostankinskogo Dvortsa-Muzeya, 1947), 2, 355, table 7.

2. Bohdan Khmelnitsky (1595–1657), son of a minor Ukrainian nobleman, early joined the Ukrainian Cossacks. In 1648 he was elected hetman (commander-in-chief) and led a rebellion against Polish rule. When compromise with Poland seemed impossible, he turned for aid to Tsar Alexei of Russia. In 1654 Ukraine was incorporated into the Russian state. This alliance led to the destruction of Ukrainian autonomy. Florinsky, *Russia,* 1: 260–263. Also, William H. Harris and Judith S. Levey, editors, *The New Columbia Encyclopedia* (New York: Columbia University Press, 1975), 545, under Chmielnicki.

Chapter 8: *1811: New Place, New Faces*

1. As early as 1721 Peter I decreed that family members must not be sold apart from one another, and in the nineteenth century Nicholas I twice forbade selling unmarried children away from their parents. Nevertheless, forced separations continued. Peter Kolchin, *Unfree Labor: American Slavery and Russian Serfdom* (Cambridge: Belknap Press of Harvard University Press, 1987), 117–119. In 1804 Count Sheremetev issued an order forbidding serfs to purchase widows and girls. Nevertheless, at the beginning of the nineteenth century, on the Sheremetev estate in Ivanovo, Vladimir province, a trade in the sale of girls in the marketplace developed. They were brought for sale from Ukraine, and many wealthy serfs of Count Sheremetev bought them in the pomeshchik's name. K. N. Shchepetov, *Krepostnoe pravo v votchinakh sheremetevykh* (Moscow: Trudy Ostankinskogo Dvortsa-Muzeya, 1947) 2: 103–104.

2. Advertisements listed serfs for sale in the *Moscow News* (*Moskovskie Vedomosti*) in 1797:

- For sale: a waiter, 25 years old, with his wife and a minor son. A very good weaver; can also shave and draw blood. The wife can look after the mistress and is capable of any work. Also for sale in the same place: a . . . carriage, not much used, of the best workmanship.
- At house no. 352, 4th block, 6th ward, there are for sale: a good hairdresser for men and women; height above average, of fairly good figure, also useful as a valet for the bedroom, waiter, or footman, 27 years old; his wife, 24 years old, a laundress and needlewoman, with a daughter over 2 years old; both of good conduct. Lowest price for the lot, 1,000 rubles.
- For sale: 3 horses . . . They can be seen and inquiry made about the price, at house no. 260, block 1, ward 8. In the same house there is for sale a musician who plays the bassoon and is beginning to sing in a bass voice. Very well trained in reading and writing. 15 years old.

Daniel H. Kaiser and Gary Marker, *Reinterpreting Russian History: Readings, 860–1860s* (New York: Oxford University Press, 1994), 295.

3. Alexander Petrovich Sumarokov (1718–1777), one of the leading writers of the eighteenth century, wrote in many genres. Not only did he write plays, but he composed two operas, fables, comic odes, songs, etc., and was also a journalist. Nikolai Ivanovich Novikov (1744–1818) was a journalist, editor, and publisher of a series of journals that were shut down by Catherine the Great because of their liberal content. He condemned the system of serfdom. He was arrested, and imprisoned until the death of Catherine. Nikolai Gavrilovich Kurganov (1725 or 1726–1796), educator and writer, embraced the philosophy of the Enlightenment, an eighteenth-century movement that encouraged the questioning of traditional values and doctrines, emphasized the free use of reason, inclined toward individualism, and attacked intolerance, dogmatism, censorship. Fyodor Alexandrovich Emin (1735–1770), author of tales of romance and adventure, was the first Russian author of prose fiction to spurn anonymity. Mikhail Matveyevich Kheraskov (1733–1807) was a prolific writer who wrote in all the genres characteristic of that period. In his day he was known as the Russian Homer. Mikhail Vasilyevich Lomonosov (1711–1765), of humble origin, was one of the foremost minds of the Enlightenment. He was a scholar and a scientist. In two works, *Rhetoric* (1748) and *Grammar* (1757), he established rules for the Russian language. Denis Ivanovich Fonvizin (1745–1792) was the leading Russian playwright of the eighteenth century. His satires hold the stage even today. Fonvizin contended that a writer should be "the first guardian of general welfare, and raise his voice against abuses and prejudices." Garvriil Romanovich Derzhavin (1743–1816), from an impoverished noble family, was the greatest Russian poet of the eighteenth century. "Felitsa," a satirical ode to Catherine the Great, won her favor. A classical poet, he became poet laureate and held high government posts. For Derzhavin, Fonvizin, Emin, Kheraskov, Lomonosov, Novikov, and Sumarokov, see Mark Slonim, *The Epic of Russian Literature* (New York: Oxford University Press, 1964); also, William E. Harkins, *Dictionary of Russian Literature* (Paterson, N.J.: Littlefield, Adams, 1959). For Kurganov, see A. M. Prokhorov, ed., *Bol'shaya Sovetskaya Entsiklopediya,* 3rd. ed. (Moscow: Izdatel'stvo Sovyetskaya Entsiklopediya, 1970–1981) 2: items no. 65, 373; 22: item no. 775; 27: item no. 649; 29: item no. 1265.

Chapter 9: *Our Life in Pisaryevka, 1812–1815*

1. Gideon Ernest Laudon, Baron of Laudon (also spelled Loudon) (1717–1790), an Austrian field marshal, was one of the successful Hapsburg commanders during the Seven Years War (1756–1763) and the Austro-Turkish War of 1787–1791. *Encyclopedia Britannica,* 15th ed., 7: 189.

2. Napoleon invaded Russia on June 12, 1812, and entered Moscow on September 14, 1812, leaving the city virtually destroyed. With troops decimated, his prospective winter quarters burned down, and his supply line overextended, he began his fateful retreat on October 19, 1812.

Chaper 10: *School*

1. Ladizhka is a variation of a game of great antiquity that has been played around the world. In different cultures, stones, animal bones, and seeds have all been used in the game, with or without a ball. The U.S. equivalent is the children's game jacks, played with six to twelve or more six-pronged metal jacks and a small ball. After the jacks are strewn on the floor, the player tosses the ball in the air and then tries with one hand to pick up the jacks and catch the ball. In the Russian variation, Nikitenko and his friends used the ankle bones of animals. In Russian, *ladizhka* means ankle bone. Such objects have been found in prehistoric caves in Kiev. For variations of ladizhka and jacks, see *Encyclopedia Britannica,* 15th ed., 6: 460.

2. Radcliffe, born Ann Ward (1764–1823), was known for her tales of terror in the convention of the Gothic novel. *The Mysteries of Udolpho* was her most popular novel. Jean de La Fontaine (1625–1695), a French author, had a highly productive literary career. Best known for his fables, he was a prolific writer in many genres: comedies, lyrics, elegies, ballads, and licentious tales.

3. Finals and graduation: The date of his graduation, 1815, may be incorrect. At the end of Chapter 4, Nikitenko writes that he was born in 1804 or 1805. Reference sources are unsure of his birth year and list it as 1804 or 1805. In this chapter he writes, "I was only thirteen years old when I graduated," which would establish 1817 or 1818 as his graduation year, rather than 1815.

Chapter 11: *Fate Strikes Again*

1. State peasants, under the superintendence of the state, lived on state and crown lands. Unlike serfs, they were not owned, yet they were not free and had to fulfill certain obligations. Still, they had more control than serfs over their own lives. They paid a "soul" tax and obrok (quitrent) as well as a small levy to the provincial government; they also paid special local taxes and a communal tax. Like serf communes, they had to provide recruits for the army. There were many categories and subclasses of state peasants. Jerome Blum, *Lord and Peasant in Russia: From the Ninth to the Nineteenth Century* (Princeton: Princeton University Press, 1961), 475–503. One category of state peasants was the military settlers, colonists on military borderlands. Troops were settled on land, combining soldiering with farming and, to some extent, crafts and manufacturing. Hugh Seton-Watson, *The Russian Empire, 1801–1917* (Oxford at the Clarendon Press, 1988), 161–162. For Nikitenko's description of some military settlers and the wealth they had acquired as traders, see Chapter 13.

Chapter 14: *My Friends and Activities in Ostrogozhsk*

1. Vladimir Ivanovich Astafeyev was an Ostrogozhsk pomeshchik who played an important role in helping Nikitenko to gain his freedom in 1824. On April 6, 1826, when Nikitenko received the news of his friend's death, he made the following entry in his diary: "I received sad news from Little Russia. I was informed of Vladimir Ivanovich Astafeyev's death. He was one of my closest friends and instrumental in bringing about the happy change in my fate. I was terribly upset about the news of his passing. I shall always revere his memory. He was, in the full sense of the word, a second father to me. My first father gave me life, while my second made it possible for me to live as it should be lived." Helen Saltz Jacobson, editor and translator, *The Diary of a Russian Censor: Aleksandr Nikitenko* (Amherst: University of Massachusetts Press, 1975), 6–7.

2. Count S. S. Uvarov (1786–1855), minister of education from 1832 to 1849, was appointed by Nicholas I. An entry in Nikitenko's diary on May 14, 1832, describes a meeting he had with Uvarov. "We have a new Deputy Minister of Education, Sergei Semyonovich Uvarov. He asked to see me, and I did today. He spoke to me for a long time about political economy and literature. The university wants to offer me a position in literature. I've been hoping for it for a long time. Uvarov is a man educated in the European tradition who has long been considered enlightened. With his help a 'purification system' has been adopted which is now operating at the universities, that is, incompetent professors are being dismissed." For Uvarov's political philosophy and role in censorship, see Nikitenko's commentaries in his diary. Jacobson, *Diary of a Russian Censor,* 38, 62, 105. For more about Uvarov's role as minister of education, see Hugh Seton-Watson, *The Russian Empire, 1801–1917* (Oxford at the Clarendon Press, 1988), 218–226.

3. Kharkov College was founded in 1721 in Belgorod and transferred to Kharkov in 1726. In 1805 Kharkov University was founded. S. V. Utechin, *A Concise Encyclopedia of Russia* (New York: E. P. Dutton, 1964), 267.

4. Alexander Ypsilanti (1792–1828) was a member of a prominent Greek family that fought for the independence of Greece.

5. Merchants as serf owners: Dolzhikov was a wealthy merchant. A series of laws enacted between 1730 and 1762 limited ownership of settled estates with peasant inhabitants to members of the nobility. Wealthy merchants were not permitted to acquire serfs, although from the early eighteenth century they could employ "assigned" peasants in their manufacturing establishments. Peter Kolchin, *Unfree Labor: American Slavery and Russian Serfdom* (Cambridge: Belknap Press of Harvard University Press, 1987), 39, 40.

6. Johann Heinrich Jung-Stilling (original name Johann Heinrich Jung), also called Heinrich Stilling (1740–1817), was a German writer best known for his autobiography, *Leben* (Life), published in 1806. Raised in great poverty, he became a schoolteacher at age fourteen, and after great difficulty and deprivation was able to achieve his goal of becoming a doctor. He studied medicine in Strasbourg, where he met Goethe, who was very impressed

by him and published the first, and best, two volumes of Stilling's *Jugend* (Youth), in 1777. *Encyclopedia Britannica,* 15th ed., 6: 654.

Chapter 15: *My Friends in the Military; General Yuzefovich; The Death of My Father*

1. Mikhail Matveyevich Kheraskov was the author of *Rossiada* (1779) an epic poem, describing the conquest of Kazan in 1552 by Ivan the Terrible, and *Vladimir Reborn* (1785), concerned with the introduction of Christianity in Russia.

2. Vladislav Alexandrovich Ozerov (1769–1816) was a leading representative of sentimentalism in drama. In *Oedipus in Athens* he portrayed Oedipus as a sentimental Christian. William E. Harkins, *Dictionary of Russian Literature* (Paterson, N.J.: Littlefield, Adams, 1959). Also, Mark Slonim, *The Epic of Russian Literature* (New York: Oxford University Press, 1964), 54. Konstantin Nikolayevich Batyushkov (1787–1855) was a Russian elegiac poet whose sensual and melodious voices were said to have influenced the great Russian poet Alexander Pushkin. His collected works appeared in 1817, and shortly afterward he ceased writing. Suffering from mental illness, he was sent abroad in hope of a cure, which was never achieved. *Encyclopedia Britannica,* 15th ed., 1: 966. Nikitenko describes in his diary entry of August 13, 1834, his first meeting with Batyushkov when a relative of the poet offered to introduce Nikitenko to him. At that time the poet was suffering from mental illness. Helen Saltz Jacobson, editor and translator, *The Diary of a Russian Censor: Aleksandr Nikitenko* (Amherst: University of Massachusetts Press, 1975), 53. Vasily Andreyevich Zhukovsky (1783–1852), a Russian poet and translator, was one of Pushkin's most important precursors in forming Russian verse style and language. The bulk of his work consisted of free translations. He introduced into Russia the works of German and English contemporaries, as well as classic works such as Homer's *Odyssey. Encyclopedia Britannica,* 15th ed., 12: 914. Nikitenko's diary (1826–1877) contains many entries concerning Zhukovsky, including a discussion of the poet's role in securing the freedom of Nikitenko's mother and brother. Jacobson, *Diary of a Russian Censor,* 60, 71, 72, 77, 80–81, 93, 105, 130, 131, 132.

3. Kondraty Fyodorovich Ryleyev (1795–1826), a poet and one of the principal leaders of the December Uprising (1825), played a major role in securing Nikitenko's freedom from serfdom. In 1826, following the failure of the Uprising, he was hanged along with four other leaders. Harkins, *Dictionary of Russian Literature,* 342. For more about Ryleyev's poetry and participation in the Uprising, see Mark Slonim, *The Epic of Russian Literature* (New York: Oxford University Press, 1964), 75, 77–80, 102, 112, 139. For his role in Nikitenko's life, see Jacobson, *Diary of a Russian Censor,* pp. viii, xiv, xv, 2, and 11.

4. Alexei Fyodorovich Merzlyakov (1778–1830) was a poet, critic, translator, and professor at Moscow University. Although an adherent of classicism, at the same time he is noted for his songs stylized in the folk manner. Some of them have become popular songs. B. A. Vvedenskii, ed., *Entsiklope-*

dicheskii slovar' v dvukh tomakh (Moscow: Gosudarstvennoe Nauchnoe Izdatel'stvo, 1963), 2: 20. Also see Mark Slonim, *The Epic of Russian Literature* (New York: Oxford University Press, 1964), 54.

Chapter 16: *Farewell, Ostrogozhsk*

1. Count Alexei Andreyevich Arakcheyev (1769–1834) became Alexander I's war minister in 1808. His name became a symbol of intolerable despotism. He supervised the creation of military settlements, a system of military-agricultural colonies where settlers combined soldiering with farming. This involved turning entire peasant villages into army camps. For more about Arakcheyev and military settlements, see Hugh Seton-Watson, *The Russian Empire, 1801–1917* (Oxford at the Clarendon Press, 1988), 161–162. For Alexander I's orders on the establishment of military settlements and for abstracts from a charter for the inhabitants of Chuguyev district (December 19, 1817), see George Vernadsky, senior editor, *A Source Book for Russian History from Early Times to 1917*, vol. 2, *Peter the Great to Nicholas I* (New Haven: Yale University Press, 1972), 503–504. For Arakcheyev's cruel measures in Chuguyev, see *Up from Serfdom*, chap. 16.

Chapter 18: *The Dawn of a New Day*

1. Bible societies: In December of 1812 Tsar Alexander I authorized the founding of a network called the Russian Bible Society and named Prince A. N. Golitsyn its first president. For more about Prince Golitsyn, see Chapter 19.

2. The Holy Alliance was an agreement among the sovereigns of Prussia, Austria, and Russia to preserve the social order. The written agreement was particularly the product of the religious zeal of Tsar Alexander I, who drafted the text in December of 1815. The monarchs, he wrote, were to "take for their sole guide the precepts of the Christian religion." Hugh Seton-Watson, *The Russian Empire, 1801–1917* (Oxford at the Clarendon Press, 1988), 175.

3. Ultramontanists were in favor of greater or absolute supremacy of papal authority over national or diocesan authority in the Catholic Church.

4. The era of the Runichs and Magnitskys: Mikhail Leontyevich Magnitsky (1778–1855), as superintendent of Kazan school district (1819–1826), directed a purge of free-thinking professors at the University of Kazan in 1819. Other universities followed suit. Dimitry Pavlovich Runich (1780–1860), as superintendent of the St. Petersburg school district, organized a purge in 1821 of the most progressive and talented professors. Seton-Watson, *The Russian Empire*, 168–169.

Chapter 19: *St. Petersburg: My Struggle for Freedom*

1. Prince Aleksandr Nikolayevich Golitsyn (1773–1844) was minister of spiritual affairs and education from 1816 to 1824. While generally tolerant of all religious groups, including sects of Christianity, he was certainly not a lib-

eral, and his ministry was dominated by extreme obscurantists. He acquired many enemies. In 1824 he resigned his post. Hugh Seton-Watson, *The Russian Empire, 1801–1917* (Oxford at the Clarendon Press, 1988), 164–171.

2. *Nestor:* Friar Nestor, a monk of the Kiev Crypt Monastery at the end of the eleventh century and the beginning of the twelfth century, was a chronicler whose writings are considered a valuable historical source.

3. Yevgeny Abramovich Baratynsky (1800–1844), the foremost Russian philosophical poet, was a contemporary of Pushkin. When Nikitenko met him, the poet, a former army officer, had been reduced in rank to private after his expulsion from the Cadet Corps for theft. Later, Baratynsky received a commission. One of the poet's masterpieces was "On the Death of Goethe." Modern critics value his thought more highly than did his contemporaries. *Encyclopedia Britannica,* 15th ed., 1: 884. Also, Mark Slonim, *The Epic of Russian Literature* (New York: Oxford University Press, 1964), 128–131; and William E. Harkins, *Dictionary of Russian Literature* (Paterson, N.J.: Littlefield, Adams, 1959), 15–16.

4. Name day is the day of a church feast day for the saint after whom one is named.

Glossary

The term "peasant" in this glossary and in Nikitenko's memoir applies to privately held peasants—that is, serfs. There were other categories of peasants who were not free, but most of the peasants in Russia then were serfs.

barshchina Labor obligation of peasants to their pomeshchik.

meshchane Nikitenko defines a certain group of serfs in the sloboda as "so-called meshchane." They were a class of serfs who gained considerable wealth as small traders dealing mainly in grain, tallow, and skins.

mir A peasant commune, a form of peasant self-government on the pomeshchik's estate. The elected commune assembly was responsible for collecting taxes, distributing land allotments, recruiting conscripts, and other matters related to peasant households and peasant welfare.

Moscal A pejorative for Muscovite.

obrok Quitrent, in cash or kind, paid by peasants to their pomeshchik.

pomeshchik A noble landowner (male).

pomeshchitsa A noble landowner (female).

sloboda A large village near a town. Not to be confused with the historical meaning of sloboda, a settlement or territory exempted from state obligations.

verst A measure of distance equaling 0.66 miles or 1.067 kilometers.

votchina Hereditary landed property of a noble.

Index